MODERN SOCIAL THEORY
THEORY
From Parsons to Habermas

MODERN SOCIAL THEORY

From Parsons to Habermas

Second edition

IAN CRAIB
University of Essex

New York   London   Toronto   Sydney   Tokyo   Singapore

First published 1992 by
Harvester Wheatsheaf
Campus 400, Maylands Avenue
Hemel Hempstead
Hertfordshire, HP2 7EZ
A division of
Simon & Schuster International Group

Typeset in 10/12pt Ehrhardt by
Keyset Composition, Colchester

Printed and bound in Great Britain by
Biddles Ltd, Guildford and King's Lynn

British Library Cataloguing in Publication Data

A catalogue record for this book is available from
the British Library

ISBN 0–7450–1087–3 (hbk)
ISBN 0–7450–1088–1 (pbk)

2 3 4 5 96 95 94 93

For Benji

Theory is good but it doesn't prevent things from existing

(Reported comment by Charcot to Freud, quoted in Roazen, P. (1970)
Freud and His Followers, Allen Lane, London, p. 91.)

CONTENTS

Preface to the Second Edition   *ix*

PART I   INTRODUCTION   **1**

1   *What's wrong with theory and why we still
    need it*   *3*
2   *Cutting a path through the jungle*   *15*

PART II   THEORIES OF SOCIAL ACTION   **33**

INTRODUCTION   35

3   *Parsons: Theory as a filing system*   *37*
    I: Structural-functionalism   *37*
    II: Neofunctionalism and conflict theory   *56*
4   *Rational choice theory: 'The price of everything . . .*   *69*
5   *Symbolic interactionism: Society as conversation*   *85*
6   *Society as a conspiracy: Phenomenological
    sociology and ethnomethodology*   *97*
7   *Structuration theory: There is no such thing as
    society; there is such a thing as society*   *111*

PART III   FROM ACTION TO STRUCTURE   **125**

INTRODUCTION   127

8   *The world as a logical pattern: An introduction
    to structuralism*   *131*

9 *Structuralist Marxism: The world as a puppet
theatre*   149
10 *Post-structuralism and postmodernism:
The world gone mad*   177

PART IV   FROM STRUCTURE *OR* ACTION TO
STRUCTURE *AND* ACTION   197

INTRODUCTION   199

11 *The Frankfurt School: There must be some way
out of here*   203
12 *Jürgen Habermas: Back to the filing cabinet*   231

Conclusion: Playing with ideas   247

Index   259

PREFACE TO THE SECOND EDITION

During one of my more irritable moments when revising this book, my wife, Fiona Grant, suggested that it must be like altering a kilt: multiple pleats have to be carefully undone and sown in again. This seemed the perfect metaphor, with the added difficulty that this particular kilt has to fit a body growing in strange directions. Some pleats have almost disappeared: conflict theory and the work of Lukács are now small parts of larger pleats; while new pleats – rational choice theory and structuration theory – have appeared. Others – ethnomethodology, symbolic interactionism, structuralism, structuralist Marxism, and critical theory – have been 'let out' a little, while yet others – functionalism, post-structuralism, Habermas – have required larger alterations.

I do not spend as much of my time as I used to teaching social theory, but, to my delight, I found that the discussions and arguments that I had with my students ten years ago have continued in my head, taking in new material as it arrives. I hope the same is true for them. Discussions with my colleagues continue in the outside world, and I am especially grateful to David Lee, Lidia Morris, Rob Stones and Tony Woodiwiss, all of the Sociology Department at Essex University, for reading and commenting on various chapters. Finally, many thanks to Marion Haberhauer, who knitted the first edition onto disc and made my needlework a lot easier, and to the Fuller Bequest Fund, administered by the Essex Sociology Department, for financing the exercise.

PART I

―――

INTRODUCTION

Chapter 1

WHAT'S WRONG WITH THEORY AND WHY WE STILL NEED IT

INTRODUCTION

The very word 'theory' sometimes seems to scare people, and not without good reason. Much modern social theory is unintelligible, banal, or pointless. The reader does not feel that she is learning anything new or anything at all; there is certainly no excitement. Even for the specialist sociology student or teacher, it requires a lot of hard work, with the minimal result of simply being informed. Few people feel at home with theory or use it in a productive way.

When I prepared the first edition of this book, there had been an explosion of theoretical work in sociology; much of this has now subsided. Nevertheless, theory is always there. It might seem that this is the result of a highly developed society allowing people to earn sizeable incomes from playing complicated games, but it would not happen if there were not real problems which force people to turn to theory. Indeed, the problems that force people to theory do not belong solely to sociological research; they are problems we all face in our everyday lives, problems of making sense of what happens to us and the people around us, the problems involved in making moral and political choices.

So somewhere there are real reasons leading people to produce theoretical work, and there must also be reasons why the result is so often unhelpful. The journey between the problems and the results is undertaken on sociological theory courses as well as in producing theory, and it has the same pitfalls. It is not made any easier by the fact that in teaching theory, we start with the result. The nature of

3

sociology is not such that we can move directly from the more practical and informative studies of the social world to social theory. Social theory is, by definition, *general*; it claims some relevance to all the separate areas studied by sociologists. We cannot move directly from, say, a study of workers' attitudes to a theory, since any worthwhile theory must deal with much more than workers' attitudes. We have to bring the two together, use our studies of the real world as the raw material of theory and use our theory to help us understand the results of our studies of the real world. But when we learn theory, we must start with theory, and that makes life difficult.

Other things make it difficult as well. Ours is not a culture that easily accepts theory in its more elaborate, worked-out form. Most of us learn, almost unconsciously, to distrust it, or we become convinced that it is beyond us. *Social* theory generates its own special prejudices. Most of us know little about the natural sciences, but we will, none the less, accept that theoretical physics is a 'good thing': it seems to have useful practical results, and even if we know in advance that we cannot understand it, those few clever souls who can ought to be encouraged. On the other hand, social theory appears to have no practical results. Worse, it takes something we know about already in intimate detail – our own social life – and makes of it unintelligible nonsense.

If this were not enough, the teaching and learning of social theory itself operates within, and helps to create, a peculiar mystique which in turn creates a disturbing environment in which to study. The teacher of theory who, for example, is concerned only or primarily with theory tends to receive from her colleagues a grudging respect combined with a barely veiled hostility. In departments where it is the researcher into the real world who attracts money and reputation, the theorist is a luxury, an amusement and a nuisance. On balance, she is lower rather than higher in the unofficial order. Many people who see themselves primarily as theorists react to this by building a protective arrogance, returning twofold any scorn they might receive. They refuse to compromise their concerns and, indeed, retreat perhaps even further into the obscure and the difficult. The process frequently starts amongst postgraduate students, and it serves to make the necessary gap between teacher and student much wider than it need be at all levels. Amongst students themselves, because theory is so obviously difficult, the theorist takes on an aura that sets her apart from others; she is seen as somehow brighter, better, more able. I have no doubt that many students (and teachers) deliberately deploy this advantage, half-consciously seeking more obscure ways of expressing themselves, adopting the latest translations from Europe before anybody else, puffing out their theoretical feathers.

All these problems are there before we even start the journey. My guess is that most people start it because they have no choice – it comprises a compulsory course at some stage in their student career, and they grit their teeth and get on with it. What can be done about it? It is no use pretending that theory can be made easy, but it can be made easier.

THEORETICAL THINKING

The first step is to look again at the way we approach the subject. Because we start with the result, it is too easy for students and teachers to imagine that the whole process is a matter of learning what various theorists have said – of learning *theories*. It is that, of course, but in one sense that is the least important aspect. It is possible – in fact quite easy, once you get used to long words – to know what Talcott Parsons has to say and to reproduce it in acceptable form in essays and examination papers. And apart from the purpose of passing examinations, it is quite useless. Theory is a help only if we can learn from it, and we can learn from it only if we can use it.

Another way of putting this is that it is less a matter of learning theory than of learning to *think* theoretically. We could liken it to learning a new language in a particularly difficult way – not by gradually building up vocabulary and learning the various grammatical rules, but by listening to the language being spoken, in all its complexity, its slang, dialects, and so on. It is only just an exaggeration to liken it to being carried off to a very different society – a tribal village in New Guinea, say – where much of what happens is unfamiliar, and having to learn the language there by listening to people speak it.

Such a process can be made easier if we have some insight into the purposes of the inhabitants, and I said above that the problems which lead people to theory are problems we all face in our everyday lives. I think the truth is that we all think theoretically, but in a way of which we are not often aware. What we are not used to is thinking theoretically in a systematic manner, with all the various constraints and rigours that involves; when we do see such thinking, it is at first foreign to us.

What, then, are the problems in response to which we all think theoretically without realising it? Most of us are affected in some way by events over which we have no control and the causes of which are not immediately obvious. Some of these are unexpected, some happen at first in a slow and less noticeable way. A member of the family might be made unemployed, for example, or fail to gain an expected place at university or college; some product or service might suddenly become unavailable because of a strike, or because of government or local-authority economies; over a long period, an income – wage, social security benefit, unemployment pay, pension, student grant, or whatever – might buy less and less. We can do things to alleviate the effects of all these, but they happen whether we as individuals like it or not, and it is by no means clear why they happen. There are similar, more intimate events in our personal lives: the slow changes in the relationship between parents and children, or between lovers, which no one wills but which, none the less, happen. I might suddenly find that a friend has turned hostile for no obvious reason. On an even more personal level, I might fall in love at the most inconvenient and unexpected time, or find myself in the grip of some other violent emotion which comes from nowhere and seems to dominate my life. Or – an example I will continue to develop – I might find myself caught in something with a physical as well as a psychological manifestation: sexual impotence, perhaps.

In all these situations, we try to find some explanation. Often it takes the form of blaming somebody or something, frequently unfairly – I lose my job because of all the blacks coming over here; I'm unhappy because my mother dominates me; I'm impotent because my wife is frigid. Sometimes the blame is closer to the mark: I lose my job because of an economic situation largely created by government policy; I'm heading for a nervous breakdown because I cannot admit to certain feelings which I none the less have; I'm impotent because women – or a particular woman – scares me. Sometimes the explanations are more sophisticated, but my point is that as soon as we start thinking about and trying to explain something which happens to us, over which we have no control, we are beginning to think theoretically. When something happens over which we do have control, there is no need for an explanation; it happens because I want it to happen and do something to make it happen (or do not do something which would stop it happening). There is another way of putting this that takes us closer to 'theory' as it is presented in theory courses. Theory is an attempt to explain our everyday experience of the world, our 'closest' experience, in terms of something which is not so close – whether it be other people's actions, our past experience, our repressed emotions, or whatever. Sometimes – and this, perhaps, is the most difficult – the explanation is in terms of something of which we do not and cannot have any direct experience at all, and it is at this level that theory really tells us something new about the world.

This will become clearer if we investigate this everyday theoretical thinking more closely. Pushing the sexual impotence example further: it might be something which happens to me unexpectedly, and perhaps I might not want to admit to it for a while. Eventually, however, I am forced to recognise it and begin thinking about it. Then I might have, as my first reference, some previous similar experience of my own or of a close friend who has found himself in the same position. I look for common features in the situation: perhaps it is a matter of being under particular pressure at work; perhaps it happens when my wife is particularly successful in her work or gets a wage increase; perhaps if I am very frightened by the experience, and need urgently to place the blame elsewhere, I might attribute it to some more intimate feature of her behaviour.

There is a second 'resource' for my explanation, which I will probably use anyway, and particularly if I have no previous experience of impotence – mine or anybody else's. I can draw on some very general ideas about the world which do not come from my direct experience in anything like the same way. For example, I might assume that sexual potency – indeed, a permanent readiness to exploit any opportunity that presents itself – is a fundamental part of being a man; my impotence means that I am unmanned, I no longer fall into that category. This is not an idea that comes from my experience. I do not have knowledge of the sexual cycles of all men, or any man other than myself. I have not been taught the idea in any direct way, although it might be possible to identify situations in which I have unconsciously learnt it. My main point, however, is that in making sense of the world, I draw on experience and on ideas about the world that have no direct relation to experience. The two intertwine: my fear and shame at being unmanned might lead me to look for something about my wife that I can blame.

Social theory is employed for the same purposes: to explain and understand experience on the basis of other experiences and general ideas about the world. Given this, it is possible to look at some differences between everyday theoretical thinking and social theory. The first is that social theory attempts to be much more systematic about both experience and ideas. In sociology the real systematisation of experience often takes place in the supposed absence of theory, and there is considerable debate about whether this is possible or desirable. I suspect that it would now be generally recognised that some simple 'objectivity' or completely 'unbiased' organisation of facts is not possible, but in any case, the steady and systematic attempt to gather knowledge about people's experience can in itself produce knowledge which is, at first sight, strange. If I extend my concern about my impotence into a study of male sexuality even just in my own society, I might find that impotence is a 'normal' condition in that most men experience it at some time in their lives, and I will certainly find that all sorts of behaviour that I consider unmanly are engaged in by men. General ideas, on the other hand, are systematised through subjecting them to rules of logic – the ideas in a theory should follow from each other, not contradict each other: at the very least they should have clearly defined relationships to each other. It is important to realise that there is no conclusive end to this process on either level: we can always discover more about our world and organise it in different ways, according to different principles.

This brings us to the second difference. In the course of systematisation, what I will call 'second order' problems arise, problems about the best way of carrying on the systematisation, only indirectly connected with explaining our experience as such. An example would be debates about what we mean by 'explanation' – when is an explanation adequate, and when is it not?

The third difference has already been mentioned. The various processes of systematisation might lead us to the conclusion that things exist in the world of which we have no direct experience and, on occasion, that these things are the opposite of what we might expect from our experience of the world. It is perhaps more difficult to accept this in the case of the social world, but we already accept it about the natural world, and that should at least suggest that we should keep an open mind. If we believed only what we see by just looking, nobody would believe that the earth was round or that it travelled round the sun. For most of our history, nobody did believe it (as far as we know).

Returning to our example of sexual impotence, our various systematisations might lead us to the conclusions that in most societies female sexuality has been controlled by men, and that whatever men believe about themselves, women get the blame if those beliefs are disturbed. We might then be struck by the similarity between this situation and some of the abstract ideas put forward by Marx about the relationship between social classes, and set about refining and modifying Marx's ideas so that they help us to make sense of the relationship between men and women. We might go further and integrate some general ideas taken from Freud, and end up with a theory of something called 'patriarchy' – a model of social organisation in which men systematically oppress women. This is the opposite of my experience of impotence: my experience – and my first reaction – is that my wife is exercising power over me by denying me something, she is making my life miserable. The theory of patriarchy enables me to reinterpret this reaction: what is really happening is that my wife is, in some way, threatening my power; perhaps she is too independent, perhaps she is simply fighting back with the weapons at hand. By blaming her, and particularly by trying to persuade her to accept responsibility, I am trying to reassert that power.

Whether or not you accept such an explanation (and there is plenty of room for debate), every social theory considered in this book makes some propositions which are counter to our immediate experiences and beliefs, and this is, in fact, the way in which we learn from theory. The punk might believe that she is in full rebellion against the culture of her parents and authority, yet for the functionalist theorist she is setting in motion a series of adjustments by means of which that culture and society continue to survive in a smoother-running way than before. The worker might believe she is getting a fair day's wage for a fair day's work, but for the Marxist she is being systematically exploited. When I fail a student's examination paper, I might believe that I am applying a rule and upholding academic standards: she does not come up to some predetermined standard, in the same way that I might say a piece of wood is not long enough for my purpose. The symbolic interactionist and (in a different way) the ethnomethodologist would say that I am creating a failure. If we are honest, most of us would accept that there have been occasions on which we were really doing the opposite of what we thought we were doing; for this reason alone we should tolerate the apparent strangeness of social theory.

I said above that social theory can only be made easier, not easy. For example, it is not possible to trace the theories examined in this book back to everyday problems; the problems had already been subjected to many centuries of philosophical thought and developments in knowledge before the theories arose. Nevertheless, they can be seen as asking sensible questions about the world (even if the answers are not always sensible). Perhaps the best way to learn 'theoretical thinking' is not just by reading and understanding theory but by asking the theory questions and speculating on the answers. That is the way in which the book will proceed: What questions does the theory ask? What questions can we ask the theory? It should be (or begin with), above all, an imaginative game. Having some idea of what Parsons says, can we, for example, explain the election of our government in Parsonian terms; or can we use Parsons to understand the increasing divorce rate or changes in the level and nature of crime? The first step is always to speculate, to try to *invent* an answer. The rigour of logic and facts will follow on all too quickly. The pay-off is that if we can do it well, if we can use our theory to find out about the world, then our range of effective action increases; we become more free.

All this could be read as an apologia for theory, a justification of its obscurities and difficulties. None the less, I meant what I said at the very beginning – that much modern theory is unintelligible, banal, or pointless. In the process of theoretical thinking, a number of things can go wrong.

THEORETICAL TRAPS

The first trap lies prior to theory proper and there have been times, including the present (1992), when sociologists have seemed especially prone to falling into it. This is the trap of empirical sociology by itself. It may take the form of only collecting facts, of becoming absorbed in technical debates about methodology and statistical correlation, or of relying on empirical sociology to 'expose' the reality behind popular mythology. Gordon Marshall's book *In Praise of Sociology* (1990) deals with a number of studies which have been significant in revealing aspects of British society, but he has nothing to say about theory. The real function of theory has to do with the interpretation of whatever facts we might be able to discover and agree on, and indeed, it will become apparent that in some cases we need a theory to tell us what those facts are. All the studies Marshall discusses are dependent on theory, even if it is not explicit, and as at least one reviewer has pointed out, without some attempt at overall theory, sociology remains an empirical adjunct to other disciplines.

The first truly theoretical trap is what I shall call the '*crossword puzzle trap*'. One of the most influential books in sociology in the last thirty years has, paradoxically, not been a work of sociology at all but a study of the history of the natural sciences: Thomas Kuhn's *The Structure of Scientific Revolutions* (1970). Kuhn makes a distinction between what he calls 'revolutionary' and 'normal' science, and it is the latter which is important for my present point. Normal science is routine science. The scientist is in possession of accepted theoretical knowledge, routine experimental procedures, and the instruments necessary to carry them out. These (together with other elements) comprise what Kuhn calls a 'paradigm'. Her scientific activity consists of trying to manipulate certain features of the natural world, suitably isolated in experimental situations, to fit the paradigm. In the same way as a crossword puzzle provides a frame and a set of clues, so the paradigm gives us a general framework and indications of what the world should be like, and the scientist sets about filling in the squares in detail. Now I think there are a number of reasons why the social scientist should not employ theory in this way, however productive it might be for the natural sciences, and that is a matter of debate. The complexity of the subject matter of social science, the impossibility of isolating significant aspects of the social world in order to carry out experiments, the fact that human activity is self-conscious and reflective, all combine to make such puzzle-solving activity damaging – what some people call 'reductionist': it reduces the complexity of the real world to a set of theoretical concepts.

For example, we do not learn much about my reaction to impotence by sticking the label 'patriarchy' on it; we need to show not only how the nature of patriarchy conditions and determines both my impotence and my reaction to it, but also how these processes interact with others (for example, a changing labour market which gives greater opportunity for women to embark on full-time careers) in order to understand the full complexity of the situation. Otherwise, something is lost. We need, then, to take account of all the various links ('mediations') between what the theory tells us and the experience or event we are trying to understand.

The second trap I shall call the *'brain-teaser trap'*. I mentioned above that in systematising our ideas about the world, a number of second-order problems arise, not directly connected with explaining something. I gave as an example what we mean by 'explanation'. Many such problems are very important, and without doubt a number will arise in the course of this book. But many might be unsolvable, or bear little relation to what we are trying to do; they are, none the less, fascinating problems, and I know from my own experience that a great deal of pleasure can be derived from tackling them – the same sort of pleasure that can be derived from the 'brain-teasers' sometimes found in the quality Sunday papers. I think this is a 'permissible' activity as long as it is recognised for what it is: when it is mistaken for the theoretical enterprise as a whole, that theory seems to be (and is) irrelevant.

A good example is the debate, imported into social theory from British analytical philosophy, about whether or not a person's reasons for their actions are to be considered as causes of their actions. There is a crucial issue here to do with the very nature and possibility of a social science, but the terms of the debate are so limited in their scope and exclude so many dimensions of human action that it seems to me that the real problem disappears. Indeed, I think it is possible to establish elegant solutions on either side, none of which is much concrete help to social analysis, and none of which is conclusive.

Thirdly, there is the *'logic trap'*. This might sound odd, since I have already suggested that a central aspect of theoretical thinking is the attempt to achieve logical coherence between different parts of a theory. My point is that it is possible to take this to an absurd extreme. In the course of this book there will be several examples of the way in which a theory might be demolished on logical grounds which, if taken to the extreme, would mean that no theory at all was possible. The main point here is that whilst a theory must strive for internal coherence, for logical order, the world itself is often illogical or logical in a different way to the theory, which must be capable of allowing for this difference. There are a number of examples of supposedly theoretical arguments which are really competitions in logic that have long left behind any concern with explaining or understanding the social world.

Finally, there is the '*description trap*'. The difference between an explanation and a description will be discussed in Chapter 2. For the moment it is sufficient to say that an explanation tells us something we didn't know and couldn't discover simply by looking; a description tells us only what we can discover by looking. A great deal of modern theory seems to me to describe something, often something we know very well, in abstract theoretical terms, and then pretend that it is an explanation. It is perhaps this which contributes most to the bad name of theory: endless pages of long words which, when we translate them, tell us the obvious. We shall see that Talcott Parsons is particularly vulnerable on this point, but much postmodernist theory also chatters on in a jargon which adds little or nothing to our knowledge.

So – I have tried to show why theory is necessary, and some of the traps into which it can fall. However, social theory is frightening for another reason: there is so much of it, and there are so many different types. I want now to spend some time looking at the range of theories with which sociologists are currently working, and at possible ways of organising them to make the task easier.

Chapter 2

CUTTING A PATH THROUGH
THE JUNGLE

WHY CONFUSION IS NECESSARY:
DIMENSIONS OF THEORY

This book is based on the premiss that theory is useful and necessary, and that it is incurably confused and confusing, and incurably fragmented: sociology, by its very nature, cannot develop one overarching theory that embraces the whole discipline. It is useful to think of social theory as having at least four different dimensions, and of theorists as doing four different things at the same time. In the first chapter, I was talking about theory as a way of establishing knowledge about the social world. This is its *cognitive* dimension, and most of this book will be concerned with it. We can trace 'cognitive fault lines' in social theory which help to make sense of the process of fragmentation, and I will be returning to this in the last part of this chapter. For the moment, I want to concentrate on the remaining three dimensions.

To begin with, the sociologist is caught up with the problem she is trying to theorise, not just as a sociologist but as a person. There is a strong argument that – however obliquely – the social theorist's experience of the world enters into her theory, can leave her blind to certain aspects of the world or affect the way in which she deals with problems. Perhaps 'her' is the wrong pronoun here, since the clearest example is the way in which the mainly male sociological community has ignored or misdefined the place of women in our society. It has been usual, for example, to place a family in the stratification system according to the occupation of the male. Sexual stratification has received very little attention until recently – apart from Parsons's work on the family, where the woman's traditional role was barely questioned. In a more immediate way as well, a number of quite personal hopes and fears are embodied in the work. Alan Dawe, following the American sociologist Alvin Gouldner, has likened some theoretical work to prayer. This second dimension of theory, then, is the *affective* dimension: theory embodies the experience and the feelings of the theorist, and any theoretical debate involves more than rational argument. It involves the desire to *know* and to *be right*, and these desires can outweigh the evidence of external reality.

This second dimension muddies the waters: it contributes to the obscurities of the arguments and sometimes to the overemphasis of differences.

The third dimension I call the *reflective* dimension. By this I mean that sociology and social theory have to be part of the world as well as a way of understanding the world: they must reflect what is going on 'out there' and what is happening to all of us. This dimension has become increasingly important over the last decade, and it is bound up with what sociologists have had to say about the nature of the modern or (as some would say) the postmodern world. One feature of present-day Western society is an accelerating rate of change, technological change in particular. This affects, in turn, geographical and social mobility, career structures (in that the skills with which we enter employment can become outdated before half of our working lives are over), the range of roles we have to play and the speed at which we have to change roles. One way of putting this is to say that our lives are becoming increasingly fragmented. At the same time, our societies and the organisations for which we work are becoming increasingly complex, and perhaps experienced as more beyond our control than ever before. Social theory reflects some of this, both in its own fragmentation and in other ways to which I will return at the end of this chapter.

The fourth dimension, the *normative* dimension, exaggerates the effects of the third. Any theory of the way the world is must make implicit or explicit assumptions about the way the world ought to be. Alvin Gouldner has referred to these as 'domain assumptions'. It follows that a theory must always have certain implications about political action, about what sort of actions are possible, and which are desirable. Social theory, then, is not only *about* social processes, conflicts and problems; it is also *part* of those processes, conflicts and problems. I do not think that this is a bad thing; indeed, such assumptions should be made as explicit as possible, because if they are not argued out rationally in an academic setting, they are unlikely to be argued out anywhere. This process brings out an important aspect of any theory: its *flexibility*. A theory is always open to being used to argue different points in different ways in different situations, and the flux of normal social and political life will ensure that most theories are pushed in different ways. Marxism is the obvious example, but most of the theories we will be looking at here have become involved in debates that go well beyond their immediate cognitive dimension. Social and international conflicts always push their way into theory, often in disguised form, and sometimes split it down the middle. To develop this any further would require a political sociology of the discipline; I want to concentrate on the cognitive dimension, and that involves a short excursion through the philosophy of science.

WHAT DO THEORIES EXPLAIN?

At first glance, the philosophy of social science might be even more frightening than social theory. Whereas the word 'theory' sometimes holds out the hope that it might be understood, the word 'philosophy' by itself defies understanding. And if theory is such a mess, would not philosophy be even more of a mess?

The simple answer is no. Perhaps the best way of looking at philosophy is as a sort of 'theory of theory', and simply because it is more abstract, certain things appear more clearly and simply. Of course, what I called the 'brain-teaser trap' is more pronounced, and the more technical the philosophical argument, the greater the danger. However, apart from general background details, I do not want to go into the arguments. Indeed, I will avoid most of them altogether – if you want to find out what they are, a number of references can be found in the Further Reading at the end of this chapter. Instead, I want to concentrate on one recent development.

The philosophy of social science concerns itself with two issues: first, the nature of the world: what sort of things exist and what are the different forms of existence – for example, do human beings exist in the same way as inanimate objects, and if not, what are the differences? These questions can be classed under the heading *ontological* questions, and you might think, with some justification, that the answer to the example I have just given would be obvious to anybody but a philosopher. Secondly, it concerns itself with the nature of an explanation: what methods must be employed to arrive at an explanation, what logical structure must it have, what proofs are required? These are *epistemological* questions – about the way in which we know our knowledge *is* knowledge.

In the case of the social sciences, and sociology in particular, these issues have been discussed in the context of a debate about whether the social sciences and the natural sciences are similar – whether social science should employ the same methods as the natural sciences. For a long time there were two alternatives: yes or no. Then, beginning with the work of Thomas Kuhn – which I mentioned in the last chapter – it was realised that the natural sciences themselves were more difficult and complex animals than had hitherto been supposed. This opened up a third alternative: yes *and* no. In some ways the social sciences are like the natural sciences, in other ways they are not.

The arguments are, of course, still continuing, but I want to concentrate on one comparatively recent development most generally known as realism, particularly as developed in the work of Roy Bhaskar, which, I think, throws some light on the fragmentation of social theory in a way that the others do not. Bhaskar is concerned to demonstrate that ontological and epistemological questions are interrelated in the sense that the way we gain knowledge about the world, what comprises an adequate explanation, depends on the sort of beings that exist in the world: to put it another way, the object we are studying determines the knowledge we can have of it. This should become clearer shortly.

One of the more traditional ways of dividing up social theory was to make a distinction between 'holistic' theories and 'individualistic' theories. The former start with 'society' as a whole, regarding it as something more than the sum of the individuals who make it up. The actions of individuals are then seen as in some way determined by the society of which they are a part. The latter start with individuals and see society as the product of individual actions. There were also those who argued that both processes go on at the same time: individuals make societies and societies make individuals. Now Bhaskar argues that all three of these positions are mistaken in so far as they regard societies and individuals (agents, in his terminology) as beings of the same type, so that one can determine the other or there can be a process of mutual determination. Societies and agents are beings of a radically different type; they have different properties. The next step is to investigate those different properties.

Beginning with societies: it is possible to talk of a society as something greater than the individuals who make it up. A society exists in its own right – or *sui generis*, to use Durkheim's term. Durkheim put forward the argument for this view a long time ago, as a demonstration that we need such a discipline as sociology to study societies. There are certain features of social existence which precede an individual's birth and continue after her death, and into which that individual has to fit. We can draw an analogy with language. The English language was in existence long before I was born, and will continue in existence long after I die. If I want to communicate with any or most people in my society I must learn to speak it, and nothing I do will alter that. I do not create the language, nor does anybody else; it has, in *this* sense, an independent existence. We will see later that there is also a sense in which societies and agents *depend* on each other, without determining or creating each other.

The first property of societies is that they are *relational*: they are comprised of enduring relationships between agents and each other, and the material objects that also make up the social environment. It must be remembered that relationships outlast any particular agents engaged in them, so it is more useful and accurate to talk of relationships between positions rather than agents. Thus, for example, the nuclear family may be seen as involving relatively enduring relationships between three positions: mother, father, child(ren). There is a level at which these relationships remain the same whichever particular individuals fill the positions. Similarly, there are basic aspects of my relationship to my students which remain the same from year to year, although I teach different students each year.

A second feature of societies is that they possess what Bhaskar calls '*ontological depth*' – they have levels of existence beyond what lies on the surface, beyond what we can see, and these underlying levels are of special significance because they can explain what we see. There is an oft-quoted passage from Marx that makes the point well: 'All science would be superfluous if the outward appearances and essences of things directly coincided.'[1] There is nothing about the outward appearance of my desk that tells me it is made up of countless millions of molecules bouncing off each other. There are, I think, two evident senses in which a process of cause and effect is at work in societies. First, an underlying set of social relationships, an underlying social structure, might be seen to cause some surface set of relationships; for example, a Marxist might argue that the political arguments reported in the news each day are caused by underlying economic relationships, even if the arguments are not about economics. Second, an underlying structure might be such that it has certain laws or tendencies of development; for example, there might be some mechanism in the underlying relationships of a capitalist society that causes it to go through regular economic crises, or causes increased state intervention in economic affairs.

Turning now to agents: Bhaskar argues that human action does not create society but either maintains or changes it in some way – this is the sense in which the two are not independent of each other. Societies do not 'determine' agents, but they survive and change only through acting individuals. Bhaskar suggests a 'transformative' model of human action: societies provide the raw material, human beings act on it, and societies come out at the other end. The crucial property of human action, as far as my argument here is concerned, is that it is *intentional*; it aims at achieving something. Bhaskar makes essentially the same point in a rather different way: human beings not only monitor their action (i.e. know what they are doing) but monitor the monitoring – they can reflect on what they know they are doing, assess it, make judgements and choices. In this respect they are crucially different from societies, which are structures of social relationships.

An important point here is that there is no simple relationship between an agent's action and intention and its effect on society or a particular social relationship. A standard example, used by several writers, is that a person might marry because she is in love, wants to please her parents or wants to gain access to regular sexual relations. The effect of that action is to reproduce the enduring social relationships of the nuclear family. There is a reverse example. I might divorce my wife because I no longer love her, because I want to live with my mistress, because I don't like her or she doesn't like me. The effect on society is to contribute towards a kinship structure in which single-parent families are as common as the 'normal' lasting nuclear family. Even when my actions are directly intended to change or preserve some aspect of social structure, the result is not automatic. For example, a government might decide to reduce public expenditure, particularly on social services, to free money for private enterprise, assuming that a flourishing private enterprise society provides better living conditions for all its members. The result might be that since there is less money available to buy industry's products, an economic recession starts and many private enterprises collapse.

The social world then is made up of two distinct and different types of being: societies and agents. I said above that for Bhaskar, epistemological questions depend upon ontological questions. In other words, this has certain implications for theory.

HOW DO THEORIES EXPLAIN?

It should be apparent by now that I am suggesting that theory is *necessarily* fragmented in that we need different types of theory to explain different things. In suggesting this, I am going some way beyond Bhaskar and possibly pushing his ideas in a direction with which he would not be happy. But on the basis of his argument, I think it is possible to suggest that explanations of features of social structure and explanations of human actions are of different types. I want now to try to outline these different types of explanation, and what I am doing, in effect, is elaborating on the idea of theory that I presented in the first chapter, filling in some of the processes of theoretical thinking.

The work of theory in relation to societies is to identify underlying structures of relationships, and the first step towards this is to employ analogy and metaphor. A society is *like* something else. We can find a series of metaphors throughout social theory: sometimes society is likened to a biological organism; Marxism employs the metaphor of a building, base and superstructure; symbolic interactionism, perhaps, employs that of a conversation. In some ways this is the most imaginative stage, but it is followed by increasing precision. It is not just similarities that are important but differences as well, and as the theory develops, so concepts emerge that have little to do with the original metaphor. It is not just a matter of specifying underlying structures, however, since the theory must offer an explanation – in other words, it must have some conception of cause.

A digression on the idea of a *cause* is necessary, since in everyday life we tend to use it as if it were unproblematic: my broken leg was caused by a car crash; the cause of the break-up of my marriage was

ith my secretary; inflation is caused by high wages. A very
process is implied in each of these explanations, and a
difference between the two types of theory under con-
lies in the type of causal explanation that each offers. It is
not   cient for a theory to suggest that something causes something
else; it must stipulate how that causal process works – for example, if
a firm pays higher wages it must charge higher prices to cover costs,
hence inflation. (I do not believe that this explanation is right,
incidentally, but it is a useful example.)

In the case of societies, a *structural* notion of cause is implied. The
cause is seen not as a single event or thing, but as residing in a
particular arrangement of relationships. These relationships may be
seen as framing or constituting a 'causal mechanism' (rather like a
light switch, perhaps) which, when set in motion, produces certain
results. The theory should also stipulate what sort of conditions will
set the mechanism working, or alternatively, whether it will work
simply by virtue of the relationships that form it. This is a difficult
idea to understand in abstract terms; there will be a number of
examples in Part III, but to outline them properly would require
elaborating a whole theory, which I do not want to do at this stage.
Instead I will offer a couple of examples which have little to do with
social structures but which, I hope, will get the general idea across.

The first comes from music. If we can set aside developments such
as the twelve-tone system, all popular and most classical music we
hear in the Western world is based on a limited number of notes
which could be learnt in the abstract in a very short time. All music is
made of the same notes; what distinguishes between pieces of music
– what 'causes' different tunes, if you like – is the arrangement of
those notes. As a second example, most of us have been involved in a
close relationship with a parent or lover or friend that has 'gone
wrong' for a time, or, perhaps, for ever. We can see the surface
appearances: more or less bitter arguments, nagging irritability,
feelings of unhappiness, emptiness, even despair. On reflection, if we
can manage it, or later, when the feelings have subsided, we can
admit that it is not the fault of either partner; it is the *relationship*,
some lack of balance, some 'fault' in what goes on between the
partners. It might be, for example, that the 'causal mechanism' lies in
the relationship between my insecurity about my masculinity and my
wife's suppressed rage, which, in certain circumstances, will create a
bitter argument about who feeds the cat.

Turning now to agents: the theoretical explanation of how and why people act has an entirely different structure and a different notion of cause. Agents, remember, reflect on their actions, make decisions, have intentions. When we talk about the cause of an action in everyday life, we refer to a number of things, but the distinctive element is the agent's intention: the state of affairs that she hopes to bring about, what she wants to achieve. The technical term for this sort of explanation is teleological: the end-point, the effect, is there at the beginning, in the form of a desire which must then be put into practice. The action is explained by its end-result, in a sense, the effect is the cause. There is a great deal of debate about whether this is the right way of explaining actions or whether it is possible to construct some other more conventional causal explanation, and it is not possible to sort out all the arguments in this context. In practice, I think a teleological explanation is implied in all forms of social theory that have anything to say about action, and I do not think it could be otherwise. This is not the only difference: to understand an action properly is to understand forms of thinking, relationships between meanings in people's heads; in other words, it involves an act of interpretation in which ideas such as structural causality and causal mechanism play no role. If we are trying to make sense of a particular passage in a book, for example, these notions are of no real help.

The question remains of how we know whether a theory is right or wrong (the crucial epistemological question). The simple answer is that we don't, but we can make judgements between more or less adequate explanations offered by a theory. Such judgements are not simple, they must involve a number of aspects that are different for the different types of theory; but we must always remember that we are living in a world in which there are no final answers. As the world itself changes and becomes a different place, so the theory by means of which we understand it will change.

A number of criteria by which we can make the judgement in the case of theories of society are suggested by what I have already said. The better theory will be able to specify in more detail the causal processes at work and the situations in which causal mechanisms come into operation. Beyond this (on the side of what I referred to in the last chapter as 'general ideas'), I think logical coherence is important – a theory which regularly contradicts itself must be regarded with suspicion. On the side of 'experience' a theory must, in some way, be measured against evidence. It is, I think, a feature of the social sciences that this cannot be done in any rigorous and systematic way, but we can always discover features of experience which suggest that a theory ought to be revised or replaced by another theory. A theory could suggest that something might happen which does not happen. Much modern Marxist theory, for example, has been devoted to revising the original system of thought to explain the absence of socialist revolution in North America and Western Europe. Vice versa, something the theory suggests should not happen does happen. It is rare that a theory must be rejected – rather, it is usually a matter of revision and refinement, perhaps limiting its scope and employing supplementary explanations. All the theories we will be looking at in this book seem to me to tell us something about the world; there are some clear examples in which one theory does something better than another, but whatever their deficiencies, they all have some range of applicability.

Most of what I have said also goes for theoretical explanations of action. My points about logical coherence and the relationship to evidence can remain unchanged. Detailed specification of causal processes can be replaced by detailed specification of the interpretative processes of agents. The one additional criterion is that explanations on this level always remain rooted in agents' experience, whereas theoretical explanations of social relationships might contradict agents' experience and employ concepts which are not available to the agents themselves.

WHY DO THEORIES FRAGMENT?

I have suggested that social theory is necessarily fragmented along the lines I have been talking about (and perhaps along others as well – I will return to this shortly). But as it stands, this does not provide us with a way of making sense of the confusion. It is not possible to allocate different theories to different 'objects' – some to societies, some to agents. This sort of division would have no more success than those suggested earlier on in the discipline's history (to some of which it bears some resemblance). Perhaps it ought to be possible to carry out such a division, and if we could do so the frontiers of theoretical knowledge would be set by the problems of passing from one sort of explanation to another, of conceptualising the nature of the links between agents and societies. This is not the case, however, and these distinctions offer us an *in*direct way of making sense of the mess.

To begin with, they indicate a dilemma. Societies and agents are two different types of being, requiring different types of explanation or understanding. To understand social reality, however, we have to understand *both*: societies would not remain in existence without agents, and vice versa. Roy Bhaskar seems to try to avoid the problem by allocating different objects to different sciences: societies to sociology, agents to psychology, and the relationship between the two to social psychology. This seems to me to be a false division, since each separate science requires the others to make any sense – just as their 'objects' require each other in order to be what they are. Such an inclusive, 'totalising' theory seems to me to be implied in the very enterprise of sociology, yet at the same time it is impossible to achieve. Nevertheless, many of the theories we will be looking at have laid claims to being such a totalising theory, and that is precisely why the process of fragmentation has taken place, or why they have been fragmented from the start. In effect, they have tried to generalise a theory appropriate to one type of object in the social world to all types of objects. These attempts lead to very clear inadequacies in dealing with either agency or societies or both. Such attempts to totalise, and their results, will be a major theme throughout this book.

Beyond this, it is conceivable, although I do not think it has yet been established, that there might be other forms of being in the social world. I have three particular possibilities in mind. The first involves structures of social relationships at the surface level, as opposed to underlying structures. These include what most sociologists talk about under the name *institutions*, and they seem to combine qualities of agency *and* social structures. A political party, for example, has intentions: it develops policies that it desires to implement when it gains power. At the same time it has features that we would attribute to social structures: it is comprised of more or less enduring relationships, and it might be possible to identify underlying structures. The second example lies on the side of agents. It is conceivable that we can identify an 'ontological depth' of the agent: in other words, an unconscious. If we take Freud seriously, it would seem that the unconscious does not work in the same way as the conscious level. In both cases the form of theory we use, the way we construct theoretical explanations, might be different. Thirdly – and this will emerge in Parts II, III and IV – it seems possible to identify a level of what I will call 'general meanings' – ideas which, like language, exist over and above individuals, into which we are all socialised as we become members of society, but which are different again from societies. The chapter on structuralism in Part III will deal with this level.

The discussion of theoretical explanation in the case of societies points to another form of fragmentation, which I referred to in the last chapter as the 'description trap'. An explanation ought to identify clearly the causal processes and mechanisms involved: a description does not do this. All theories work with *generalisation* and *analytic abstractions*. An analytic abstraction identifies common features of objects which enable us to put them in the same class irrespective of other differences; the resulting class is a generalisation. For example, we can place all organisations that produce goods for sale on the market as economic organisations – 'economic organisation' becomes a class of institution. If we look at another aspect of the same organisation, we might be able to classify it as a social organisation or a cultural organisation. Descriptive theory is concerned with setting up such general classifications, and not with identifying causal mechanisms. Parsons's structural-functionalism is the main example, and these points will become clearer in the next chapter. For the moment it is sufficient to point out that without any account of causal processes and mechanisms, it is possible to make any one class more important than the others without any decisive reason to do so. It is also possible to develop the scheme of classification to take account of anything anyone might suggest. It is rather like a jigsaw puzzle where the pieces can be put together in any order, and sections added or taken away, without the final picture looking any more or less complete. It is in fact in its identification of causal processes, giving priority to one thing rather than another, that a theory gains its explanatory impact and forms a coherent whole.

The way in which social theory is caught up in the modern world has exacerbated these lines of fragmentation. The fragmentation of our experience itself has, I think, led to a general scepticism about the possibility of explanations, of a totalising theory, and this in turn has led to theory concerning itself with description; I see Giddens's structuration theory as the most recent example of this, but it applies as well to postmodernist theory, the development of 'neofunctionalism,' and symbolic interactionism. Beyond this, I think (and I am not sure whether this is crude Marxism or crude Craibism) that while societies and institutions have developed in such a way that they seem beyond human control, we have reacted, in theory and in everyday life, by persuading ourselves that we have more power over our everyday lives. We might not be able to create a just society, but we can look after our health and, in phantasy, live for ever. The growth area in social theory has been in theories of social action, which see people as creating societies rather than vice versa, and post-structuralist theories of discourse which, in effect, say that we create our world by the way we think and talk about it. Theories of society, social structure, have changed in the sense of becoming more limited.

THE PLAN OF THE BOOK

There are ways of oversimplifying the development of social theory, making out that despite the number of theories, there is none the less a steady and coherent development to the discipline. I do not think this is the case: we can trace, in general terms, a pattern of development, but this seems to me to have much more to do with what is going on in the world around us than with any increasing logical coherence and development in sociology.

Thus, it is possible to argue that there are three periods in the development of social theory since the Second World War (see Kilminster, 1991). The first, until the 1960s, was dominated by Parsons's structural-functionalism, but in the USA symbolic interactionism, despite the fact that Parsons incorporated it into his synthesis, still provided an alternative, together with a radical tradition represented by C. Wright-Mills; and in Britain conflict theory, which would often accept elements of structural-functionalism, provided another alternative. The tendency was to divide sociological theory into 'consensus' and 'conflict', but it was not always clear what belonged where.

This first period coincided with a time of comparative stability and increasing affluence in Western societies. The explosion of political conflict and change which started in the 1960s produced a corresponding explosion of sociological theories. In the USA various schools appeared, centred on understanding the social world through the eyes and activities of the social actor; ethnomethodology has proved the most lasting of these, although this period also saw

increased attention to work from the European philosophical traditions of phenomenology and existentialism, and the British tradition
of analytical philosophy. There was also a rebirth of Marxism in
Anglo-Saxon academic life. There have always been national Marx-
isms – the theory has developed in different ways in different political
contexts, and four or five different varieties of Marxist thought have
fed into the mainstream of English-language social theory. By far the
most important of these have been the French and German
traditions. In Britain the rebirth of Marxism came through the
translation into English of the work of the French philosopher Louis
Althusser; interest in Althusser's work, and the work of his pupils
and associates, brought with it and encouraged an interest in the
tradition of thought known as structuralism. Althusser's Marxism was
not the only variant of structuralism, which inspired work in
anthropology and the sociology of culture. Structuralism was always a
source of lively debate, and over the years many of its original
propositions have been turned on their heads with development of
thought now labelled post-structuralist and postmodernist.

In the USA, where it became attached to the earlier radical
tradition, and to a lesser extent in Britain, the German
Marxist tradition took root. Sometimes known as the Marxism of the
Frankfurt School, sometimes simply as critical theory, this represented a school of thought that originated with Hegel, who was a
crucial influence on Marx himself. Originally this generated a greater
interest in Hegel's thought, but this school has also undergone
significant transformations, particularly in the work of Jürgen Habermas. Habermas's work has opened up yet another philosophical
tradition to social thought: hermeneutics. Hermeneutics was original-
ly a product of debates about how to interpret sacred religious texts,
but it can now be taken as a general theory of interpretation.

The result of this explosion is still with us, in that the range and
depth of theories available to the sociologist is much greater than it
was in the 1950s and 1960s. The intense and often bitter debate
which was a background to the first edition of this book has, however,
subsided with the reduction in political conflict in the USA and
Europe, the re-establishment of right-wing governments and, over
recent years, the apparent collapse of communist societies. Of the
major traditions, Marxism has been most affected by these developments. With the waning of conflict, a potential theoretical synthesis
has emerged with Anthony Giddens's development of structuration

theory. I shall argue that it is not a synthesis, but if it were, it would be remarkable for its looseness, since it allows space for most of the theoretical traditions discussed in this book to continue in their own way; the only exception is functionalism.

As with the first edition of this book, I have not attempted to give an account of each type of theory at work in sociology. The aim, rather, is to give an initial insight into the most widely read and influential modern theorists. One theme that remains the same is that of fragmentation. I indicated above that this book will be organised around different schools or streams of theory. I think each can be seen as fragmented around the 'fault lines' I have just been discussing. Mainstream or traditional sociological theory, structural-functionalism, rational choice theory, symbolic interactionism, ethnomethodology, structuration theory, are analytic and descriptive theories that share the same basic assumption: that the proper object of sociology is social action. They then tend to generalise descriptions of social action to descriptions of social structure. Structuralism, as its name implies, tends to do the opposite – generalise explanations of social structures to agents, and the real problems of the approach arise when it does so. Finally, critical theory and hermeneutics tend to work in the same way as social action theories, but they maintain some idea of social structure existing over and above individuals: the two are brought together, but only to fall apart again.

NOTES

1. Marx, K. (1966) *Capital*, vol. 3, Lawrence & Wishart, London, p. 817.

FURTHER READING

Types of social theory

In the 1970s, there was a debate about different types of sociologies which, although dated, still provides a useful starting point for coming to grips with theory. Dawe and Benton are particularly useful. Kilminster presents a modern overview and Marshall a survey of important empirical sociology. Alexander offers a good survey.

Albrow, M. (1974) 'Dialectical and categorical paradigms of a science of society', *Sociological Review*, vol. 22, no. 2, pp. 183–201.

Alexander, J. (1987) *Sociological Theory Since 1945*, Hutchinson, London.

Benton, E. (1978) 'How many sociologies?', *Sociological Review*, vol. 26, no. 2, pp. 217–36.

Corrigan, P. (1975) 'Dichotomy vs. contradiction: On "society as construct and construction". Remarks on the doctrine of the two sociologies', *Sociological Review*, vol. 23, no. 2, pp. 211–43.

Dawe, A. (1970) 'The two sociologies', *British Journal of Sociology*, vol. 21, pp. 207–18.

Friedrichs, R. W. (1972) *A Sociology of Sociology*, The Free Press, New York.

Kilminster, R. (1991) 'Structuration theory as a world-view', in C. G. A. Bryant and D. Jary (eds), *Giddens' Theory of Structuration: A critical appreciation*, Routledge, London, pp. 74–115.

Marshall, G. (1990) *In Praise of Sociology*, Unwin Hyman, London.

It will become apparent later that Anthony Giddens has a particular axe to grind, but his version of the development of social theory is particularly important. See especially:

Giddens, A. (1977) 'Four myths in the history of social thought', in *Studies in Social and Political Theory*, Hutchinson, London, pp. 208–34.

Giddens, A. (1982) 'Classical social theory and the origins of modern sociology', in *Profiles and Critiques in Modern Social Theory*, Polity Press, Oxford, pp. 40–67.

Giddens, A. (1987) *Social Theory and Modern Sociology*, Polity Press, Oxford.

The affective and normative dimensions of theory

The most interesting work on this was produced by the political upheavals of the 1960s; the only area in which this is continued outside of specific traditions is in the area of feminist theory. Alvin Gouldner's book is the classic statement from the early period.

Craib, I. (1987) 'The psychodynamics of theory', *Free Associations*, no. 10, pp. 32–58.

Dawe, A. (1973) 'The role of experience in the construction of social theory: An essay in reflexive sociology', *Sociological Review*, vol. 21, no. 1, pp. 25–55.

Gouldner, A. W. (1971) *The Coming Crisis of Western Sociology*, Heinemann, London.

Oakley, A. (1974) *The Sociology of Housework*, Martin Robertson, London (ch. 1).

Wallace, R. (1989) *Feminism and Sociological Theory*, Sage, London.

THE SOCIAL AND NATURAL SCIENCES: REALISM

Most of the reading in this section is quite difficult. Keat and Urry's *Social Theory as Science* provides the most accessible survey of the arguments. Of Bhaskar's work, *The Possibility of Naturalism*, chs 2 and 3, are particularly important and rather more accessible than the rest of his work. *Reclaiming Reality* offers a good general survey. The debates in Lakatos and Musgrave illustrate a range of alternative positions.

Benton, E. (1977) *Philosophical Foundations of the Three Sociologies*, Routledge & Kegan Paul, London.

Benton, E. (1981) 'Realism and social science', *Radical Philosophy*, no. 27, pp. 13–21.

Bhaskar, R. (1978) *A Realist Theory of Science*, Harvester Press, Sussex, 2nd edn.

Bhaskar, R. (1979) *The Possibility of Naturalism*, Harvester Press, Sussex.

Bhaskar, R. (1980) 'Scientific explanation and human emancipation', *Radical Philosophy*, no. 26, pp. 16–28.

Bhaskar, R. (1989) *Reclaiming Reality: A critical introduction to contemporary philosophy*, Verso, London.

Harré, R. and Madden, E. H. (1975) *Causal Powers*, Basil Blackwell, Oxford.

Keat, R. and Urry, J. (1975) *Social Theory as Science*, Routledge & Kegan Paul, London.

Kuhn, T. (1970) *The Structure of Scientific Revolutions* (2nd edn), University of Chicago Press, Chicago.

Lakatos, I. and Musgrave, A. (eds) (1970) *Criticism and the Growth of Knowledge*, Cambridge University Press, Cambridge.

Outhwaite, W. (1987) *New Philosophies of Social Science*, Macmillan, Basingstoke.

PART II

THEORIES OF SOCIAL ACTION

INTRODUCTION

Part II will be concerned with theories of social action – or persons or agents. In fact, it covers most of what one might call mainstream sociological theory in a general mapping rather than a detailed exposition. Chapter 3 deals with structural-functionalism, the work of Talcott Parsons, some of his earlier critics, and more recent developments of his ideas. Parsons's work dominated social theory for several decades, and without doubt he is the most sophisticated and comprehensive theorist of this tradition. His theory is a model for the totalising ambitions of sociological theory as a whole, and one of its most interesting features is the way many of his critics can be reincorporated into it – all that is needed is a change of emphasis, a slight shift in direction. I will be arguing that it fragments as it crosses the border between human action and social systems, and the chapters that follow – on rational choice theory, symbolic interactionism, phenomenological sociology and ethnomethodology – deal with approaches which deny that a society can exist over and above the individuals who make it up, or at least maintain an ambivalent attitude to such an idea. Yet they all, in some way, assume the existence of such a society, and it always seems to be possible to overcome the problems of one theory by moving to another.

The final chapter in this part of the book looks at Anthony Giddens's structuration theory, perhaps one of the most remarkable developments in sociology over the last twenty years – or even the last ten years, for when I wrote the first edition of this book, it was by no means clear to me that Giddens was offering anything very different to what already existed in the tradition of Weberian and conflict sociology. What marks out structuration theory is the combination of, on the one hand, a rejection of functional or structural explanations and, on the other, an attempt to develop a theory which can still deal with societies or social systems. I will be arguing that Giddens does not succeed in this, leaving us with a very general theory that, in his historical sociology, also assumes, implicitly, the very idea of society that he is trying to reject.

The range of theories here, and their development – particularly the development of neofunctionalism and structuration theory – indicate a major theme in this book: the apparent difficulty of developing and holding on to a theory of a society as a whole in the classical sense that we can find in the work of both Durkheim and Marx. Paradoxically, behind many rejections of such an idea, the existence of society is implicitly assumed.

Chapter 3

PARSONS: THEORY AS A
FILING SYSTEM

Structural-functionalism

INTRODUCTION

Talcott Parsons dominated English-language social theory from the end of World War II until the mid 1960s. He produced an immense theoretical framework that claimed, in principle, to be capable of embracing everything in the social world. The basis of the system was laid during the economic crises of the 1930s. Alvin Gouldner, in *The Coming Crisis of Western Sociology* (1970), argues that in fact it was developed as a response to the challenge of Marxism: whereas Marxism was a general theory of society which condemned capitalism, structural-functionalism was to become a general theory of society which did not so much justify capitalism (although it often did) as offer an explanation and understanding of its difficulties without condemning it. As we shall see, this is achieved by seeing difficulties as part of an evolutionary process leading to greater stability and integration. Perhaps luckily for Parsons, capitalism responded in an appropriate way after World War II, and the period during which he dominated sociology corresponded with a period of comparative stability and economic expansion. Both the theory and capitalism began to run into difficulties again in the late 1960s, and within ten years it seemed that Parsons's theory was of purely historical interest. Since Parsons's death in 1979, however, there has been a major revival of interest amongst younger American sociologists in the United States, and there is now a flourishing 'neo-functionalist' school in existence.

Parson's work is notoriously difficult to understand – because of its complication rather than its profundity, I would suggest. Reading him, I am sometimes made to think of a filing clerk who is too intelligent for his work. To exercise his intelligence and overcome his frustration, he develops a new and complicated system which has a place for every document ever used by his firm. The problem is that he is the only person who can work it, and without him nothing can be found.

In his early work Parsons set out to bring together the different streams of nineteenth- and early-twentieth-century social thought into one comprehensive synthesis. There are still debates about the accuracy of his interpretations, and critics frequently point out that he barely mentioned Marx. For our present purposes the most important feature of this synthesis is that it brings together the 'holistic' and 'individualistic' theories of social action associated with the names of Durkheim and Weber, respectively, amongst the founding fathers of sociology. For Weber, sociology should be concerned with the actions of individuals directed towards each other (i.e. social action). Such action can be seen as sets of means employed to achieve particular goals – practical purposes or the realisation of some ultimate value, or a combination of both. It must be understood in terms of the meanings which individuals give to it. Durkheim was also concerned with meanings, but he saw the most important meanings as having an existence over and above individuals. They comprised a 'collective conscience' into which individuals had to be socialised. Thus both are concerned with meanings – with people's ideas – but one starts with the individual, one with the social whole. Both are theories of ideas and actions – of persons.

Here we can find Parsons's main themes. First, he sees the social world in terms of people's ideas, particularly their norms and values. Norms are the socially accepted rules which people employ in deciding on their actions; values can best be described as their beliefs about what the world should be like, and they too have a determining effect on people's actions. The most important social processes are seen as the communication of meaning, of symbols and information. Secondly, he is concerned with the organisation of individual actions into systems of action, with employing the holistic and individualistic approaches at the same time.

The idea of a system gives us the crucial analogy or metaphor in Parsons's theory: that of the biological organism or living system. He pushes this further than a simple analogy: he does not stop at saying that social life is *like* a living system, he says that it *is* a living system of a particular type. The problem with this will emerge later, but it is fair to say that it is always dangerous to push an analogy too far: there is a world of difference between saying 'My love is *like* a red, red rose' and saying 'My love *is* a red, red rose.' The idea of social life as a system – a network of different parts – explains the 'structural' part of the structural-functionalist label that is usually attached to Parsons's work. The analogy with a biological system explains the 'functionalist' part. If we take the human body as a system, it can be seen as having certain needs – for example, food – and a number of interrelated parts (the digestive system, the stomach, the intestines, etc.) which function to meet those needs. Parsons sees a social system of action as having needs which must be met if it is to survive, and a number of parts which function to meet those needs. All living systems are seen as tending towards equilibrium, a stable and balanced relationship between the different parts, and maintaining themselves separately from other systems (a tendency to 'boundary maintenance').

Parsons's emphasis is always on stability and order, and indeed, he sees social theory as attempting to answer the question 'How is social order possible?' – a problem often associated with the philosopher Thomas Hobbes, who formulated it in its clearest form. It presupposes that in the 'natural state' human beings are entirely self-seeking, that there is a war of all against all, and this natural tendency has to be moulded and limited by social organisation.

THE GRAND THEORY

Parsons's idea of theory

Parsons describes himself as an 'incurable theorist'; certainly his style conveys the sense of a terminal case. He has a particular idea of what a theory is, and this explains some of the difficulty. The world we can see is confused and confusing, and to make sense of it we must use our general ideas to organise it. Assuming that the real world is a system, the first step is to organise our general ideas into a systematic

and ordered body of abstract concepts. Only after we have done this
will we be able to make propositions about the world. An abstract
concept is a generalisation which emphasises something important
about the world. Such concepts abound in everyday life. The concept
of 'red', for example, can be seen as an abstraction from all the red
things we see around us. Now the logical ordering of abstract
concepts is not the same thing as talking about the world we can see
around us, and if this is kept in mind, then Parsons becomes
marginally easier to read.   From Parsons's point of view, the first
test for such a theory is its logical coherence. If it is, as he intends it
to be, a logically coherent theory of social science, then it should
bring together all that we already know about the social world, and
much of his work is concerned with translating other theories and
research results into his own terms, to show that they fit. The
assumption is one we will meet again: that despite appearances the
social world is organised in a logical, rational way, and a logical,
rational theory is therefore most likely to be right. Eventually, this can
be confirmed by developing testable propositions from the theory,
but that stage is some way off.

The unit act and the system of action: institutionalisation

In *The Structure of Social Action*, originally published in 1937, Parsons
argued that all the major theorists he examined could be seen as
moving towards what he called a 'voluntaristic theory of action', in
which human beings were conceived of as making choices about –
deciding between – different goals and means to achieve them. Such
a conception could be the foundation of all the human sciences, and
he suggested that it was possible to distil from their work a basic
model of human action, defining all its components in abstract terms.
This model comprises, first, the human actor and, second, a range of
goals or ends between which the actor must choose, and different
means by which these ends may be reached – again, the actor has to
choose between them. However, the choices are not made in a
vacuum. The environment is made up of a number of physical and
social factors which limit the range of choices: for example, my
eyesight is not good enough to enable me to become an airline pilot,
and in the current economic situation I cannot choose to be an
engineer because no engineering jobs are available. Most important

of all, the environment includes generally accepted norms and values and other ideas which influence our choice of goals and means. If I am a Roman Catholic and a gynaecologist I will not specialise in abortion, even if the option is open to me; similarly, I am not able to break the informal rules that govern relationships with my colleagues (e.g. about attendance at the university) without suffering punitive criticism. The most formal and universal norms are set out in a society's legal system – I always have the option of murdering my students when they hand in late work, but I am unlikely to take it, not only because I think it is morally wrong, but because there is a likelihood of severe punishment.

The 'unit act', then, is made up of an actor, means, goals, and an environment which comprises physical and social objects and norms and values. This is an abstract description of all action and the starting point of Parsons's immense scheme, most of which can be unravelled from here. The task of the social scientist is to make sense of the ways choices are made within the constraints I have just discussed. Now Parsons is not concerned just with individual action but also with systems of action, and as his theory developed, so did his idea of a system. Amongst the social objects in the actors' environment are other actors, and for Parsons a system of action is made up of relationships between actors. The emphasis of Parsons's work here changes from voluntarism, from looking at the individual actors' choices, to looking at the way systems of action limit and even determine individual choices. This has been the focus for a number of criticisms, to which I will return later. For the moment, I want to look at the way in which Parsons develops the idea of the unit act to a conception of the *social system*. This is built up around the norms and values that, together with other actors, make up part of the actors' environment. He assumes that each actor aims for maximum gratification, and if she engages in interaction with another and receives gratification, the interaction will be repeated. Each actor will come to expect certain responses from the other, and so social rules or norms will develop, together with generally accepted values, which help to guarantee those responses. A simple example would be a love affair which develops into a marriage. As the partners gain gratification from each other, so they come to expect each other to continue to act in the way which supplies gratification. The marriage will develop its own informal, and perhaps even formal, rules of behaviour. Each may come to expect the other to tolerate minor adulteries, or to share equally in the household chores, and each will come to regard this as an obligation. Both may come to believe in the 'sanctity of marriage', although before the wedding, both may have laughed at the idea.

Reverting to Parsons's terminology, a system of 'status roles' develops – a network of positions to which expectations of behaviour (and rewards and sanctions for fulfilling or not fulfilling those expectations) are attached. This process is called *institutionalisation* – a solidifying of relationships over time in such a way that the behaviour attached to each status role remains constant whoever is occupying it. Society as a whole, and different institutions in society, may be considered as a network of status roles, each governed by established norms and values.

The social system is not the only system contained in embryonic form in the unit act. The description of the process of institutionalisation and the development of the social system which I have just described presupposes three other systems. It presupposes an actor who aims for maximum gratification (i.e. a personality system); it presupposes, as far as society as a whole is concerned, a system of wider values which give coherence to the different norms attached to different status roles (i.e. a cultural system); and it presupposes a physical environment to which society must adapt (i.e. a biological organism). This is where the filing system requires at least sixty-four new filing cabinets. I will not bother with all of them.

Systems and subsystems: functional prerequisites

For Guy Rocher (1974) Parsons's theory is like 'a set of Chinese boxes – when one is opened, it contains a smaller one, which contains a smaller one still, and so on'. This is an apt description. I said above that Parsons's concepts – unit, act, status roles, social system, etc. – were abstractions, and there are different levels of abstraction. Going back to the example of red: there is a higher-level abstraction ('colour') of which red is one type, lower-level abstractions (dark red, light red, pink, etc.), and lower-lower-level abstractions, which involve adding other qualities (dark red and round). The process can be continued until we are describing a unique object (the dark red round rubber object of six inches in diameter on the floor in front of me – in other words, 'this ball'). Here there is an insight into the difficulty of Parsons's theory – much of it is equivalent to describing this ball as 'the dark red . . . etc.'.

By talking about the development of status roles and the social system, we have arrived somewhere above the middle level of abstraction. It is possible to distinguish at least the following levels:

1. The highest level: all living systems. Sometimes Parsons writes as if living systems are a subsystem of *all* systems (i.e. everything), but that is not important for our present purposes.
2. Second-highest level: systems of action, including everything in the unit act.
3. Third-highest level: the subsystems of action; the personality, cultural, biological and social systems.
4. Fourth-highest level: subsystems of subsystems. The subsystems of the social system are the political system, the socialisation system, the economy and the 'societal community' (I will explain this shortly).
5. Fifth-highest level: subsystems of subsystems of subsystems. The most clearly worked out at this level belong to the economy: the economic commitments subsystem, the capitalisation subsystem, the production subsystem, the organisational subsystem.

Presumably the process could go on *ad infinitum*, but I will concern myself only with levels 3 and 4. The first question to ask is why at each stage we find four new subsystems, and the answer brings Parsons's functionalism into play. He argues that any system, at whatever level, must satisfy four needs or requirements if it is to survive, and in each case a specialist subsystem is developed to meet each requirement. These four requirements, or *functional prerequisites*, are as follows:

1. Each system must adapt to its environment (*adaptation*).
2. Each system must have a means of mobilising its resources in order to achieve its goals and thus obtain gratification (*goal attainment*).
3. Each system must maintain the internal co-ordination of its parts and develop ways of dealing with deviance – in other words, it must keep itself together (*integration*).
4. Each system must maintain itself as nearly as possible in a state of equilibrium – the examples below and later should distinguish this from 3 above (*pattern maintenance*).

Table 3.1 shows which subsystem fulfils which functional prerequisite for the general system of action and the social system.

Table 3.1   Subsystems fulfilling functional prerequisites

Major system	Adaptation	Goal attainment	Integration	Pattern maintenance
The general system of action (described in the 'unit act')	The *biological organism*, which provides the link between the physical world and the meanings (norms, values, etc.) that make up the world of action	The *personality system*, which is formed by socialisation in such a way that it internalises general cultural values and societal norms. It thus becomes the instrument through which the major system achieves its goals	The *social system* of status roles governed by norms which define which actions are or are not allowable	The *cultural system* – the most general ideas, ideals and values of the major system, made more concrete in the norms of the social system and internalised in the personality system
The social system	The *economy*, the link between social organisation and the physical world or nature	The *political system* – including *all* forms of decision-making and resource mobilisation	The '*societal community*' – the institutions of social control – ranging from the legal system to informal rules of conduct	The *socialisation processes*, by means of which individuals are educated into the cultural values and societal norms of the system

To sum up: the unit act contains, in embryonic form, four subsystems which can be seen as developing through a process of institutionalisation; each subsystem has further subsystems of its own. At each level, the subsystems develop to meet four needs or functional prerequisites which must be met if the system is to survive. It is more important to get the general idea of all this rather than the detail.

Ways of analysing action: the pattern variables

Before moving on to look at how all this works, I want to deal briefly with one other set of variables – what Parsons calls the *pattern variables*. These illustrate even more emphatically the classifying power of his thought – on my tentative calculation, we now need 512 filing cabinets and we have not yet reached the lowest level of abstraction, and no information about the real world has yet been collected. More importantly, they bring together two different concerns in his work: the voluntaristic theory of action, concerned with individual choices, and systems theory. Both individual actions and system organisation can be seen as choosing between alternatives; remember from the original discussion of the unit act that all action involves choice. There are four major pairs of alternatives:

1. Particularism–universalism: I may treat an object as a specific, unique object, or as one of a general class – the difference between the way I treat my children and my students.
2. Affective–affectively neutral: I may allow the full range of my feelings to come into play in a relationship (my children) or I might maintain neutral feelings (my students).
3. Quality–performance: I might value an object for its own sake (my children) or for what can be done with it, its instrumental potentiality (my students).
4. Diffuseness–specificity: I might be involved in a total relationship to all aspects of an object (my children) or I might be concerned with only one activity in the relationship (my students).

This is as far as I want to go in elaborating the filing system as such; the pattern variables will not reappear until I discuss the criticisms that can be made of structural-functionalism. I have included them because they illustrate certain important features of Parsons's theory. For the time being, I want to return to systems and the relationships between them.

The cybernetic hierarchy

I said in the Introduction to Part II that Parsons's theory of social action is also a theory of meanings – of norms, values, symbols and communication. For Parsons the various systems are related through the exchange of symbolic information. A symbol is seen as something valuable not in itself but because of what can be done with it. Money is the clearest example: a coin is near to worthless as a metal object; it is valuable only because we can use it to buy things. Each subsystem of the social system has its equivalent symbol: the economy itself deals in money, the political system in power, in the societal community it is influence, and in the socialisation system, commitment. Through exchanging symbolic resources, each system remains in equilibrium with the others, whilst maintaining its own identity – maintaining its boundaries.

There is more than this to the exchanges between systems, however. Here we go back to the analogy between systems of action and all living systems – in fact *all* systems, because Parsons draws on cybernetics, the science of systems. This suggests that any system is controlled by that subsystem which is the highest on information and lowest on energy, and we can thus construct a hierarchy of subsystems, the lowest being that which has most energy but least information. Parsons himself provides the useful example of a washing machine in which the controlling timing mechanism, which has a great deal of programmed information, uses very little energy (electricity) compared with the working parts it controls. Thus the lower subsystems push energy up through the system, the higher controlling subsystems pass information back down. We can thus order the different subsystems described in Table 3.1 in the manner shown in Table 3.2.

This ordering of systems, together with the postulate that all systems tend towards equilibrium, does – finally – enable us to approach the real world and organise it to some effect. We can put the filing system to work. We can also talk about causal mechanisms: first, the idea of a 'homeostatic loop', where change in one subsystem affects the others, which in turn react back on the first and restore the

Table 3.2 The cybernetic hierarchy

The general system of action		The social system
The cultural system	High on information	The socialisation system
The social system	High on information	The societal community
The personality system	High on energy	The political system
The biological organism	High on energy	The economic system

original situation. And, secondly, a 'feedback' mechanism, whereby those subsystems 'high' on information use that information selectively to control subordinate subsystems.

I have not described Parsons's system in anything like its full complexity – a number of the subsystems that I have only mentioned are analysed in much greater detail, and there are other aspects to the theory. However, I hope I have dealt with enough aspects to convey a general idea of the enterprise without causing too many nervous breakdowns.

Structural-functionalist explanations: change and modernity

In the following examples, I will be using the term 'explain' loosely; it will emerge later that the ability of Parsons's system to explain rather than describe is a major issue for critics. Parsons presents an evolutionary theory of change, drawing again on the analogy with biological organisms, this time on the way a cell divides and multiplies. Most people will have seen, at some time, a film taken through a microscope of a cell dividing into two and then four, and so on. For Parsons, the development of human society can be seen in the same way. Simple societies can be regarded as the single cell, which divides first into the four subsystems of the general system of action and then, in turn, each of these divides. This process involves three stages: the new subsystem differentiates itself, the new arrangement goes through a process of adaptation and reintegration, and finally there is the establishment of a more general system of values at the highest cybernetic level – a system of values which embraces the new subsystem.

A more specific example can be taken from Parsons himself: the transition from agriculture-based peasant societies to industrial societies. This involves the separation of the economic from the socialisation system. Whereas in pre-industrial societies the family unit was also the main unit of production, the family holding and working the land together – albeit with some division of labour – industrialisation separated work into factories and offices whilst family life became confined to the home. For this separation to be successful, Parsons argues that it must have greater adaptive capacity; work is carried out more efficiently and rationally in the new industrial units and productivity increases, whilst the family fulfils its socialisation functions more efficiently when it is stripped of its economic functions. The process of integration involves the co-ordination of the two subsystems (presumably such developments as the laws prohibiting women and children from certain occupations) and the development of a new economic hierarchy of control, since the father of the family no longer fulfils that role.[1] Both subsystems must be integrated into the wider societal and political communities, and finally the value system must develop to include the new status roles: the father stripped of some previous power, the new industrial managers, and so on.

A more recent example comes from an article Parsons wrote on American youth and youth subcultures (1964). In general terms he argues that the twentieth century is a period of remarkable historical change, and there are reasons why youth in particular should experience the strains of such change. The strains are seen in terms of *anomie* – a state in which values and norms are no longer clear, or have lost their relevance. The explanation begins with the cultural: a paradoxical feature of the American value system is that at its centre is the value of individual success and achievement. The paradox is that in the pursuit of this value, structural differentiation is hastened, society becomes more complex more quickly, and lower-level value patterns become outdated. At the same time, increased complexity means that individual achievement has to be limited by specialisation and co-operation.

There are various ways in which youth is made problematic by this process. Training and education take much longer, so during the period when they might once have moved into adulthood, young people are kept dependent on the family, despite the fact that at the centre of their lives are people of the same age outside the family, the 'peer group'. The increased specialisation has isolated the nuclear family and young children are thus made more dependent on it, and this can create problems later when it is time to begin leaving the family. Traditional ties are weakened by the increased complexity of social relations, and this is reflected in changes in sexual behaviour, where the contrast with traditional values is most marked.

In this context, youth subcultures have destructive and progressive functions. On the one hand they can be simply rebellious, rejecting traditional values and the central value system and offering nothing in their place. They can also be means by which the traditional value systems are transformed and brought up to date and new values established, and they provide social support for the individual in the long period when she has outgrown her own family but is not in a position to form a family of her own. Most youth subcultures in fact display both aspects, and both are likely to entail conflict.

Thus change and conflict are explained in terms of continuing evolutionary adjustment of different subsystems to each other. This analysis encapsulates the tensions of the modern world: it involves living in larger and larger communities, undergoing constant differentiation and acting rationally, orientated only by the most universal norms and values; the attempt to find a specific individual and communal identity in this context is not only an explanation of youth culture.

CRACKS IN THE GRAND THEORY

I said above that Parsons developed the most comprehensive and worked-out form of action theory, and there is a sense in which the other variants may be seen as fragments of his system. Now I want to look at the main fault lines along which this fragmentation occurs. In the period up to his death, there were three main lines of criticism. Many critics distinguish between the logical and substantive problems with the theory, but I do not think this is very helpful: a logical problem in a theory's explanation is also a sign that it misconceives what it is trying to explain. There are also a number of common criticisms that boil down to saying that the theory does not generate testable propositions about the world; this might be true, but as I have pointed out before, this is not the only criterion by which theories can be judged, and in the case of the social world, complexity and the inability to experiment make the formation of testable hypotheses very difficult.

Here, I will concentrate on the imaginative or creative aspect of the theory, the employment of the biological systems analogy, on the generalisation from action (persons) to system (societies) and the explanatory power of the theory.

Structural-functionalism as Utopia: the problems of conflict and change

It was often argued that Parsons's model of social life, with its emphasis on equilibrium, balanced exchange and functional relationships, cannot make sense of social change and conflict. Dahrendorf likened it to a literary Utopia, a vision of a perfectly good or perfectly bad society, a world of balance, with no sense of history and without any source of change inside the society. Such criticism is frequently extended to argue that the theory has an in-built conservative bias: inequalities of wealth (social stratification) are seen as functional, an efficient way of keeping the system going, as are differences in status; power is distributed in the way that is most functional for achieving the system's goals; everything is perfect.

I deliberately employed the example of historical change and youth subcultures to illustrate that this sort of criticism is misguided. In fact, throughout the time when Parsons was writing, others were using the same framework to understand change. Robert Merton, for example, argued that the emphasis on functional unity and equilibrium tends to direct attention away from questions about the *degree* of unity and equilibrium and the processes by which they come about. He also made important distinctions between manifest and latent functions (similar to that between intended and unintended consequences) and function and dysfunction (the opposite of function), both of which can be deployed to make sense of change and conflict. Alvin Gouldner (1970) pointed out that system integration may involve anything from complete dependence of the parts on each other to comparative independence. Both writers tended towards a less general level of theorising than Parsons. Merton called it middle-range theory, dealing with different parts of the system rather than the system as a whole. Finally, Lewis Coser, in *The Functions of Social Conflict* (1956), argues that the occurrence of social conflict can be seen as having a vital integrating effect through releasing tension and setting in motion a chain of adjustments; this is along the same lines as the youth-culture example.

If Parsons takes the analogy between a social system and a biological system to its extreme, these criticisms – particularly those of Merton and Gouldner – can be seen as drawing back from identifying the two and exploring the differences.

Teleological and functional explanations

The important criticisms seem to me to have to do with structural-functionalism's failure, at least in Parsons's theory, to explore the differences between biological, living systems and social systems: it results precisely in a generalisation of a theory of persons to a theory of societies. Persons are, amongst other things, biological organisms; it does not automatically follow that the same is true of societies.

One line of argument is that we cannot claim that social systems have needs which must be met in order to survive. Parsons's critics argue that in practice this is meaningless. To establish that it is true, we would need examples of societies which did not survive and we would have to show that they did not meet all the functional requisites. Now excluding very simple societies, it is difficult to find an example. It seems that what usually happens is that a society less well adapted to its environment is absorbed through military or economic conquest by a better-adapted society. It does not disappear but remains, perhaps in a modified form, as part of the better-adapted society. Thus some native American tribes were wiped out by military conquest, but others remain today as a clearly identifiable part of American society. The difference between those that were wiped out and those that survived seems to depend as much on the political processes of the conquering whites as on anything else; and the sense in which those that remain have 'survived' is itself debatable. An even clearer example is the way in which peasant agriculture in South and Latin America has been integrated into the industrial system of North America and Europe. In fact the Parsonian position would be tenable only if different societies were like different animal species battling for survival: only the fittest would survive.

Second, the critics argue that to say that a social system has needs does not explain how those needs are met. It might be true, for example, that modern industrial societies need complicated education systems. Yet Britain, France and America, all societies at approximately the same evolutionary stage, have different education systems. A need can be met in any number of ways, and simply stating its existence does not explain anything about how it is met. Third, Anthony Giddens argues, against functionalism, that proper explanations involve reference to actors and actions, and that functionalist explanations can be rewritten in such terms. Thus, to explain the existence of something by the function it fulfils is to make a nonsense of the idea of cause. A function is not fulfilled until something exists. If the function is the cause of its existence, then the effect – existence – must come before the cause – the function. In other words, time seems to be reversed.

I said that the first criticism would not apply if social systems were like animal species. The second and third would not apply if social systems really were like individual actors. If a social system had sense organs that could experience the need for, say, an education system as the body can experience hunger; if the experience could be communicated to a system brain, translated into symbolic thought, pondered and analysed; if the social brain could decide what sort of education system it wants and then transmit the appropriate messages along its nervous system so that an education system were constructed, then – and only then – would these criticisms not apply. But social systems do not have needs and goals like individuals.

The difference is that the human organism is made up of parts which are not capable of independent reflective thought and are controlled by a part that is. It is only in *Peanuts* cartoons that the stomach argues with the feet and the tail demands higher status. Social systems are – according to Parsons himself – made up of parts which are capable of reflective thought as they occupy their status roles; the organic link is very different to that between parts of the body. Yet the implication that a social system is consequently different from other living systems is not taken up.

Material and normative interests

Here I want to draw on two papers by David Lockwood, written during the period when Parsons was the dominant figure in sociology. In the present context, they emphasise the difference between persons and societies by pointing to features of the social world which exist but cannot be understood by structural-functionalism.

I have emphasised throughout that at the centre of Parsons's theory are meanings: norms and values, around which the action system and the social system are organised. Lockwood suggests that there is another factor at work in social life, what he calls the 'material substratum':

> the factual disposition of means in the situation of action which structures differential (life-chances) and produces interests of a non-normative kind – that is interests other than those which actors have in conforming with the normative definition of the situation. (Lockwood, 1964: 284)

Thus social life is structured by people's access to goods and property and the life which goes with the possession of goods and property. For example, it is possible to argue that the distribution of property (including skills) is such in both Britain and the USA that blacks have different material interests to whites. The white material interest might be in maintaining a system of racial discrimination which keeps blacks out of certain types of jobs, and this might outweigh adherence to a core system of social values which includes racial equality. Similarly it might be suggested, with some evidence in support, that people go to work not because they adhere to a system of norms and values that says work is a good thing, but because they have a material interest – at the lowest level, that of not starving. Think about it: why do *you* work?

In a second article, Lockwood (1964) distinguishes between what he calls *social* integration, which is a matter of relationships between actors, and *system* integration, relationships between different parts of the system. We can talk about societies manifesting social or normative integration, but not manifesting system integration. An economic crisis, for example, may certainly be taken as an indication of a system imbalance, a lack of integration; however, people may still adhere to the values and norms of the society, despite the economic hardship they suffer. We can add to this the idea of material interests, and it becomes apparent that the normative system may be used to achieve certain material interests. It may be in the material interests of large business corporations to reduce the taxes they pay, necessitating cuts in government expenditure on social services. The central normative and value system – which, for example, may involve a strong belief in private enterprise and the absence of state interference – may persuade those who suffer from the cuts that those cuts are justified.

Parsons's theory, and structural-functionalism in general, seems to me to be incapable of grasping such eventualities, despite the fact that they are immediately plausible. It can see social life only as a normative and value-controlled system, not as also a 'material' system. To do that, to make a distinction between social and system integration, it is necessary to make a distinction between persons and societies.

Can structural-functionalism explain?

When I gave some examples of structural-functionalist explanation, I said that I was using the term 'explain' loosely. I have indicated some problems with functional explanation, and now I want to suggest that by its very nature the theory is descriptive rather than explanatory. This is indicated by the possibility of writing out vast complicated passages of Parsons's work and then rewriting them in common-sense language, adding to the clarity, not losing any ideas, and taking up only a few lines. C. Wright Mills does this brilliantly in *The Sociological Imagination*. It seems to me that this is possible because of the very meaning Parsons gives to theory – we break everything down into its component parts and then add them together: 'this ball' becomes the dark red round rubber object on the floor. My relationship with my employer is particularistic, affectively negative, performance-orientated and specific: I don't like her, but I'm having an affair with her in the hope of promotion.

If an explanation involves identifying causal processes and causal mechanisms, then the theory cannot explain. Its concepts – systems, subsystems, and so on – are abstractions; causal processes and mechanisms are real. If you go back to my earlier 'explanations', I think it should be clear that they are really elaborate descriptions with an element of explanation provided by the idea of a cybernetic hierarchy and a process of evolution attached to it. It might be said that Parsons is a 'cultural determinist' as opposed to Marx's economic determinism. On closer examination, however, even this is ambiguous. Wolf Heydebrand points out (1972) that the flow is two-way: energy from below, information from above; and both could be regarded as determining or causing. Taking Heydebrand's example of the police force: this must be geared to enforcing the cultural values and social norms of a society (i.e. controlled from above). At the same time its very existence depends upon an economic system which produces enough to keep a police force in existence. We cannot assign any causal priority.

I think this throws light on another criticism of Parsons already touched on several times: that as his theory develops, it changes from an individualist theory talking about actors' choices, as in the model of the unit act, to a holistic one dealing with the way systems determine actors' choices. The vast majority of his ideas, and most of his work, have been concerned with systems rather than individuals, and the criticism is usually made from the point of view of an action theory which concentrates on individual action and interaction. However, I do not think this criticism is justified. Parsons deals with both, and the importance of the pattern variables – the reason why I listed them earlier – is that they enable him to deal with both. However, he cannot do so at the same time – he must switch from one point of view to the other – and this is precisely what the different variants of action theory do: structural-functionalism and conflict theory are concerned in different ways with systems of action; symbolic interactionism and more recent variants with individual interactions. Parsons cannot give priority to one or the other; in one sense, the system is the individual writ large; in another, the individual is the system writ small. No causal priority is, or can be, assigned. Consequently, it is possible for variants of action theory to emphasise either side over the other and, indeed, for Parsons to do the same at different stages in his career.

Neofunctionalism and conflict theory

NEOFUNCTIONALISM: BREAKING OPEN THE FILING CABINETS

When Parsons died, it was common to dismiss his theory as of only historical interest. Even a sympathetic commentator like Peter Hamilton referred to him as an 'overturned patriarch' (1983). Rather like Freud's original patriarch, who was overthrown and murdered by his sons (so that they could get their hands on the women), he has come back to haunt us, in the shape of a substantial body of work known as 'neofunctionalism'. The way in which Jeffrey Alexander, the most sophisticated member of the neofunctionalist school, has dealt with the criticisms is simply to accept them. This has produced some interesting work, but it seems to me like a sort of internal fragmentation of the system: it is as if somebody has broken into Parsons's filing cabinets, jumbled up the contents and claimed that it does not matter what order the files are in.

In his introduction to *Neofunctionalism* (1985), Alexander jettisons even the minimal dimension of causal explanation involved in the idea of a cybernetic hierarchy, claiming that we should regard social development as open-ended and the result of many determinations. Neofunctionalism provides a general *descriptive* account of interrelations and uses the idea of equilibrium as a reference point, not as something that really exists in the world – equilibrium is always a moving equilibrium. Parsons's distinctions between culture, society and personality are important, as is the idea of differentiation as a mode of social change – but Alexander, unlike Parsons, is saying only that these are important, not that they provide a complete understanding of everything.

This modification and opening up of structural-functionalism is perhaps best understood in the context of Alexander's ideas about what social theory should do – what he calls its 'multi-dimensionality'. In the first volume of his massive *Theoretical Logic in Sociology* (1984), he argues that we must take into account three sets of opposites: first, theory and fact (the metaphysical and empirical dimensions of sociology); second, individual volition and collective domination; and third, normative and instrumental action. In his volume on Parsons he argues that Parsons tends to collapse the empirical and the theoretical, ignoring the collective imposition of norms and values and the material aspects of action. His big advantage is that at least he is aware of all these dimensions, and he therefore provides the starting point for good theory. This approach enables all sorts of ideas to be brought into Parsons's work: Gould (in Colomey, 1990), for example, argues that Marxism can be seen as a voluntaristic theory of action (and thus integrated into Parsons's system), and Sciulli (in Alexander, 1985) argues that we can find the basis for a critical theory in Parsons's work.

CONFLICT THEORY

The power of Alexander's thought is shown in his critique of conflict theory, the first opposition to emerge as the dominance of structural-functionalism came to an end. I suggested that structural-functionalism could take account of social conflict and change; conflict theory insists that it cannot, and in this respect I think it is simply wrong. However, it is important because the arguments it put forward have directly or indirectly informed much empirical research in sociology, particularly in the Weberian tradition. The major figures included Dahrendorf (1959) and John Rex (1961) as well as David Lockwood, whom I have already discussed.

Percy Cohen (1968: 167) represents the opposition of structural-functionalism and conflict theory as two models making a series of apparently mutually exclusive assumptions about society and social life, and this provides an excellent starting point, as shown in Table 3.3.

Apart from purposes of comparison, I have said all I want to say about the left-hand side. On the right-hand side, the key terms are evidently 'interest' and 'power', and I suggested that Lockwood's use of the concept of interest presents structural-functionalism with situations it cannot explain. I will argue that conflict theory fails to build on this; so it is open to Alexander's arguments. In the end the theory remains within the orbit of structural-functionalism, compared to which it is less systematic and less inclusive. In other words, it can be seen as a fragment of structural-functionalism.

I will concentrate on Dahrendorf's work. Dahrendorf emphasises

Table 3.3   Consensus and conflict theories

Consensus theory	Conflict theory
1. Norms and values are the basic elements of social life	Interests are the basic elements of social life
2. Social life involves commitment	Social life involves inducement and coercion
3. Societies are necessarily cohesive	Social life is necessarily divisive
4. Social life depends on solidarity	Social life generates opposition, exclusion and hostility
5. Social life is based on reciprocity and co-operation	Social life generates structural conflict
6. Social systems rest on consensus	Social life generates sectional interests
7. Society recognises legitimate authority	Social differentiation involves power
8. Social systems are integrated	Social systems are malintegrated and beset by con- tradictions
9. Social systems tend to persist	Social systems tend to change

from the beginning that his theory is not intended to replace consensus theory. Each deals with a different set of problems. Both employ the same concepts, but in opposite ways – every social element has a function, but it also has a dysfunction; consensus and coercion exist side by side. Different theories organise the same world in different ways, according to the sort of problem we want to solve. Conflict theory is just a way of looking at the world. On Friday afternoon, the world is bright and happy; on Monday morning, it is grey and miserable.

Conflict theory thus engages with no clear metaphor for building its picture of the social world. It is none the less possible to suggest one from the outside: society is like a more or less confused battleground. If we watch from on high, we can see a variety of groups fighting each other, constantly forming and re-forming, making and breaking alliances. For conflict theorists closer to

Marxism, like Rex, the groups are rather more clearly defined and the pattern of conflict is more stable; others see more of a kaleidoscope. Dahrendorf falls into this latter category.

For Dahrendorf, the biological analogy, and the idea of a social system itself, is replaced by a conception of an 'imperatively co-ordinated system'. Taken from Weber, this is, as far as I can see, a complicated term for 'authority' system or 'power' system. In some contexts, the distinction between authority and power is important: power tends towards reliance on force; authority is legitimated power – power which has achieved general recognition. In the present context, the distinction is rather less important. The crucial point is that an 'imperatively co-ordinated association' is any organisation in which authority exists (which must include practically all organisations), and that the very existence of authority (or power) creates the conditions for conflict. The starting point for looking at power and authority is not very different from Parsons's: both see it as a necessity, although Dahrendorf would not look favourably on the term 'functional prerequisite'. Both would agree that a 'function' of power is to integrate a unit, ensuring compliance where norms and values fail. But whereas Parsons emphasises the integrative aspect, power and authority meeting the needs of the whole system, Dahrendorf argues that it is also divisive, because it engenders conflicting interests and role-expectations. Power and authority are scarce resources, and those who hold them have an interest in maintaining the status quo; those who do not possess them have an interest in their redistribution, hence in changing the status quo. These, he argues, are *objective* interests, built into the roles themselves, alongside the interest or function of all roles in maintaining the organisation as a whole. The social world is thus structured into *potential* conflict groups: what Dahrendorf calls *quasi-groups*.

This is really as far as the theory goes as a theory; the next step consists of generalised empirical propositions about the conditions under which quasi-groups become conflict groups; the different conditions which result in different types of conflict; and the conditions that determine the ensuing results. Compared to structural-functionalism, then, Dahrendorf's theory is a low-level one in two parts:

1. A central theoretical proposition: that role structures generate conflicting as well as complementary interests.
2. General descriptions of conditions producing conflict.

All variants of conflict theory have a similar structure, and the reason they have generated so much empirical research is that they encourage investigation into the general descriptive statements that qualify the theoretical insight.

My own criticism of this is that it does not explain anything. If we look again at the two parts of the theory listed above, it is apparent that if we are to explain a real conflict, we have to describe the real conditions that produce it. The theoretical proposition tells us only that conflict is possible. Since it also tells us that consensus is possible, it does not tell us very much: the same thing causes opposite results. Hence we have no causal theoretical explanation at all, and we can see how the approach has directed attention to empirical research. Alexander (1987) offers a criticism of conflict theory which, I think, elaborates on this. Conflict theories are action theories – voluntaristic theories in Parsons's terms – and the explanation of social stability faces them with a dilemma: either they must explain stability by some form of coercion, giving up voluntarism, or they must embrace what he calls a 'multi-dimensionality' – that is, take into their theory all the elements of Parsons's functionalism that they want to reject. There is a sense in which Dahrendorf does this by claiming that we need one theory to explain stability and another to explain conflict, but at the same time his theory offers the possibility of explaining both. Alexander argues that the dilemma is resolved by resorting to *ad hoc* empirical factors to explain stability, thus surrendering the possibility of systematic theory. In Dahrendorf's case, he suggests, 'pluralisation' has separated authority structures in such a way as to make serious conflict less likely. Alexander points out – correctly, I think – that this moves towards Parsons's notion of differentiation. Overall, his argument is that the conflict theorists use Parsons's own biases to construct an inaccurate straw target, and that the issues they deal with can be dealt with equally well within Parsons's theory, even if Parsons himself does not deal with them. On the other hand, we cannot fit structural-functionalism into Dahrendorf's framework, simply because the latter is neither as systematic nor as wide-ranging. We can push an extra coat into a suitcase, but we can't fit a suitcase into the coat pocket. This form of conflict theory is best seen as a special case of structural-functionalism: a fragment.

NEOFUNCTIONALISM AND MODERNITY

Why should Parsons's theory open up like this and become the source of such wide-ranging work? It seems to me that there are two answers. The first is the realisation, expressed most cogently in Alexander's work, that social theory is multidimensional, and that Parsons's Grand Theory at least recognised the dimensions, together with the acknowledgement that there are multiple causal processes at work in social life. This amounts to saying that the world cannot easily be organised into a filing system with one specific key. On the other hand, the search for any sort of key seems to be surrendered – description is embraced with the assumption that causal processes can be identified empirically. The *theoretical* identification of causal mechanisms and processes seems to be lost, and we are left simply with the idea that the world is a complicated place. This leads to the second answer – that we are seeing an effect of the apparently incomprehensible nature of modernity, a part-surrender of the attempt to find any underlying coherence in the world. This has been followed through in two papers by Frank J. Lechner (in Alexander, 1985 and Robertson and Turner, 1991), who argues that Parsons was able to recognise the fundamental problems of modernity, that social action not only inherently creates order but also creates disorder, and Parsons's four dimensions of order are also dimensions of disorder. He also argues that Parsons recognised that the complexity of the modern world involves recognising and valuing a range of different interpretations of reality, yet paradoxically – or even contradictorily – implied that his theoretical system was *the* one. He aimed at a totalising system which, in effect, showed that totalising systems of thought were no longer possible. In this way, we can see the breaking down of Parsons's system as an inevitable outcome of the processes that Parsons himself was trying to understand.

The paradoxes of social theory are underlined by attempts to return to Parsons as *the* important theorist of modernity. Hoiton and Turner, for example, argue (1986) that the most striking aspect of Parsons's work is that he presents a theory of modernity which emphasises the values we must accept to make modernity work. Unlike other sociologists he does not seek, or yearn after, a return to or resurrection of pre-modern values. Following on from this, Robertson and Turner argue (1991) that Parsons should now be read as a theorist of modern capitalist societies in a situation where there is now no credible alternative to capitalism – his suggestion that the socialist nations faced disaster has proved more than the Cold War phantasy it was once taken to be.

It is also argued that Parsons now represents the 'moral high ground' of pluralistic liberalism, encouraging tolerance and openness; certainly in the USA the neofunctionalism of Alexander has become associated again with the progressive liberalism with which Parsons once associated himself. These various political interpretations of Parsons seem to me to have much more to do with the political context in which we read him than with anything inherent in his thought, but it does raise explicitly the moral/political dimension of social theory which I discussed in Chapter 2, and to which I will shortly return.

A BRIEF CONCLUSION

Parsons's system is in many ways a lesson in the activity of theorising and its dangers. Beyond this, however, it does emphasise the large-scale systematic aspects of social existence, which for a while seemed to disappear from popular forms of action theory. In fact, I suspect this is the reason why younger American sociologists have returned to it: it has its faults, but at least it is a theory of society as a whole. I have argued that the source of the main problem lies in generalising from the actor to the social system; in doing so, an understanding of the depth of individual action and the depth of society is lost, and neofunctionalism's attempts to reintroduce these dimensions involves surrendering the idea of an explanatory theory in favour of treating Parsons's categories as simply enabling description.

The system does seem to me to provide, potentially, an understanding of one realm of social existence. In Chapter 2 I mentioned an 'intermediate realm', an area of reality which displayed features of persons and societies. Organisations such as political parties, religious groups, some business enterprises, can be seen as having an independent existence and as possessing aspects of human action – goals, norms and values which unite the people involved. It might be possible to understand these organisations as forms of biological systems, and to identify with some precision the functional prerequisites, examples which disappear because they do not fulfil those prerequisites, the processes by which they are fulfilled, mechanisms of adjustment and integration, and so on. In other words, there are occasions when groups of human beings acting together (not whole societies) can be likened to other living systems, including individual human organisms, without the dangers and inadequacies I have been discussing.

One way of looking at the difficulties with structural-functionalism is in terms of the dangers of metaphor. The creative or imaginative aspect of the theory lies in its use of metaphor – social systems are like biological systems. Parsons, however, pushes this to an extreme which I pointed out above - social systems are a type of living system. There seems to me to be no reason to push the metaphor this far; to do so is to make an unjustified metaphysical assumption about the nature of the world, and I think it does serve to direct attention away from things like conflict and change. Both Merton and Gouldner can be seen as developing the metaphor further, to the stage of drawing distinctions and identifying differences between social systems and other living systems, and the neofunctionalists take this much further. Functionalist explanations that fail to do this certainly tend towards conservative bias, but this is not a necessary part of structural-functionalist theory. There is an important lesson for theoretical thinking here: metaphors and analogies serve to draw attention not only to similarities but to differences, and the latter are as important as the former.

Finally, the unjustified use of the metaphor also carries with it an endorsement of the universalistic values of the system, the commitment to modernity without, as Turner and Holton put it, 'nostalgia'. It seems to me that perhaps this is the least desirable aspect of Parsons that we should take up. I discussed social phenomena such as youth subcultures above, and the reappearance of various nationalisms in Eastern Europe indicates that the universalistic values of modernism are not by themselves sufficient to attract and hold personal commitments; nor, I suspect, should they be: they are essential for a liberal society of any sort, but by themselves they contribute to the forms of 'homelessness' that undermine liberalism. To endorse Parsons for his uncritical acceptance of modernity could leave us in the position of saying that, despite everything, the *Titanic* was a wonderful ship.

Given that the starting point is action, it seems to me that any form of action theory is likely to be incorporated into the structural-functionalist framework, especially when it gives up its main explanatory thrust; the alternative is to surrender any notion of a society as a whole existing over and above individuals and groups. The forms of action theory that I will be looking at in the next chapters often make such a denial, or offer alternative ways of explaining social cohesion as a product of individual action and relationships. They do not cross the bridge from the acting individual to society.

I do not believe, however, that these are the only alternatives. We can find in Lockwood's argument the idea of *material* interests; Rex, too, incorporates the idea into his conflict theory, and its links with Marxism are fairly clear. As long as such interests are dealt with as an aspect of voluntaristic theory, however, we are left with the dilemma that Alexander so acutely identifies. If, however, material interests can be seen as concerning a deeper and more complex relationship between human beings and the material world, then a different conception of society can emerge. This will be encountered for the first time in the chapter on structuralist Marxism.

NOTES

1. As far as I know, Parsons mentions only the second of these.

FURTHER READING

Very little of Parsons's own mammoth output makes easy reading; I have found the following comparatively accessible and, at least, comparatively short:

Parsons, T. (1961) 'An outline of the social system', in Parsons, T., Shils, E., Naegele, A. and Pitts, J. (eds), *Theories of Society: Foundations of modern sociological theory*, The Free Press, New York, pp. 30–79.
Parsons, T. (1964) *Social Structure and Personality*, The Free Press, Glencoe, NJ.
Parsons, T. (1966) *Societies: Evolutionary and comparative perspectives*, Prentice Hall, Englewood Cliffs, NJ.
Parsons, T. (1970) 'Some problems of General Theory in sociology', in McKinney, J. C. and Tyriakian, E. A. (eds), *Theoretical Sociology: Perspectives and developments*, Appleton-Century-Crofts, New York, pp. 27–68.

Parsons, T. (1971) *The System of Modern Societies*, Prentice Hall, Englewood Cliffs, NJ.

His most important books are:

Parsons, T. (1949) *The Structure of Social Action*, The Free Press, New York.
Parsons, T. (1951) *The Social System*, The Free Press, New York.
Parsons, T. and Shils, E. (1951) *Toward a General Theory of Action*, Harvard University Press, Cambridge, MA.

The following are secondary sources; Rocher is the clearest:

Adriaansens, H. P. M. (1980) *Talcott Parsons and the Conceptual Dilemma*, Routledge & Kegan Paul, London.
Bourricaud, F. (1981) *The Sociology of Talcott Parsons*, University of Chicago Press, Chicago.
Colomy, P. (ed.) (1990) *Functionalist Sociology*, Edward Elgar, Aldershot, Hants.
Devereux, E. C. (1961) 'Parsons' sociological theory', in Black, M. (ed.), *The Social Theories of Talcott Parsons*, Prentice Hall, Englewood Cliffs, NJ, pp. 1–63.
Hamilton, P. (1983) *Talcott Parsons*, Ellis Horwood, Chichester/Tavistock, London.
Holton, R. J. and Turner, B. S. (1986) *Talcott Parsons on Economy and Society*, Routledge & Kegan Paul, London.
Merton, R. K. (1968) *Social Theory and Social Structure*, The Free Press, Glencoe, NJ.
Mills, C. Wright (1980) *The Sociological Imagination*, Penguin, Harmondsworth.
Moore, W. E. (1978) 'Functionalism', in Bottomore, T. and Nisbet, R. (eds), *History of Sociological Analysis*, Heinemann, London, pp. 321–61.
Robertson, R. and Turner, B. S. (1991) *Talcott Parsons, Theorist of Modernity*, Sage, London.
Rocher, G. (1974) *Talcott Parsons and American Sociology*, Nelson, London.

The most useful critical essays are:

Burger, T. (1977) 'Talcott Parsons, the problem of order in society, and the program of analytic sociology', *American Journal of Sociology*, vol. 81, pp. 320–34, plus the following debate: Parsons's 'Comment', ibid., pp. 335–9; Burger's reply in vol. 83, no. 2, (1978), pp. 983–6.
Coser, L. (1956) *The Functions of Social Conflict*, The Free Press, Glencoe, NJ.

Dahrendorf, R. (1964) 'Out of Utopia: Toward a reconstruction of sociological analysis', in Coser, L. and Rosenberg, B. (eds), *Sociological Theory*, Macmillan, New York, pp. 209–27.

Demereth, N. J. and Peterson, R. A. (eds), (1967) *System, Change and Conflict: A reader on contemporary sociological theory and the debate over functionalism*, The Free Press, New York.

Giddens, A. (1977) 'Functionalism: Après la lutte', in *Studies in Social and Political Theory*, Heinemann, London, pp. 96–134.

Gouldner, A. W. (1970), *The Coming Crisis of Western Sociology*, Heinemann, London.

Heydebrand, W. and Toby, J. (1972) 'Review symposium on Parsons' *The System of Modern Societies*', *Contemporary Sociology*, vol. 1, pp. 387–401.

Homans, G. C. (1964), 'Bringing men back in', *American Sociological Review*, vol. 29, pp. 809-18.

Lockwood, D. (1964), 'Social integration and system integration', in Zollschan, G. K. and Hirsch, W. (eds), *Explanations in Social Change*, Routledge & Kegan Paul, London, pp. 244–57.

Lockwood, D. (1964) 'Some remarks on *The Social System*', in Demereth, N. J. and Peterson, R. A. (eds), pp. 281–92.

Schwanenberg, E. (1970/71) 'The two problems of order in Parsons' theory: An analysis from within', *Social Forces*, vol. 49, pp. 569–81.

Turner, J. H. (1978) *The Structure of Sociological Theory*, Dorsey Press, Homewood, IL.

For the development of neofunctionalism, see:

Alexander, J. (1984) *Theoretical Logic in Sociology: The modern reconstruction of classical thought: Talcott Parsons*, Routledge & Kegan Paul, London.

Alexander, J. (1985) *Neofunctionalism*, Sage, London.

Alexander, J. (1987) *Sociological Theory since 1930*, University of Columbia Press, New York.

Colomy, P. (ed.) (1990) *Neofunctionalist Sociology*, Edward Elgar, Aldershot, Hants.

Conflict theory

The central works are:

Dahrendorf, R. (1958) 'Toward a theory of social conflict', *Journal of Conflict Resolution*, vol. 2, pp. 209–27.

Dahrendorf, R. (1959) *Class and Class Conflict in an Industrial Society*, Routledge & Kegan Paul, London.

Rex, J. (1961) *Key Problems in Sociological Theory*, Routledge & Kegan Paul, London.

Useful commentaries:

Binns, D. (1977) *Beyond the Sociology of Conflict*, Macmillan, Basingstoke.
Cohen, P. (1968) *Modern Social Theory*, Heinemann, London.
Turner, J. H. (1978) *The Structure of Sociological Theory*, Dorsey Press, Homewood, IL.

Chapter 4

RATIONAL CHOICE THEORY: 'THE PRICE OF EVERYTHING . . .'

INTRODUCTION: METHODOLOGICAL INDIVIDUALISM

Following Alexander, it is perhaps now generally recognised that Parsons's achievement was to bring together into a systematic theory the two ends of a continuum, or the two sides of the opposition, identified by the terms action and structure, individual and collective. As I emphasised when I discussed neofunctionalism and conflict theory, Parsons's theory was none the less voluntaristic – it began with the acting individual choosing between options in a specific environment, and attempted to move from there to the analysis of social systems. My argument is that this movement is not possible, but at the same time we cannot avoid taking account of both.

If we make our starting point a voluntaristic theory of action, then there are a number of stances that we can take towards Parsons's attempt at synthesis. The first is that it is weighted too far in one direction or the other, but in general the weighting can be corrected, either by a new theory altogether (the impetus behind conflict theory) or by an adjustment of perspective that reduces bias – the position of Alexander. These two options eventually fail – the first (conflict theory) because it can easily be reintegrated into Parsons's system; the second (Alexander's) because it entails surrendering the explanatory duty of theory in relation to societies or social structures. There are, however, other options based on sticking to the voluntaristic starting point and denying the existence of society or social systems as entities in their own right. All the rest of the approaches discussed in

69

Part I adopt this position, and they all have to find some answer to the question: if a society does not exist in its own right, then how does the regular patterning of relationships that enables us to identify apparent social wholes come into existence? Such a position has become known as methodological individualism.

One answer, which has a long and respectable – if implicit – history in sociology, originating most clearly in the work of Max Weber, is that human social relationships are patterned and stable because people act rationally. It is not claimed that all action is rational – Weber himself distinguished between four types of action: traditional action, affective action, action orientated to ultimate values, and action orientated to practical goals in this world. Only the last of these is rational in the fullest sense, and with the development of capitalism, and industrial society as a whole, it is increasingly dominant. Weber, however, was aware of all sorts of other things going on in social life. The conception of society as made up of individuals acting rationally has been most explicitly developed by economics and latterly in game theory. Anybody who has taken an economists course will recognise this view behind the assumption of the perfect market or perfect competition: a number of suppliers and buyers with equal information are brought into contact on the market, and their preference choices determine prices, which adjust supply and demand. Stability and order are brought about by individuals making free rational choices. The systematic nature of society is then seen as the result of what Adam Smith called a 'hidden hand', what is often encountered in the literature as 'unintended consequences'.

RATIONAL CHOICE THEORY

One reaction against Parsons's structural-functionalism that became important in the United States went under the name of 'exchange theory', associated in the 1950s with the names of George Homans and Peter Blau. Exchange theory involved a rejection of 'grand theory' and, in Homans's case, the attempt to build up a deductive theory based on simple first principles, those of behaviourist psychology. People will engage in behaviour that brings rewards, satisfies needs – this is the level of Parsons's unit act, at the beginning of his analysis of institutionalisation. The idea of exchange as a source of or means to social solidarity has a long tradition in social anthropology, and the exchange theory picture of society is one in which people exchange activities seeking to maximise profit; attention is given to the rational procedures by which people decide on actions. Although this approach rejected anything like Parsons's systems theory, it developed in a Parsonian environment and paid more attention to the idea of society than does modern rational choice theory.

The statement 'There is no such thing as society' is more readily associated with Margaret Thatcher than with sociologists, who, if they can be expected to believe in anything, might be expected to believe in the existence of society; however, such an idea has come to have its place in modern social theory in several forms. For rational choice theory, it is a firm, even dogmatic, starting point. In some forms it is connected with right-wing opinions, but the 1980s in particular saw the rise of a rational choice Marxism, emphasising again that there is no inherent link between a theory and a political position; however, I think one could argue quite strongly that there is a link between the nature of modernity and rational choice theory: it will become evident throughout this book that it is increasingly difficult to hold on to the idea of society as an object of study, or as an object that actually exists.

Perhaps the easiest way of characterising rational choice theory is in terms of its attempt to build up models of what the individual does if she acts rationally in a particular situation. I know what my income is, I know what goods and services are available to me, and I have a scale of preferences; thus I can rank the options open to me in order of preference. There is a clear utilitarian dimension to rational choice theory: I choose what brings me most satisfaction or most utility, and there is an assumption that I know what my situation is – although it is a matter of debate, within the theory, how much information I need to make a rational choice. A rational choice explanation is an intentional explanation, in that it assumes that an individual's desires and beliefs are reasons for her action, but it goes further in the claim that they are also the causes of her action – this takes us back to the philosophical debate to which I referred in the opening chapters. Much work in rational choice takes up such philosophical issues or is concerned with the complexities of ordering preferences. I do not intend to go into these issues here, but it is important to note – and I think it helps to understand the arguments – that it is, as Jon Elster (1986b) presents it, a *normative* theory: it points to the most efficient way of reaching a given goal in a given situation. Many of its contributions have been concerned with, for example, ways of constructing political systems.

An example of a sociological explanation along rational choice lines, discussed by Lydia Morris (1990), is Gary Becker's 'New Home Economics'. This turns out not to be an updated version of what, in my schooldays, girls used to do instead of woodwork; interestingly, however, it does have distinct affinities with the attitudes behind those courses. For Becker, the division of labour in the household is seen as the result of rational choices of how to maximise utility by allocating time to the market or to household activities. As far as I understand it, since men, as a rule, can command higher wages on the market, it is rational for them to devote most of their energy to market work rather than household work, whereas the opposite is true for women – although changing market conditions can change the situation. The possibility of women achieving higher earnings is thus seen as a cause of higher divorce rates, since it becomes less rational to choose the traditional role when others are available. Morris makes two major criticisms of this type of explanation: first, it assumes that the household is a consensually operating unit – i.e. that there is an agreement between members – and this is not necessarily true; secondly, it does not deal with the constraints that the household encounters in developing its strategies. Thus, using a combination of emotional blackmail and physical force, I might prevent my wife from realising her full earning capacity; or, if we decided that we should, we might still find that the absence of reasonably priced nursery care might make it uneconomic. Beyond this, of course, the structure of the labour market does not allow the range of choices that Becker assumes. I will return to this example and the criticisms later. For the moment, I will turn to another form of rational choice theory.

RATIONAL CHOICE MARXISM

On the face of it, Marxism seems directly opposed to the assumptions of rational choice theory, identified as it often (and often wrongly) is with determinist explanations. Rational choice Marxism can, perhaps, be seen as a reaction to the apparent determinism of structuralist Marxism in the 1970s, but it is also a response to the resurgence during the 1980s of right-wing, free-market politics which shares the assumptions of methodological individualism – a matter of meeting the enemy on their own ground. A number of theorists are important here; the best-known (although in my opinion least close to Marxism) is Jon Elster. Here I am going to follow an excellent, readable account by Alan Carling (1986), who draws on the work of John Roemer (1982).

Carling introduces at the beginning the notion of scarcity, which seems to me to be implicit anyway in the notion of choice: if we did not have limited resources, we would not need to choose how to use them. From choice and scarcity we can derive a very elementary theory of history – that rationality is at work 'indirectly' in the choice of social relations that will further productive techniques. The free exchange on the market becomes exploitation through one agent taking unfair advantage of unequal access to resources – such access, as far I understand it, being contingent. Oppression is defined as unfair exclusion from access to resources. Different forms of exploitation are identified which fit very roughly into the Marxist theory of history – feudal, capitalist and socialist (the last having to do with unequal access to status).

Thus, an understanding of exploitation and oppression can be built into the theory. Elster – in an argument that appeals to Erik Olin Wright, a much more orthodox Marxist – offers a solution to what at first glance might appear to be the thorny problem of class formation. Social class must be seen as some form of coalition of individuals, not as any form of entity over and above individuals. But if each individual acts to maximise utility to themselves, how can they operate together? In games theory, this is known as the 'free-rider' problem – basically: 'Why the hell should I do anything?' If, for example, I receive any pay increase negotiated by the Association of University Teachers (my apologies for the far-fetched example), whether or not I am a member of the Union, why should I even bother to pay my subscription? Other people are paying and doing the work, and my contribution would make no practical difference. On the other hand, if nobody else is active in the Union, which is slowly disappearing as people leave, or retire, or whatever, there is no point in my taking unilateral action.[1]

There are various ways round this. In its right-wing versions, collective actions, or coalitions, are regarded with some suspicion – they are the result of special interests which interrupt the working of the free market; hence suspicion of professional associations and political activists as pursuing their own self-interest. Where concern is for widespread involvement in social processes, in democracy, it is often suggested that some incentive or compulsion is needed. It is in my interest not to bother to vote – my vote will make no difference to the eventual result, it will simply be swallowed up with all the others; why should I waste my energy? However, if voting were a legal requirement and I would be fined for not voting, then I might change my mind. I might also change my mind if somebody offered me money to vote.

Elster prefers to see this problem in terms of the 'assurance game', on the basis of what he calls a 'conditional altruism'. I will decide that I will participate if other people will. This, however, requires access to information about other people's intentions, and possibly negotia-tion, but it does provide a basis for analysing the formation of collective action, or the failure to act collectively, an idea which Wright seems to use in his book on social classes (1985).

To return to my example of the household division of labour: we now have some way of dealing with at least one of Morris's criticisms. Either the household decisions are negotiated and agreed to maxi-mise the utility to each of its members, or one partner – whom we might imagine, in the case of male/female households, is usually a man – employs a given inequality in access to resources to his own advantage. We might even argue that this given, unexplained inequality is a result of oppression in that women are unfairly excluded from some resources. We can also, perhaps, begin to make sense of the feminist movement in terms of the assurance game. Such an explanation raises interesting questions about the scope of explanations offered by rational choice theory.

The scope of rational choice explanation

Alan Carling (1990) is refreshingly modest about the claims of rational choice theory, arguing that it does not and cannot explain everything, and rejecting the tendency present in much Marxist (and much sociological) theorising which sees a failure to understand or explain one feature of social life as a failure to explain anything. In his terms, rational choice theory is a 'special' not a general theory, dealing with actions taken in given contexts and according to given preferences. The nearest it gets to a general theory is his proposition about the combination of rationality and scarcity. It does not explain contexts, or non-rational motivations; nor, he argues in his earlier paper (1986), can it deal with gender and ethnic differences. There seems to be general consensus around this point, although Peter Abell (1991) claims that there is no *a priori* reason why contexts and preferences should not eventually be brought within the scope of the theory, since they too might be seen as the result of previous rational choices. He acknowledges that this cannot be done at the moment and I shall argue later that there is in fact an *a priori* reason why it cannot be done.

For the moment, however, I want to try to specify more closely what is going on in a rational choice explanation. Perhaps the first point to make is that it does not imply that all actions are rational, that all human beings act rationally. It seems to me that there are two claims: one is that enough people act rationally enough of the time to make the theory a workable proposition; another is that we should, when trying to understand human action, give priority to rational explanations and rational models. Returning to Abell (1991): he points out a range of strategies that are possible if an explanation in terms of rational action fails. These include working with a broader assumption of self-interest, and introducing subjective elements into our understanding of the ways in which people realise what resources are available to them and judge courses of action to be feasible. There are, in fact, quite complex and subtle ways of looking at assessment of situations and choices which expand on more narrow ideas of self-interest. Sen (1977), for example, introduces the idea of sympathy (roughly, it might be in my self-interest to reduce the sufferings of others) and commitment – I might be committed to another person in such a way as to put her interest before mine. I suspect that anyone who has agonised about whether their love is selfish will recognise that many apparently generous actions can be interpreted as being in one's self-interest. Elsewhere (1983) he suggests that each individual might have different sets of preference rankings which can themselves be ranked. Elster (1989a, b) seems increasingly to give a much more important place to the irrational, which leads on to my next point.

A more sophisticated claim would be that by privileging rational action we open the way to looking at other motivations. In this sense the theory comes much closer to Weber's notion of an 'ideal type' – by looking at the way in which reality differs from what we might expect if individuals were acting rationally, we can discover the underlying – or at least the non-rational – aspects of their behaviour. This, I think, is a very strong defence of rational choice explanation, but it does assume that we see ourselves as looking for more complex understandings than are offered by rational choice theory alone – something I suspect its adherents would be reluctant to do.

I shall argue later that the more modest the claims of rational choice theory, the more it is worth taking seriously; before I do that, however, I want to look at the main lines of criticism, the first of which follows on directly from what I have just been discussing.

The limits of rationality

By far the most comprehensive critique of rational choice theory is Barry Hindess's *Choice, Rationality and Social Theory* (1988); I have a number of disagreements with the position from which he argues, but what follows takes up several of the points he makes. In relation to the issues I have just been discussing, he points to the claim that on the basis of very simple assumptions about human behaviour, large areas of social activity can be understood. This claim, it seems to me, has much to do with model-building and then taking the model as a reality. Using Hindess's argument with my own example, it is quite possible that a rational choice model of household decision-making succeeds very well in explaining why, under certain conditions, women concentrate on domestic work and men on paid employment outside the home. Whether it is an understanding of reality is another matter, because in fact it tells us nothing about the real motives of real actors. I might work and my wife might stay at home: this might be the rational choice, but in practice my wife might want to work and I might beat, browbeat or blackmail her out of it; on the other hand, she might not want to work outside the home whatever improvements in our income it might bring; or I might prefer a lower standard of living and staying at home looking after the children, but she might insist, browbeat or blackmail me into keeping my job. All sorts of decision-making processes are compatible with the rational outcome.

We could go so far as to say that this model is not an explanation of rational choices but a rationalisation of what happens, and perhaps of what would happen despite the real motivations of individuals. As Abell (1991) puts it: 'Will we not always, *post hoc*, be able to find some motive/preference which will fit the case?' (p. xi). His answer to his own question is that this becomes much more difficult when we look at individuals' interdependencies rather than at individual actions as such, and the main contribution of sociological theory is to model these structures. I am by no means clear why this should be so – we can just as easily construct *post hoc* motives for interdependent individuals as we can for individuals acting alone. Going back to my comments about ideal types, it seems that the rational choice models have to be the basis for investigation whether or not their predictions or explanations seem to fit what really happens. They are a way into reality, but no more than that.

The remaining two criticisms show the limits of rational choice theory rather than rule it out of court. I have already touched on them in citing Carling's argument that rational choice theory is a 'special' theory, dealing with action in given circumstances with given ranges of preference. Abell suggests that in principle the circumstances themselves can be explained as the result of previous rational choices, but in my own view this is not possible – we are left with an infinite regress: we might be able to explain how one particular set of circumstances comes about, but that set emerges out of another. Short of recounting the whole of human history in terms of rational choices by individuals in varying relationships to each other, we *have* to assume a given set of circumstances.

This has an interesting consequence, as Hindess points out: it introduces, undercover, a form of structural determinism; comparing the two sorts of explanations, he writes:

> In both cases, actors are creatures of their situations and they act accordingly: in one case because they pursue the most rational course of action given the situation in which they find themselves and in the other because they have internalised the appropriate norms and act on them. In fact ... it would not be difficult to develop an account of the emergence and perpetuation of norms in a rational choice framework once the nature of incentives involved in repeated patterns of interaction are taken into consideration. The mechanism by which individuals are subordinated to their situations may be different in the two cases, but the overall result is the same. (Hindess, 1988: 39)

In fact, as we have seen, Parsons did precisely what Hindess is talking about: he began with individual action in relation to other individuals and moved from there to the development of systems, and at times a structural determinism. The question of norms has always haunted liberal political theory, and it haunts rational choice theory. Even Adam Smith recognised that self-interested individuals must also be governed by some connection to the social order as a whole – this was an origin of economic 'prudence' in the self-interested individual, and Elster, in one of his most recent works (1989b), suggests that 'social norms provide an important kind of motivation for action that is irreducible to rationality'. My main point, however, goes beyond collective norms – or 'general meanings', as I referred to them above – to structure and structural determinism. It seems that from the above emerges a *prima facie* case for the existence of a form of structural determinism: we are positioned, and certain courses of action seem to follow from that position – the actions that we choose to call 'rational' – although interestingly, the rational outcome might follow whatever our motivations.

There is a further point here. Hindess argues that it is a mistake to assume that the only actors in the social world are individuals. There are 'social actors': business firms, political parties, governments, who have concerns and objectives that cannot be reduced to the concerns and objectives of the individuals who make them up. The organisation of individuals within 'social actors' can be treated as part of their conditions of action, so once again, even within the framework of rational choice theory, we find we can refer to more than the individual.

My third argument here I will take from Hindess: the assumption that actors' modes of reasoning are transparently rational removes the possibility of looking at the techniques of reasoning they use. This is a far-reaching criticism not only of rational choice theory but of any model of the individual of what Hindess calls the 'portfolio' type:

> It treats action as resulting for the most part from intentions that are themselves the product of a portfolio of beliefs and desires which the actor carries around from one situation to another. Actors sort through their portfolios for the beliefs and desires that seem to be relevant to their situations and use them to identify possible courses of action and to choose between them. In this model, the content of the actors' portfolio may change from time to time, but at any given moment they are to be regarded as relatively stable. (Hindess, 1988: 48–9)

Now Hindess points out that when we make a decision in many areas, we use specialised techniques of reasoning: a trained accountant, for example, will audit a set of accounts according to a set of procedures that might have little or nothing to do with his personal desires or beliefs (except, perhaps, in the most abstract sense of the desire to earn a living and the belief that these procedures will avoid mistakes). Something else intervenes between desire/belief on the one hand and action on the other. It is the assumption of a simple relationship between two ends of a continuum, where the only thing that intervenes is the actor's rationality, which gives us the crude distinction between rational and irrational action. The implication of Hindess's argument is that if we take techniques of reasoning into account, we can see all action as rational in one sense or another; the particular techniques of reasoning themselves define what is rational or irrational. What might be rational in one technique of reasoning might not be so in another. In the classic example, we can make sense of the Azande's belief in witchcraft if we know how they see the world.

Translating Hindess's argument into my own: rational choice theory directs us away from the ethnographic detail that actually enables us to understand how people think, how they see and, in one sense, actually construct the world they live in. And this would include the way in which they construct their beliefs about the world, the information on which their decisions are based. It is not simply a matter of knowing or not knowing about one's situation; there are different *ways* in which one may know about it. However sophisticated the portfolio model of the actor, it assumes a fairly straightforward form of beliefs (they can only be right or wrong), a straightforward view of our desires (I wonder whether we often know what we want) and a comparatively simple connection between the two.

CONCLUSION

It might sound as if these criticisms undermine the approach altogether, but I do not think they do. If we take rational choice theory, in Carling's terms, as a special rather than a general theory, and avoid the tendency apparent in Abell, for example, to try to make it into a general theory, then it seems to me that it does capture one dimension of human action, one that is perhaps more important in modern societies than others. The simple form of rationality that it assumes – often referred to as instrumental rationality – is one technique of reasoning that we do use in our everyday lives. We do many other important things as well, and these are ignored by the theory, but we do employ instrumental rationality. And although the models it constructs do not necessarily tell us anything about the world, they do offer a way into the world, a sort of grid against which we might begin to discern complexity. This seems to be the way in which Elster's work has developed – to the point where, for example, he seems to suggest that the assumption that there are rational solutions to problems is itself irrational.

Thus, if we return to Becker, his model doubtless describes what goes on in some families, but not in all. It assumes the structural determinations – or limitations – on choices by members of the household, and in that sense there is an implicit structural determinism. In fact, as I read more around rational choice theory, its most interesting possibility seems to me to be that it shows one of the ways in which existing structures of relationships reproduce themselves. And if we take it as offering an ideal-type rationality, then we can use it to look not only at actions which do not fit, but also at the possibly multiple ways in which non-rational choices (in the terms of the theory) have the outcome that would be there if the actions were rational.

It is fairly straightforward to see how rational choice theory, like conflict theory, can be reintegrated into Parsons's system, in which the notion of instrumental action actually plays an important part; and however strongly the approach insists on methodological individualism, we have seen that it is pulled all the time towards taking account of the society as a whole, and of various collective levels. For sociologists who see their concern as *society*, or at least supra-individual entities, it is perhaps too easy to reject rational choice analysis. If we are positioned within a social system, then rational choice is one of the ways in which the system works and reproduces itself.

NOTES

1. Many of the arguments here owe much to Olson's 'social choice' theory – see Further Reading.

FURTHER READING

Rational choice theory

Key texts in the approach include:

Becker, G. S. (1976) *The Economic Approach to Human Behaviour*, University of Chicago Press, Chicago.
Becker, G. S. (1981) *A Treatise on the Family*, Harvard University Press, Cambridge, MA.
Downs, A. (1957) *An Economic Theory of Democracy*, Harper, New York.
Fishburn, P. C. (1973) *The Theory of Social Choice*, Princeton University Press, Princeton, NJ.
Hardin, R. (1982) *Collective Action*, Johns Hopkins University Press, Baltimore, MD.
Margolis, H. (1982) *Selfishness, Altruism and Rationality*, Cambridge University Press, Cambridge.
Olson, M. (1965) *The Logic of Collective Action*, Harvard University Press, Cambridge, MA.
Olson, M. (1982) *The Rise and Decline of Nations*, Yale University Press, New Haven, CT.
Sen, A. (1977) 'Rational fools: A critique of the behavioural foundations of economic theory', *Philosophy and Public Affairs*, vol. 6, pp. 317–44.
Sen, A. (1983) *Choice, Welfare and Measurement*, Basil Blackwell, Oxford.

The following readers are particularly useful, and the Abell introduction, and Elster's introduction to *Rational Choice*, make good starting points:

Abell, P. (ed.) (1991) *Rational Choice Theory*, Edward Elgar, Aldershot, Hants.
Elster, J. (ed.) (1986a) *Foundations of Social Choice Theory*, Cambridge University Press, Cambridge.
Elster, J. (1986b) *Rational Choice*, Basil Blackwell, Oxford.

For 'New Home Economics', see:

Becker, G. (1981) *A Treatise on the Family*, Harvard University Press, Cambridge, MA.

and the discussion in:

Morris, L. (1990) *The Workings of the Household*, Polity Press, Cambridge.

The major works of rational choice Marxism are:

Elster, J. (1985) *Making Sense of Marx*, Cambridge University Press, Cambridge.
Przeworski, A. (1985) *Capitalism and Social Democracy*, Cambridge University Press, Cambridge.
Roemer, J. (1982) *A General Theory of Exploitation and Class*, Harvard University Press, Cambridge, MA.
Roemer, J. (ed.) (1986) *Analytical Marxism*, Cambridge University Press, Cambridge.
Ware, R. and Neilson, K. (eds) (1989) *Analysing Marxism*, University of Calgary Press, Calgary, AB.
Wood, A. (1981) *Karl Marx*, Routledge & Kegan Paul, London.
Wright, E. O. (1985) *Classes*, Verso, London.

The best and most readable introduction to the approach is:

Carling, A. (1986) 'Rational choice Marxism', *New Left Review*, no. 186, pp. 24–62.

Criticisms

By far the best and most systematic is:

Hindess, B. (1988) *Choice, Rationality and Social Theory*, Unwin Hyman, London.

Marxist critiques of the approach:

Levine, A., Sober, E. and Wright, E. O. (1987) 'Marxism and methodological individualism', *New Left Review*, no. 162, pp. 67–84.
Wood, E. M. (1989) 'Rational choice Marxism: Is the game worth the candle?', *New Left Review*, no. 177, pp. 41–88.

See also the discussion by Carling *et al.* in *New Left Review*, no. 184, (1990), pp. 97–128.

For Jon Elster's latest work, questioning the limits of rationality, see:

Elster, J. (1989a) *Solomonic Judgements*, Cambridge University Press, Cambridge.

Elster, J. (1989b) *The Cement of Society*, Cambridge University Press, Cambridge.

For an excellent discussion of these and other works by Elster, see:

Ryan, A. (1991) 'When it's rational to be irrational', *New York Review of Books*, vol. 38, no. 15, pp. 19–22.

Chapter 5

SYMBOLIC INTERACTIONISM: SOCIETY AS CONVERSATION

INTRODUCTION

Symbolic interactionism is the least-developed theory discussed in this book. Paul Rock (1979) calls it a 'deliberately constructed vagueness'; there are several varieties and for a long time the existence of the approach seems to have depended more on informal verbal tradition than on established textbooks. Over the past decade, however, there have been attempts at institutionalising and systematising the approach (documented in Plummer, 1991) which seem to me to detract from some of its value. The centre of its development was the University of Chicago Sociology Department around the 1920s, and amongst the founding thinkers – whom I will not discuss – were Robert Park and W. I. Thomas. It drew on the uniquely American philosophical school of pragmatism, on a sociological interpretation of ecology (the study of the relationship between an organism and its environment), and on the field methods developed by anthropology, now generally known amongst sociologists as participant observation. As later functionalists noted, it was strong on empirical research and weak on theory. As the anthropologist will live with a tribe in New Guinea, so the interactionist will find and live with a social group in her own country. In so far as it has a founding thinker who can be regarded as the major theorist, it is George Herbert Mead. All modern discussions of the approach give Mead a central place, and the vagueness I referred to is best illustrated by the fact that his central work, *Mind, Self and Society* (1934), was compiled from his students' lecture notes after his death.

To place symbolic interactionism in the context of the previous chapters, we should once again go back to Parsons and the idea of the unit act. This involved a set of assumptions about the social actor: she makes choices between goals and means towards these goals in a situation of both physical and social objects – the latter including social norms and cultural values. The process of institutionalisation involves actors gearing their actions to each other to provide mutual satisfaction, and if that is successful, their actions become stabilised into a pattern of status roles – a role structure. These are seen in terms of the expectations that people have of each other (i.e. in terms of meanings or symbols). Now I have argued that the approach can focus on either role structures and social systems or role behaviour and social action. I suggested that there is some difficulty in bringing these together in any sort of overall causal explanation (even if the desire is there), because the theory could not properly separate them from each other. Social systems and role structures were sometimes seen as the result of social action and sometimes vice versa, but they are basically the same thing: a theory of persons generalised to a theory of societies. Symbolic interactionism does not make this switch: it stays with social action, and although implicitly it sees social structures as role structures in the same way as Parsons, it does not concern itself with analysis on the systems level. Like rational choice theory it stays with the unit act, but it is concerned less with choice between preferences than with the construction of meanings in terms of which preferences might be expressed.

There are several forms of interactionism, but I will concentrate on the tendency known as the Chicago School, because I think it offers the most distinctive contribution and the one that is most difficult to assimilate to structural-functionalism, even though it shares the same propositions. Here the analogy of the conversation is most appropriate: the social world shows the same qualities of flow, development, creativity and change as we would experience in a conversation around the dinner table or in a bar (at least in the early stages). In fact, the world is made up of conversations, both internal and external. This tendency is, I think, closer to the spirit of the originators of the approach, with their optimism about social progress and democracy, and their view that social development is caused by and causes the development of individual creativity. It is also closer to its social basis in American life, with its emphasis on egalitarianism, individual liberty and social mobility. How close it is to the full reality of social life is, of course, another matter.

THE ASSUMPTIONS OF SYMBOLIC INTERACTIONISM

The most economical formulation of interactionist assumptions comes from Herbert Blumer (1969):

1. Human beings act towards things on the basis of the meanings that the things have for them.
2. These meanings are the product of social interaction in human society.
3. These meanings are modified and handled through an interpretative process that is used by each individual in dealing with the signs each encounters.

These correspond roughly with the three sections of Mead's *Mind, Self and Society*. Mead's starting point is the discussion of the crucial feature that separates human beings from other animals. Like many other thinkers, he settles on language, or the 'significant symbol', and he is concerned to elaborate the implications of this. Animals engage in conversations of gestures, but it would be wrong to say that they communicate like human beings. When one dog snarls at another and the other backs away, one dog is feeling aggressive and the other is feeling scared, but there is no mutual understanding. When I want to warn off a student, perhaps because she is taking up too much of my time, I do not (usually) bare my teeth and snarl; I present her with a reason which I believe she will understand. The difference is that the significant symbol, unlike the animal gesture, brings out the same reaction in myself as it does in the other, and vice versa – each of us, in the exchange, puts ourself in the position of the other. Dogs, as far as we know, are not capable of identifying with each other in this way, and it is language, the significant symbol, that makes the difference.

Another way of putting it is that the significant symbol is shared meaning. It is developed in the course of interaction, which itself is a matter of people seeking to achieve practical results in co-operation with each other. Mead is describing something like the process of an intimate relationship between two people where the participants develop an almost private language in the course of their daily activities – but for him, this is a general social process. Social interaction produces meanings, and meanings make up our world. There is a sense in which we create our world by giving meaning to it: a piece of wood is a piece of wood; in our daily activity it becomes a table. The word 'table' means the role it plays in our interaction: something to eat off, work on, use as a barricade against the bailiffs. Such meanings change and develop, and as they do so the world changes and develops.

The significant symbol provides humans with the ability to 'pause' in their reaction and to rehearse it imaginatively. The symbols enable us to stand back from the objects in the world and carry out thought-experiments; that is what is happening every time we think about doing something. It is the existence of language which enables us to stand back, to consider and choose. This brings us to the interpretative process mentioned in Blumer's third assumption. So far I have been talking about 'external conversations' – the processes of interaction in which we create, together, our shared world. The internal interpretative process is also a conversation, between two different parts (Mead called them 'phases') of the self. The significant symbol, remember, brings out the same reaction in myself as it does in others; it enables me to look at myself as others look at me. The 'Me' is precisely that: myself as others see me; the second phase, the 'I', is the part that looks at myself ('I am thinking about myself'), and Mead sees this as the source of originality, creativity and spontaneity. The internal conversation provides a channel through which all the external conversations, or patterns of interaction, must pass. This conception of the self also involves a description of the process of socialisation. In the life of the infant, initially random gestures are narrowed as she comes to recognise those that have a meaning for others. Then, through play, she learns to take the role of individual others, and as she grows older she learns, through games, to co-ordinate her activities with others, and to see herself as the group sees her. Through peer groups (friends) she comes to see herself in an increasingly wider context until she takes on what Mead calls the 'role of the generalised other'; until she can view herself as the society as a whole views her. Another way of putting it is that she takes on a sort of social conscience.

The various forms of symbolic interactionism place emphasis on different parts of the theory. The Chicago School concentrates on the flow of interaction and interpretative processes, looking at the way in which meanings develop and change; the 'Iowa School', whose leading figure is Manfred Kuhn, tries to change these insights into measurable variables, assuming that the self is stable and relatively unchanging. His Twenty Statements Test (the 'Who Am I?' test) asks people to choose the series of twenty statements which most accurately describe themselves, and he proceeds to relate the results to the respondents' social positions. Mead's ideas are not really used as a theory, to explain what is observed, but rather as a simple description of what is observed. Another variation, usually labelled 'role theory', looks at the way in which the internal conversation of the self mediates the presentation of the self in role structures. Ralph Turner's work is the most systematic in this area.

As an example, however, I will look briefly at the work of Erving Goffman, who falls halfway between the Chicago School approach and the more systematic form of role theory. His approach is often labelled the 'dramaturgical approach', a term which he himself applies. Roles – the expectations which others have of our behaviour in specific circumstances are like scripts which we then enact, and Goffman is concerned to show how we act, the way in which we manage our performance. Thus, in the 1950s, American women at college would act stupid to impress their boyfriends; the inhabitants of the Shetland Islands, where Goffman did much fieldwork for his most famous book, *The Presentation of Self in Everyday Life* (1971), would let the outward appearance of their cottages decay lest the landlord assume they were wealthy enough to pay higher rent. All aspects of life, from the most private to the most public, are seen in these terms. It is not just after she has spent the afternoon in bed with her lover that my wife tries to impress me with her care and concern for me when I get home. That 'impression management' is going on all the time, as if we were all advertising agents for ourselves. We use our physical surroundings as props and maintain areas of privacy 'backstage' where we can relax from our performances (the toilet, for example).

This can be seen in the context of Mead's discussion of the 'I' and the 'Me'. Goffman is describing the ways in which the 'I' presents the 'Me'. The difficulty is that we never find out what the 'I' is – and Mead did not tell us either, beyond saying that it was the source of creativity and originality. Everything is reduced to acting: the self has no substance beyond what is expected of us on different occasions, and we have as many different selves as there are different occasions. This leads on to one of the main criticisms of symbolic interactionism, which I will discuss shortly.

Goffman's work is mainly descriptive: *The Presentation of Self in Everyday Life* is a classification of the techniques and strategies of acting. This indicates something of the nature of interactionism as a theory: it is not rigorous and does not involve logical deduction. Rather, it provides a series of ideas which the researcher may use in her work as very general guides. The explanation that the researcher develops is of a comparatively low level; in Goffman's case it simply presupposes Mead's I/Me distinction without discussion, and then employs it to redescribe various actions using the theatrical analogy.

Goffman, at least, sees all action in these terms. Many other interactionists would argue that any explanation can be appropriate only to the particular situation which it explains; we cannot make generalisations about social life. Society seen as a conversation is in constant flux, and cannot be forced into generalised abstractions. Nevertheless, it does seem to me that Mead's insights provide a basis for an elementary teleological explanation of human action, revealing a logic to what people do that is not at first apparent. The sociologist can show the way in which people assess the world and choose between different courses of action when often, to the immediate perception of the observer, no choice is involved. Thus, in *Outsiders* (1963), Howard Becker is able to show how marijuana use is less a matter of physical addiction than a learning process – people have to learn from others what the effects are before they themselves can experience them. We can then describe this learning process in terms of new meanings developing from the interactions and choices of the new and experienced smokers. Interactionism looks for what Paul Rock (1979) calls the 'occasional rationality' of the action, the specific perspectives, meanings and choices involved in each situation.

ARE SYMBOLIC INTERACTIONISTS BLIND AND STUPID?

The most regular criticisms you are likely to come across in the rapidly growing literature on symbolic interactionism are that it ignores the wider features of social structure and therefore cannot say anything about power, conflict and change, that its theoretical formulations are hopelessly vague, and that it provides an incomplete picture of the individual. These points are usually made as if they were self-evident: any idiot can see social structures and their effects, only a fool would be content with vague theoretical formulations, and sociology clearly needs a complex theory of the individual.

As a rule, none of these arguments takes account of the

interactionists' defence of their position. If we start with the argument that interactionism's concepts are vague, it seems to me that in fact this is a necessary aspect of the approach's distinctive contribution to sociology. If the aim is to reveal the 'occasional' logic of people's action, and if it is true that social interaction is in constant flux, then the theoretical starting point must be flexible and 'sensitising' (i.e. vague), or we would lose vital aspects of what we are studying. It is at this level of analysis that we are most in danger of doing violence to what we are studying if we have to force it into a well-worked-out, elaborate theory.

Whereas the role-theory tendency in interaction does take account of social structures, from the point of view of the Chicago School an explicit case can be made against taking social structures into account. They are abstract entities, the argument goes; we can engage in abstract and interesting arguments about them (the brain-teaser tendency), and we can reinterpret the world in their terms (the crossword puzzle tendency) but we can never arrive at any satisfactory conclusions about them, and we are likely to miss what is going on under our noses. Paul Rock makes the point clearly:

> The character of society is so obscure that scientific attempts to discuss it are generally absurd. Although loose working definitions might be used to guide analysis, it is misleading to assume that larger systems of society can ever be mapped. Indeed, it is not entirely reasonable to suppose that society and its 'structures' are organised. If they are, then they can be known only to analytic *a priori* conjectures which are forever uncertain or to synthetic *a priori* understanding which is entirely unscientific. The sociologist, therefore, hesitates to write off society as a viable analytic topic at all. When he does so, it may only be to represent it as a shapeless conglomeration of fluid exchanges. (Rock, 1979: 227–8)

This, I think, is a strong case. It corresponds with my argument in the Introduction to Part II: that, at least to begin with, a theoretical explanation is a matter of imaginative explanation. I argued that this could be made less speculative as it is subjected to criteria of rationality and evidence: Rock does not believe that this can be done in any useful way.

How do we decide? I think the argument against Paul Rock can be based on something that he himself says. He acknowledges that sometimes the people we study might employ the term 'society', and we can investigate its meaning to them, and the way the meaning of the term develops in their interaction. I said in the opening chapter that everybody, in their day-to-day lives, is a theorist and in day-to-day interaction it is reasonable to suggest that people talk about 'society' because they are aware of the effects of something they cannot identify in any clear experiential way. To suppose 'society' to be a fiction, to suppose that it is unorganised, and so on, is to ignore the experience of its effects amongst those we study. In other words, it is to do precisely the opposite of what symbolic interactionism sets out to do. We can grant to Rock that our knowledge of 'society' will always be somewhat tentative, and that we should not absorb processes of interaction into a rigid theory, but not that we should have no theory of society. From my introduction it would follow that the criticism that symbolic interactionism does not take into account wider social structures might be true, but how they should be taken into account is a major problem area – not a simple matter, as the critics suppose it to be.

I said that it *might* be true; in fact it is not true. There are clear tendencies in interactionism that concern themselves with structure and associated issues such as power and, interestingly, they seem to me to focus on certain areas that can be defined within Parsons's framework. There have been elaborations around the area of role-taking and role-making, which is perhaps the most 'structural' aspect of the approach (Stryker, 1980; Stryker and Serpe, 1982) – Meltzer and Herman (in Reynolds, 1990) link this approach with the Iowa School, and it certainly seems to bring out the more behaviourist aspect of symbolic interactionism. More consistent with the Chicago School are many studies of large and small structural contexts which emphasise the *negotiated* order of social relations within such contexts. The idea of negotiation is applicable to a range of situations and can show, for example, how power relations operate 'on the spot' in the detail and language of interaction, and how social order – at this level, at any rate – is negotiated as part of the ongoing social conversation. One might also see it as one of a set of *formal* concepts which can provide a sort of general theory of interaction along lines advocated by Glaser and Strauss in *The Discovery of Grounded Theory* (1967).

The sort of exercise that is possible can be seen in Hosticka's (1979) study of lawyer–client relationships, where he shows the means by which the lawyers were able to define both what had happened to their client and what might be done about it; they were certainly not setting about discovering what 'really' happened. One way of looking at this study could be to say that it shows how structured inequalities of power appear in social interaction and reproduce themselves (and the legal system) in the process. Although this concerns the *negotiation* of order, there is also an implicit structural determinism behind it that is similar to an element I noted in discussing rational choice theory. Whereas rational choice theorists would perhaps see the interaction as a matter of choice of the most useful course of action, symbolic interactionism sees it in terms of a negotiated reality in which one partner has rather more power than the other; the outcome, however, is (we may assume) the same, and in each case the structure is presupposed. Because interactionism does not insist on the methodological individualism of rational choice theory, it is easier for it to move in the direction of social structure, as represented in Stryker's work, and perhaps it is easier to see it as a micro-study within a Parsonian framework.

In relation to the criticism that symbolic interactionism does not offer a full conception of the personality, Ken Plummer has commented (in a seminar, although not, as far as I know, in print) that this is an odd criticism for a sociological theory – one would not normally expect sociology to concern itself with the personality in the same way as psychology. A standard criticism along these lines is that it cannot make sense of emotions, but in recent years this too has been shown not to be true. The classic study here is Hochschild's *The Managed Heart* (1983), a study of the management of emotion by flight attendants and bill collectors. As the title indicates, this concerns the conscious use of emotions in interaction; other work tries to distinguish physiological or social aspects, the social rules which govern the experience and/or expression of emotions and their social effects. At one extreme, symbolic interactionism moves in a realm often referred to as 'social constructionism' where – with ethnomethodology, semiotics and post-structuralist approaches – it sees our experience in general as a result of a social process.

Yet it remains a cognitive approach to the personality – thought and thought processes remain the centre of its concern: we understand people when we understand what they think they know about the world, their meanings and self-conceptions. If we accept the existence of unconscious processes as well, then we might argue that a theory of persons must also deal with different levels of the personality and relationships between them; in other words, the personality needs to be given substance. We can acknowledge, with Goffman, that we act, but we are more than actors. Even when we deal with meanings and symbols, some approaches I will be looking at later show that interactionism underestimates the complexity of meaning formation.

In the next chapter it will become apparent that the way people form and develop their view of the world can be seen as subjected to certain rules, and that there are general processes of meaning formation that are not investigated by interactionism. And in Part III it will become apparent that meanings or symbols themselves might be seen as possessing an organised structure, even as comprising yet another type of reality in the social world.

Generally, then, interactionists choose to remain closer to the flux of interaction processes at the expense of developing their theory further, and that, perhaps, is a necessary choice – at least given the present state of knowledge in the discipline as a whole. The danger, however, is that the choice tends to leave them, in some cases, engaging in purely descriptive work, assuming the existence of social structure. In the case of Goffman, for example, there is the central theoretical insight about self-presentation followed by a catalogue of different ways in which people present themselves in different contexts. If Parsons's work can be likened to a filing *system*, then Goffman's sometimes seems like a collection of index cards that can be arranged any way we want. All actions can be understood via the theatrical analogy, and we may list them in any order we desire.

SUMMARY AND CONCLUSION

Symbolic interactionism, then, is a theory of persons, of social action, which in its most distinct form does not attempt to become also a theory of society. Its explanation of action – its theoretical component – remains fairly simple, but this can be seen as a conscious choice in favour of grasping some of the complexity of real situations. The theoretical task to which it points is the development of a more sophisticated theoretical explanation, which takes in more aspects of people's actions without losing the complexity of the real world.

FURTHER READING

Central works of symbolic interactionism

Included here are each of the three tendencies I identified. Mead and Blumer are the best starting points.

Blumer, H. (1969) *Symbolic Interactionism: Perspectives and method*, Prentice Hall, Englewood Cliffs, NJ.

Denzin, N. (1971) *The Research Act in Sociology: A theoretical introduction to sociological methods*, Butterworth, London.

Glaser, B. G. and Strauss, A. L. (1967) *The Discovery of Grounded Theory: Strategies for qualitative research*, Weidenfeld & Nicolson, London.

Kuhn, M. H. (1964) 'Major trends in symbolic interaction theory in the past 25 years', *Sociological Quarterly*, vol. 5, pp. 61–84.

Manis, J. G. and Meltzer, B. N. (1972) *Symbolic Interaction: A reader in social psychology*, Allen & Bacon, Boston, MA.

Mead, G. H. (1934) *Mind, Self and Society*, University of Chicago Press, Chicago.

Rose, A. M. (1962) *Human Behaviour and Social Process: An interactionist approach*, Routledge & Kegan Paul, London. (See particularly the paper 'Role taking: Process vs conformity', by R. H. Turner.)

Useful introductions and critical discussions

Meltzer and Petras and Reynolds are the most useful and accessible; Rock is comparatively advanced but provocative; the Plummer volumes provide an excellent collection.

Fisher, B. M. and Strauss, A. L. (1978) 'Interactionism', in Bottomore, T. B. and Nisbet, R. (eds), *A History of Sociological Analysis*, Heinemann, London, pp. 475–97.

Meltzer, B. W. and Petras, J. W. *et al* (1975) *Symbolic Interactionism: Genesis, varieties and criticisms*, Routledge & Kegan Paul, London.

Plummer, K. (ed.) (1991) *Symbolic Interactionism*, Edward Elgar, Aldershot, Hants.

Reynolds, L. T. (1990) *Interactionism: Exposition and critique* (2nd edn), General Hall Inc., New York.

Rock, P. (1979) *The Making of Symbolic Interactionism*, Macmillan, Basingstoke.

Turner, J. H. (1974) 'Parsons as a symbolic interactionist: A comparison of action and interaction theory', *Sociological Inquiry*, vol. 44, pp. 28–94.

Critical papers are included in the Manis and Meltzer reader and the Plummer volume; there are useful references in Meltzer and Petras and Reynolds. On Goffman, see:

Ditton, J. (ed.) (1980) *The View from Goffman*, Macmillan, Basingstoke.

Interactionist studies which make good starting points are:

Becker, H. (1963) *Outsiders: Studies in the sociology of deviance*, Macmillan, Basingstoke.
Goffman, E. (1968a) *Asylums*, Penguin, Harmondsworth.
Goffman, E. (1968b) *Stigma: Notes on the management of spoiled identity*, Penguin, Harmondsworth.
Goffman, E. (1971) *The Presentation of Self in Everyday Life*, Penguin, Harmondsworth.
Humphreys, L. (1970) *Tearoom Trade: A study of homosexual encounters in public places*, Duckworth, London.
Plummer, K. (1975) *Sexual Stigma*, Routledge & Kegan Paul, London.

A selection of interactionist studies of social structure:

Couch, C. (1984) *Constructing Civilisations*, Jai Press, Greenwich, CT.
Fine, G. A. (1983) 'Symbolic interaction and social organisation: Introduction to the special feature', *Symbolic Interaction*, vol. 6, pp. 69–70.
Hosticka, C. J. (1979) 'We don't care about what happened, we only care about what is going to happen: Lawyer–client negotiations of reality', *Social Problems*, vol. 26, pp. 599–610.
Strauss, A. (1978) *Negotiations*, Jossey-Bass, San Francisco.
Stryker, S. (1980) *Symbolic Interactionism*, Benjamin Cummings, Menloe Park, CA.
Stryker, S. and Serpe, R. T. (1982) 'Commitment, identity, salience and role behaviour', in Ickes, W. and Knowles, E. (eds), *Personality, Roles and Social Behaviour*, Springer-Verlag, New York, pp. 199–218.

On emotions, see:

Denzin, N. K. (1984) *On Understanding Emotion*, Jossey-Bass, San Francisco.
Hochschild, A. R. (1983) *The Managed Heart: Commercialisation of human feeling*, University of California Press, Berkeley.
Kemper, T. D. (1978) *A Social Interactional Theory of Emotions*, John Wiley & Sons, New York.
Shott, S. (1979) 'Emotion and social life: A symbolic interactionist analysis', *American Journal of Sociology*, vol. 84, pp. 1317–34.

Chapter 6

SOCIETY AS A CONSPIRACY: PHENOMENOLOGICAL SOCIOLOGY AND ETHNOMETHODOLOGY

Symbolic interactionism is the longest-standing sociological tradition concerned with looking at day-to-day social interactions. I have suggested that it can fairly easily be built into a macro-sociology that makes social action its starting point. An alternative – and in many ways very different – concern with interaction emerged during the late 1960s. This chapter will be primarily concerned with ethnomethodology, just one of a number of approaches that emerged during that period and later – phenomenological sociology, existential sociology, the sociology of everyday life – none of which really consolidated itself as a major school, although many of their insights have become common currency. I think this flourish can be seen as part of the general trend that I have already mentioned: away from any attempt to conceive of society as an 'entity' over and above individuals and towards an emphasis – what I regard as a gross overemphasis – on the ways in which human beings create their social worlds: a response to modern conditions that ignores what it is unpleasant to see. Ethnomethodology and the others are part of a swing to 'social constructionism' over the past quarter-century. Many of these approaches were motivated by a general and rather vague humanist and liberationist spirit, and it is interesting that – at the moment, at any rate – the most rigorous and least political one has proved most hardy. I will approach ethnomethodology initially through its philosophical background – European phenomenology and linguistic philosophy.

THE PHILOSOPHICAL BACKGROUND

Phenomenology

The founding father of phenomenological philosophy was Edmund Husserl, whose most important work was published in the last decade of the nineteenth century and the first decades of this century. Husserl was concerned to develop a radical philosophy in a literal sense of the word: a philosophy that goes to the roots of our knowledge and experience. In particular, he argued that scientific knowledge had become divorced from the everyday experience and activities in which it is rooted, and he saw the task of phenomenology as restoring that connection. Half a century later, sociologists were to use the same argument against established social theory, in particular structural-functionalism: it had become divorced from everyday social experience.

Phenomenology is concerned solely with the structures and workings of human consciousness, and its basic – though often implicit – presupposition is that the world we live in is created in consciousness, in our heads. Of course, it would be absurd to deny that there is an external world, but the argument is that the outside world has meaning only through our consciousness of it. The sociologist – or any scientist, for that matter – is interested only in the world in so far as it is meaningful, and she must therefore understand how we make it meaningful. This is achieved through setting aside what we normally assume we know and tracing the process of coming to know it. This setting aside of our knowledge is referred to sometimes as the 'phenomenological reduction', sometimes as 'bracketing', and in the more technical literature as the *époché*.

Phenomenological sociology
To begin with, I want to make two points. First, I must emphasise the similarity between the approaches I have discussed so far and the concerns of phenomenology. They all see meanings – norms, values, beliefs, etc. – as the central focus of the sociological enterprise. They are all theories of persons and of action. Secondly, I think that phenomenology, in its sociological form, loses some of its most interesting aspects. I have discussed it so far purely as a theory of cognition, of knowing: many phenomenological philosophers, including Husserl, have concerned themselves with a much wider range of

experience – with emotions, the imagination, hallucination and so on. This side has been lost in phenomenological sociology.

The most prominent phenomenological sociologist was Alfred Schutz, a pupil of Husserl who emigrated to the USA after the rise of fascism in Europe and made a career as a banker and part-time teacher. He came under the influence of pragmatist philosophy and symbolic interactionism, and his classic work, *The Phenomenology of the Social World* (1972), was concerned with combining the insights of phenomenology with sociology through a philosophical critique of the work of Max Weber. He attempted to show how we build our knowledge of the social world from a basic stream of incoherent and meaningless experience. We do this through a process of 'typification', which involves building up classes of experience through similarity. Thus, in my stream of experience, I notice that certain objects have particular features in common – that they move from place to place, perhaps, whilst their surroundings remain constant. This gives me the most abstract category of 'living beings'; then I notice that amongst these there are some who emit consistent noises of a type of which I am capable; thus, from 'living beings' I sort out 'other people'. I then distinguish different classes of other people: blacks and whites, men and women. Finally, I identify those characteristics which distinguish specific others: my mother, my friend. Thus we build up what Schutz calls 'meaning contexts', sets of criteria by means of which we organise our sense experience into a meaningful world and stocks of knowledge, which are not stocks of knowledge *about* the world but, for all practical purposes, the world itself. Action and social action thus become things that happen in consciousness: we are concerned with acts of consciousness rather than action in the world, and the social world is something which we create together.

This is the basis of our social world: taken-for-granted, common-sense knowledge. We each organise the world of common-sense knowledge on the basis of the 'here and now', of what we are doing in a particular time and place, or – to use another of Schutz's terms – on the basis of our 'project'. The sociologist is distinguished from other people by her own project and consequent organisation of the shared stocks of knowledge. Her project is to construct a rational, and therefore objective, account of the social world. To do this, she must construct 'second-order typifications': typifications of our common-sense typifications which order the social world in a rational way; we can then use this rational model to predict how people behave if they behave rationally, and to indicate the irrationality of their action if it does not fit the model. Schutz talks about social theory as creating a world of rational puppets who can be manipulated by the theorist to provide knowledge about the real world: we can say that if people have certain goals and behave rationally, then they will act in such a way; if the situation changes, then their action will change in this or that way. Again the cognitive emphasis of Schutz's work is clear, and, paradoxically, we arrive at a version of rational choice theory. It is, however, a more complete version, showing how the situation of choice is constructed and giving a more elaborate analysis of motivation: Schutz, for example, distinguishes between 'because motives', what we know might happen on the basis of experience, and 'in order to' motives, the state of affairs we want to achieve.

Generally Schutz's work has been used to provide further sensitising concepts, often implicitly. I am not aware of any one empirical study that uses it systematically except through the development of ethnomethodology, which I will be discussing shortly. There is, however, one writer, Peter Berger, who has made systematic attempts to extend phenomenology to a theory of society. The central work, which he wrote with Thomas Luckman, is *The Social Construction of Reality* (1967), which explicitly sets out to combine a holistic and individualistic analysis. Berger and Luckman still see shared, taken-for-granted, common-sense meanings as the basis of social organisation, but they are more concerned with shared and explicit overarching meanings that develop out of common-sense meanings. They argue that human beings have very few stable and specific instincts; the stability of social life must therefore come from the social environment which they themselves create, and in this environment it is the overarching values and meanings, initially religious, which provide the real focus of social organisation and are shared by everybody. Berger and Luckman are concerned with the way in which these meanings develop and are 'objectivated' in social institutions, and thus socialise new members of a society. Overall, this leaves us with an approach similar to structural-functionalism. Ideas, cultural values and norms are seen as the centre of social organisation, into which new members are socialised. Berger and Luckman spend rather more time talking about the development of these values out of the social interaction of individuals, but the end-picture of social organisation is the same. The crucial difference is that structural-functionalism has a great deal to say about institutional organisations and the systematic relationships between institutions, whereas for Berger and Luckman these tend to be secondary. It is fairly simple to place this approach in a structural-functionalist context as yet another fragment, concerned with the cultural system, which for Parsons is one of four systems, even if it is the most important. I said above that once phenomenology has placed action 'inside the head', it finds it difficult to break out again; and indeed, in the sociological literature Berger is regarded primarily as a sociologist of knowledge, rather than a theorist of society.

Linguistic philosophy

Ethnomethodology provides our first encounter with what has become known as the 'linguistic turn' in modern philosophy: an increasing concern with the nature of language as somehow providing the key to the world; in different ways, British analytical philosophy and European philosophy have focused on language, and this concern has fed through to sociology – primarily through ethnomethodology and Giddens's structuration theory, but also in the form of post-structuralism.

Here I am concerned with the former, and I will approach it through the work of Peter Winch, whose *The Idea of a Social Science* (1958) has had a sort of underground influence in sociology, rarely acknowledged by sociologists. For Winch, society – or social relations – and the way we conceive of social relations are the same thing; the task of philosophy and of social science is the same: to elaborate the 'form of life' of a particular society, the way in which that society conceives of its social relations. He employs a now popular analogy with language, taken here from Wittgenstein. What is interesting about language is that there is no substantive definition of a word which covers all its uses. Wittgenstein talked about 'language games', and the word 'game' is a good example. Netball is a game, so is chess and so is Snakes and Ladders; but I can also talk about the 'sociology game'; people can 'play games' with me, or vice versa, and – at least during the 1960s – a 'game bird' could mean, in different contexts, a pheasant, a partridge, a grouse, or a woman who was willing to engage in sexual intercourse. There is no definition of the word that could link all these usages. Rather, there are rules which govern the

use of the word, implicit rules which we none the less all share –
rules which, for example, would leave people looking puzzled if I
talked about having had a 'game shave' this morning.

We can look at social action in the same way: it is rule-following,
and the elaboration of a 'form of life' is the elaboration of the rules
governing a culture or subculture, the rules governing the way we
conceive of – effectively, the way we create – our world. This leads to
a fairly thoroughgoing relativism. No one form of life takes priority
over another, none is more 'true' – in the classic argument, science
and witchcraft are alternative forms of life, there are no external
standards by which we can judge one to be better than another.
However, the fact that we are all human, that all cultures have to deal
with the fact that we are born, we die, and we have to organise our
sexual relations, means that there is a basis for mutual understanding.

ETHNOMETHODOLOGY: DOING

For some time, ethnomethodology was a thorn in the side of the
sociological establishment; it appeared to undermine all existing
forms of sociological work and indirectly challenge the integrity of
established sociologists. There was a period at the beginning of the
1970s when a number of sociology departments in universities in the
USA and Britain were split by arguments, and there are stories of
ethnomethodologists being fired from their jobs simply because they
were ethnomethodologists. After an initial cult popularity the movement subsided somewhat, and although a number of sociologists still
identify themselves with the approach, it has settled into being
another of the discipline's many aspects. The analogy I drew with
viewing society as a conspiracy is even more apt in the case of
ethnomethodology. Like phenomenology, ethnomethodology sees
social organisation as something which has to be established out of
different individuals' different experiences. However, whereas Schutz
would argue that order is the result of shared common-sense
knowledge, ethnomethodology argues that such knowledge is itself
inherently unstable, something which is created anew in each new
encounter. We conspire together to create the impression of shared
common-sense knowledge. In a classroom we all assume that we are
reasonably intelligent people engaged in a process of learning and
teaching and rarely, if at all, do we need to articulate those

assumptions. For Schutz the existence of such assumptions explains the orderly proceeding of the class. For an ethnomethodologist, such assumptions do not exist in any substantial way, and in each and every class we are conspiring together – of necessity in a taken-for-granted way – to give each other the impression that they do exist. We are 'doing' a class – my students are 'doing' being students and I am 'doing' being a teacher. Every stable social interaction is an *achievement*, something done, and ethnomethodology seeks to discover how it is done. Hence the name: *ology*, the study of, *ethno*, peoples, *method*, methods – for creating social order.

It used to be common to distinguish between 'situational' and 'linguistic' ethnomethodology, but I think such a distinction is misleading, since the central insights of the approach have to do with our use of language to make situations stable, although certainly linguistic concerns have tended to be more narrow and have less connection with sociology in a wider sense. Paradoxically, the clarity of expression associated with linguistic philosophy is transformed by ethnomethodology into the most convoluted jargon to have appeared in an area where jargon is the norm. As time has passed, it has become clear that all this verbiage hides two important ideas which have led to some interesting work and a lot of nonsense – or, more charitably, a lot of routine work dressed up in a jargon that makes it seem nonsense. These ideas are built into a criticism of established sociology, and this provides a good entry to the substantive contribution of ethnomethodology.

The usual way of putting this criticism is that conventional sociology takes as a resource what should be taken as a topic. At some level, different in each case, the meanings employed by those we study – their norms, values, attitudes and beliefs; the rules which govern their conduct – are treated as if their meaning were unproblematic. The work of explanation then employs those very same meanings as its basis – the sociologist conspires with the people she studies to produce yet another impression of social order. This is where the important insights of ethnomethodology come into play. The first is the inherent *indexicality* of meaning. Language works rather like an indexing system in a library, constantly referring us to other works on the same topic, works by the same author, and so on; the meaning of each term in a language refers us to its context, the situation in which it is used and the words around it. This is most obvious with pronouns such as 'you' – which 'you' I am talking about is clear only in the situation in which I use it. However, the same is true of any word or statement; when we listen to somebody talk, we are always having to wait to understand what they are saying: if you go back and read the first sentence of this paragraph, it is by no means clear what I am talking about; in the process of reading you suspend judgement until I explain what I mean. However, the same is true of any sentence or phrase taken in isolation, and the process of explanation has no end. It is always possible to ask, 'What do you mean?' to any reply you get. We cannot, therefore, take any meaning for granted, yet we all behave as though we can. This is essentially the same insight into the nature of language as that provided by Peter Winch.

The second significant idea approaches the question of how we can behave as though meaning were clear: it points to the *reflexivity* of our talk about our actions and situations. When we describe a situation, we are simultaneously creating it, making it appear solid, meaningful and rational. When I write: 'I am writing a book on sociological theory', I am not just describing what I am doing, I am simultaneously justifying what I am doing, telling myself and others how to approach what I am doing, removing areas of doubt and uncertainty. The term 'reflexivity' sums up the activities that we employ in everyday interaction, to correct 'indexicality' and establish a sense of social stability. Harold Garfinkel, the generally recognised founder of ethnomethodology, first followed Schutz in referring to them as 'background expectancies', taken-for-granted forms of common-sense knowledge. His earlier work took the form of experiments to establish the existence of such expectations, and of indexicality. He would send his students out to do things that would challenge background expectations – for example, to go into a department store and try to bargain for goods, or to go back to their family home and behave as if they were lodgers. He regarded the resulting social disorder as proving his claim. To demonstrate indexicality he asked them to clarify the meaning of a transcribed conversation between a husband and wife, and of course no complete clarification was possible. He could always ask, 'What do you mean by this?'

Later he came to talk less about background expectations and more about 'practices' and rules, emphasising the point that maintaining an impression of social order is a never-ceasing activity. Such activities are difficult to grasp at first, simply because they are, in

Garfinkel's view, a taken-for-granted basis to all our actions; it is rather like paying constant attention to the process of breathing or the way in which we put one foot in front of another. A couple of examples should suffice. The first is 'glossing'. If we use the word at all in our everyday speech, glossing usually refers to something like 'avoiding the issue', trying to talk our way around the issue. The first part of this paragraph is glossing – I could not give a literal definition of these practices, so I talked about how hard it is to understand them. If the argument about indexicality is correct, then all talking is glossing. One of the most interesting ethnomethodologists, Aaron Cicourel, sums it up thus:

> We can perhaps achieve glimpses of our glossing activity by making it clear that every attempt to stimulate or avoid the glossing activity is itself a glossing operation. This means showing the absurdity of efforts to be uncompromisingly literal in our description of observed events or activities in which we participate. (Cicourel, 1973: 109)

In the process of glossing, it seems we have recourse to certain implicit and taken-for-granted rules (as opposed to taken-for-granted substantive knowledge). An example of such a rule is the *et cetera* clause, an addendum to all rules of social behaviour which says something like 'except in reasonable circumstances'. For example, when I give a lecture, there is an informal (and sometimes formal) rule that I am the one who does the talking and everybody else keeps quiet. The *et cetera* rule allows people to break the first rule 'in reasonable circumstances': by asking a question, perhaps, or carrying on a short whispered conversation with a neighbour, or pointing out that the room is on fire. The next step would be to look at ways in which the *et cetera* rule is invoked.

Again we are left with a low-level theory – a few theoretical insights which point towards empirical investigation. Although there have been attempts to develop the theory further – I shall look at these shortly – the emphasis of ethnomethodology has been on empirical work. It involves a sort of empirical application of the phenomenological reduction: the researcher pays no attention to the substance of what people say (that would be to engage in the conspiracy of giving an impression of social order) but looks at the way they say it, trying to identify the rules and practices by means of which the impression of order is given. The result is a startling departure from what would normally expect. Another early ethnomethodologist, Harvey Sacks, employed his research time in a Suicide Prevention Centre studying the way in which people opened telephone conversations. Much ethnomethodological research seems to spend a great deal of time and energy to come up with taken-for-granted rules that are, in fact, no surprise to anyone: amongst Sacks's conclusions, for example, were the propositions that in conversations, generally only one person speaks at a time and when more than one person speaks at a time, it will be only briefly. There are, I think, good reasons for this comparative poverty of research findings: reflexivity refers to a process in which the product is a sense of order, of apparently substantive meanings, and the starting point is the absence of that sense. We can find out very little about the process itself without already knowing about the starting point and the end-point. To try would be like trying to understand the production process in a factory without bothering to find out what raw materials are used and ignoring the finished product; and in this case there would appear to be no raw materials. This is precisely what a lot of empirical ethnomethodology manages to do, and for this reason a lot of sociologists dismiss it. I think this is a mistake: like any other theory, ethnomethodology opens some doors and closes others. I want now to examine its theoretical status rather more closely.

THE WAY OUT OF COGNITION

I think the best way to approach ethnomethodology is as a theory of 'social cognition', which in turn must have its place in a general theory of persons or actions. It is a theory of the way in which we come to agree on what makes up the social world. Aaron Cicourel seems to me to have made the most theoretical progress in this direction, and his work points to more interesting possibilities. He argues that the sense of social structure we seek to establish in our interaction is the product of what he calls 'surface' and 'interpretive' or 'deep' rules (drawing here on the work of the linguist, Noam Chomsky). Surface rules are the norms of social life that the other theoretical approaches have taken for granted. Ethnomethodology has, I think, established conclusively that such rules cannot be taken for granted but are at least interpreted and reconstructed in different ways in different situations. This reconstruction is carried out by an underlying structure of interpretative rules which, Cicourel seems to think, are innate properties of human beings. We do not learn them; instead, they are the basis for learning. This in itself is sufficiently interesting, but Cicourel goes further in indicating why such an underlying structure of interpretative rules should be necessary. Our perception of the world works through all our five senses: we can see the world, hear, feel, taste and smell all at the same time, and the things and events of the world are perceived simultaneously. Language, however, enables us only to talk about one thing at a time, and there is a process of translation from our other non-linguistic experiences of the world into our descriptions. This is why describing an event is always creating that event, never simply a matter of recording it. Here, at last, there is a pointer out of cognition, since not just our minds but our emotions are involved in our experience of the world. The connections between the word and the perception, and the word and the feeling, have been barely touched on by social theory; yet all empirical investigations concerned with what people say assume that these relations present no problems.

CONCLUSION

One of the points to emerge from phenomenological sociology in general, and from Cicourel's work in particular, refers to another part of the social world which seems to comprise a separate area of study: the realm of general meanings. The existence of such a realm is disputed by ethnomethodology in some of its forms; to accept a realm of general meanings is seen as entering into the conspiracy to give an impression of social order. However, whilst it might be true to say that an impression of social order is constructed afresh in each social interaction, we do not invent meaning each time; what we do is give a specific situation-related version of a general meaning. General meanings are tools we employ in different ways in different circumstances, rather as we might use a hammer for knocking in a nail, pulling out a nail, or smashing a window to escape from a fire. These general meanings are Cicourel's surface rules or Berger and Luckman's overarching symbols, socially shared and established, similar to language itself. Thus ethnomethodology, if it does not exactly point beyond cognition in this respect, again indicates an area of investigation and a problem for action theory: what is involved in employing a general meaning in a particular way. Again we find that a theory of action, without a theory of society or culture, nevertheless assumes a theory of culture.

Having said all this, it is still true that ethnomethodology closes some extremely important doors. In the case of symbolic interactionism, I argued that to assume that there may be no such thing as a society when the experience of those we study suggests that there is such a thing is to do violence to the experience of those we study. Ethnomethodology deliberately sets out to do such violence: the perception of 'society' as a social structure over and above social interactions is a result of conspiracy. To investigate society in such a sense is simply to take part in the conspiracy. For reasons I have already suggested, it seems to me that we can accept that social interaction involves creating an impression of social order, but this in no way invalidates the arguments I used in the Introduction to Part II about the existence of societies as separate and different objects of study. If we accept the ethnomethodological argument on this point, then we cannot approach any of the major social problems, such as unemployment, crime or war, that are crucial features of our lives. It is not helpful if opening the door to the indexical and reflexive features of interaction closes the door to more conventional forms of sociological study; rather, it should add a new dimension to them.

In redefining social action as *activity*, as what people actually do and how they organise what they do, ethnomethodology does focus attention on areas often ignored by sociologists. As Sharrock and Anderson (1986) point out, most sociology of medicine says very little about what doctors actually do – in Goffman's essay on surgeons, for example, we learn nothing about surgery. Ethnomethodology focuses precisely on the activity of surgery and its organisation. Empirical work in ethnomethodology over the past decade has focused on, for example, what scientists, including mathematicians, *do* in the day-to-day organisation of their activities. It is in the making of these activities rationally accountable that we find the answer to Parsons's problem of order; indeed, Sharrock and Anderson present Garfinkel as radicalising Parsons, looking at day-to-day interaction and not finding the common values that Parsons suggests should be there: finding, instead, that the social is a constant creation; this is, indeed, a new dimension to sociology, but in its implicit presupposition of a culture and a shared language and meanings, it still presupposes Parsons.

FURTHER READING

On phenomenological sociology

The two books co-authored by Peter Berger are very readable starting points, but Schutz provides the real flavour of the approach. The other works listed are mainly introductory articles or readers (Psathas is more advanced) and there is little to choose between them.

Berger, P. and Kellner, H. (1974) *The Homeless Mind*, Penguin, Harmondsworth.

Berger, P. and Luckman, T. (1967) *The Social Construction of Reality*, Allen Lane, London.

Filmer, P. *et al.* (1972) *New Directions in Sociological Theory*, Collier Macmillan, London.

Lassman, P. (1974) 'Phenomenological perspectives in sociology', in Rex, J. (ed.), *Approaches in Sociology*, Routledge & Kegan Paul, London, pp. 125–44.

Psathas, G. (1973) *Phenomenological Sociology: Issues and applications*, John Wiley, New York.

Schutz, A. (1962–6) *Collected Papers* (2 vols), Martinus Nijhoff, The Hague.

Schutz, A. (1972) *The Phenomenology of the Social World*, Heinemann, London.

Winch, P. (1958) *The Idea of a Social Science*, Routledge & Kegan Paul, London.

Wolff, K. H. (1978) 'Phenomenology and sociology', in Bottomore, T. B. and Nisbet, R. (eds), *A History of Sociology Analysis*, Heinemann, London, pp. 499–556.

Ethnomethodology

Of the following introductions, Sharrock and Anderson and Livingston stand out, but all are adequate:

Attewell, P. (1974) 'Ethnomethodology since Garfinkel', *Theory and Society*, vol. 1, pp. 179–210.

Benson, D. and Hughes, J. H. (1983) *The Perspective of Ethnomethodology*, Longman, London.

Heritage, J. (1984) *Garfinkel and Ethnomethodology*, Cambridge University Press, Cambridge.

Leiter, K. (1980) *A Primer on Ethnomethodology*, Oxford University Press, Oxford.

110   *Modern Social Theory*

Livingston, E. (1987) *Making Sense of Ethnomethodology*, Routledge & Kegan Paul, London.
Sharrock, W. and Anderson, B. (1986) *The Ethnomethodologists*, Ellis Horwood, Chichester/Tavistock, London.

Useful classical texts:

Atkinson, M. and Heritage, J. (1984) *Structures of Social Action*, Cambridge University Press, Cambridge.
Cicourel, A. V. (1964) *Method and Measurement in Sociology*, The Free Press, New York.
Cicourel, A. V. (1973) *Cognitive Sociology*, Penguin, Harmondsworth.
Douglas, J. D. (1971) *Understanding Everyday Life*, Routledge & Kegan Paul, London.
Garfinkel, H. (1967) *Studies in Ethnomethodology*, Prentice Hall, Englewood Cliffs, NJ.
Psathas, G. (ed.) (1979) *Everyday Language*, Irvington Press, New York.
Schenkein, J. (ed.) (1978) *Studies in the Organization of Conversational Interaction*, Academic Press, New York.
Sudnow, D. (ed.) (1972) *Studies in Social Interaction*, The Free Press, Glencoe, NJ.
Turner, R. (1974) *Ethnomethodology*, Penguin, Harmondsworth.

Recent empirical work:

Garfinkel, H. (1986) *Ethnomethodological Studies of Work*, Routledge & Kegan Paul, London.
Lieberman, K. (1985) *Understanding Interaction in Central Australia*, Routledge & Kegan Paul, London.
Livingston, E. (1986) *The Ethnomethodological Foundations of Mathematics*, Routledge & Kegan Paul, London.
Lynch, M. (1985) *Art and Artefact in Laboratory Science*, Routledge & Kegan Paul, London.

A useful summary:

Atkinson, P. (1988) 'Ethnomethodology: A critical review', *Annual Review of Sociology*, Annual Reviews Inc., Palo Alto, CA, pp. 441–65.

Useful critical studies:

Giddens, A. (1976) *New Rules of Sociological Method*, Hutchinson, London (Chapter 1).
Goldthorpe, J. H. (1973) 'A revolution in sociology', *Sociology*, vol. 7, pp. 449–62.

Chapter 7

STRUCTURATION THEORY: THERE IS SUCH A THING AS SOCIETY; THERE IS NO SUCH THING AS SOCIETY

INTRODUCTION

It is sometimes said that someone with a paragraph to say will write an article, someone with a chapter will write a book. Having recently completed a book on the work of Anthony Giddens, I hope I am not going to prove the point. In fact, in the space of a chapter there is no possibility of conveying the full range of Giddens's work; rather, I will concentrate on looking at the central aspects of his 'structuration theory' in the context of the general arguments in *this* book.

Giddens's work is remarkable – not only for its quantity, but also for the range of ideas it brings together; not just as theory, but as studies of world history; it is remarkable, too, in that Giddens has become the first British social theorist in recent times to have an international reputation. Although his style – and, to a lesser extent, his way of thinking – is different to Parsons's, structuration theory should be considered on a par with structural-functionalism. It is an attempt to maintain a conception of society as a whole, whilst holding on to the insights of the 'linguistic turn' in philosophy, and particularly of ethnomethodology in sociology.

It is appropriate to deal with Giddens at this point. If the theories considered in the previous three chapters have maintained, to some degree, that there is no such thing as society – starting, and often ending, with individual action and social action – Giddens actually tries to rescue some idea of society: certainly he is happy to talk about

111

structures and social systems; on the other hand, he insists that society is produced and reproduced through human action, and he rejects any form of structural explanation and any notion that a society might have an existence over and above individuals. This covers any explanation which grants a society or a social system emergent properties, or talks about a society or a situation determining human action. This leads to a wholesale rejection of functionalist explanation and evolutionary theories, both of which he attributes – with some justification – not only to Parsons but also to Marxism.

The end-result is a rather abstract animal: Giddens calls it an ontology of social being, which he regards as compatible with a range of methodologies and theoretical concerns in sociology; it is not a systematic theory, nor is it explanatory – it is more of a general guide to what exists in the social world. Thus although he wishes to talk about social systems and structures, and might even be regarded as 'saving' these ideas from dissolution in action theory, he holds on to them in a rather tenuous fashion. At least, this is true in his theory; when he writes about modernity there is, behind many of his ideas, an implicit view of a social system imposing itself on us.

STRUCTURATION AND THE DUALITY OF STRUCTURE

Unsurprisingly, the central idea of structuration theory is structuration, often linked to what Giddens calls the 'duality of structure'. He argues that sociology usually sees structure as a constraining or determining feature of social life, but in fact it is also enabling. The analogy with language is very clear here: it limits what we can say, but enables us to say something. Structures are, as it were, 'enveloped' in action: they exist only in and through action, which produces, reproduces and changes them. In fact, by 'structure' he means something very different to what the term implies for structural-functionalism or structuralist Marxism. He defines it in terms of 'rules and resources'; the notion of 'rule' is most important, and it refers to something very close to the notion of 'rule' in the work of Peter Winch and the ethnomethodologists. Indeed, in his most elaborate discussions of what he means by rules (in *The Constitution of Society*, [1984]), Giddens argues that the most essential rules are like those that govern a mathematical series, such as 2, 4, 6, . . .; nobody would have much trouble in continuing such a progression, but we would need to think about – and might have difficulty in articulating – the rule we were following, just as we rarely know the rules we are following when we talk.

Giddens's debt to ethnomethodology must be evident; at this level social order, structure, consists in our routine activities. He also takes seriously the notion of reflexivity, the way in which we actually constitute our social world. When he discusses the idea of a reflexive sociology, it is in terms of the way sociological work constitutes the world it is studying, and is part of that world. He offers a three-tier model of the social actor which he compares loosely with Freud's model of id, ego and superego. In fact, he regularly draws on psychoanalytic ideas when he is talking about the actor. He suggests an unconscious level which, he argues, is not very significant on a day-to-day basis, providing only a generalised motivation, but becomes important in crisis situations; secondly, there is a level of implicit or taken-for-granted knowledge – the rules I mentioned above – and finally there is the level of conscious, reflexive knowledge. The difference between these last two can be described as the difference between 'knowledge of how' and 'knowledge of what'.

The implicit, taken-for-granted level is clearly associated with routine, which plays an important part in Giddens's theory. This in turn depends on what he calls the actor's 'ontological security': a sense of the world and the people in it remaining more or less the same from moment to moment, day to day. The all-important implicit knowledge of how to proceed is learnt during socialisation, through the 'hidden curriculum'. Giddens again turns to psychoanalytic work on the importance of routine care in early socialisation to explain this.

Where are we now? So far, social order consists in largely routine, implicit rule-following activity, and 'structure' refers to the rules that are implied in such action. It is easy to see how Giddens can claim, at this level of argument, that structure exists only in and through action, just as the structure of our language exists only in and through our speech. Such action he refers to as 'social practices', and it is by taking social practices as its object of study that sociology can overcome the traditional dualism of action and structure (the dualism, of course, around which this book is organised). In

Giddens's terms, this dualism is in fact a *duality*: there is one 'thing', one object of study, with two sides:

> The basic domain of study of the social sciences, according to the theory of structuration, is neither the experience of the individual actor, nor the existence of any form of societal totality, but social practices ordered across time and space. (Giddens, 1984: 2)

These practices, however, can be looked at from two sides, concentrating on one and bracketing the other: we can engage in 'strategic analysis', looking at what actors do, how they reflexively constitute their activity, the implicit rules they follow; or we can engage in 'institutional analysis', the analysis of social systems. So far, what I have had to say about Giddens places him firmly in the tradition of action theory without Parsons's movement to systems analysis, but going rather beyond the scope of rational choice theory, symbolic interactionism and ethnomethodology. However, Giddens wants to go further, and at first glance it is difficult to see how this could be achieved. How can we move from talking about social practices and structures as implicit rules to talking about social systems, social institutions?

INSTITUTIONS

For Giddens, a conception of institution is derived almost directly from his conception of action and rules. Institutions are the ordering of implicit rules (structures) in time and space. Giddens is using 'institution' here not in the sense of an organisation like a church or a university but in the sense that marriage is an institution, a practice that is deeply embedded through history and across space. In discussing all this he produces a host of distinctions and concepts, most of which I am going to gloss over; my main aim is to convey a general sense of what he is on about, rather than a detailed understanding.

Human actions, and therefore social practices, have certain properties on which institutions are based. To begin with, social practices imply communication – we need to talk to each other – and this involves 'structures of signification', i.e. rules which govern communication. The 'institutions' that develop from these rules are symbolic orders or modes of discourse; basically, the symbolic systems through which we organise and see the world. It is worth pointing out here that throughout his work Giddens insists on the actor's implicit and/or explicit knowledgeability of what she is doing, and whilst he recognises that symbolic systems can be used to maintain power, the possibility that such a system might be 'ideological' in the Marxist sense of false consciousness is not there for him.

Action is also transformative, changing the external world and social relations, and therefore inevitably involves power. For Giddens, power is inherent in all human relations, as is contestation of power, a 'dialectic of control'; by virtue of being human, nobody is completely powerless. This aspect of action leads to structures of domination – domination over people giving rise to political institutions, and domination over resources (the point at which resources, as well as rules, become important) giving rise to economic institutions. Finally, action is inherently normative, involving reference to implicit or explicit values. This implies the existence of structures of legitimation and legal institutions. Social systems are defined by different 'clusterings' of institutions.

Thus Giddens, at this point, is building up a model of society very much like that of Parsons; we move towards social systems through understanding the institutionalisation of social practices; unlike Parsons, however, he does not say that systems have emergent properties; there is no equivalent to Parsons's use of systems theory, which Giddens explicitly rejects. Nevertheless, he does discuss social systems.

SOCIAL SYSTEMS

I think it is difficult to discern exactly what Giddens means by 'social system'. There is a sense in which the concept possesses a quality of 'now you see it, now you don't', especially when it is taken in conjunction with his historical sociology and his book on modernity. A starting point is to be found in his distinction between social integration and system integration. We have already come across this distinction in David Lockwood's criticism of Parsons, but Giddens gives it his own meaning. For Giddens, social integration refers to reciprocity between actors in face-to-face situations; system integration, on the other hand, involves reciprocity between groups and collectives, and is something which is achieved through time and space.

A brief excursus is necessary here. Throughout his work, Giddens makes a great deal of the notions of time and space, arguing that sociology has never come to grips with their importance. I have argued elsewhere (Craib, 1992) that he deals with time and space on two different levels, and unless these are clearly separated, his work is confusing. On one level, he is taking up the phenomenology of time and space, especially through the work of Heidegger. This, I think, is the least important aspect of what he has to say. More important is his use of notions of time and space as a way of analysing, describing and classifying social systems.

The immediate problem is how we can move from reciprocity in face-to-face interaction to reciprocity across time and space – that is from action to systems. There are a number of factors at work, some of which I have already mentioned: the existence of implicit knowledge of how to go on, and routine, are clearly important. Reflexive knowledge, our reflexive monitoring of our actions, also has a role to play. Giddens also uses a notion found in rational choice theory: unintended consequences. I am particularly suspicious of unintended consequences as an explanation for the existence of ordered social systems. It reminds me of a joke I have heard attributed to W. C. Fields: 'I'm sorry I'm late; I was on my way here when I was suddenly taken drunk.' I suspect that the existence of ordered social systems is as accidental as getting drunk; if order were an unintended consequence of action, we would expect chaos to be an unintended consequence as well. I am not sure that action theory can offer an explanation of why we don't get chaos; in fact I suspect that a tenable explanation has to draw on the idea of social systems existing over and above individual and collective action, with emergent properties of their own. But this contributes more to the grinding of my own axe than it does to understanding Giddens.

And so back to the question of how we move from reciprocity in face-to-face interaction to reciprocity across time and space. Giddens's central answer can be found in his treatment of Goffman. Goffman is usually regarded as a particularly quirky writer; only he is capable of doing the sort of work he does. Giddens is concerned to portray him as a systematic social theorist, and the way in which he does so is intriguing and, I think, basically right. The key text in this enterprise is *Frame Analysis* (1974). Here Goffman is concerned with – amongst other things – the way in which what we might call 'slices' of interaction, encounters, conversations, actions, are 'framed', how we signify when something is beginning and when it is ending. On the one hand, this takes us closer to the concerns of ethnomethodology (away from symbolic interactionism, which Giddens does not seem to hold in very high esteem); but on the other hand, it gives us an apparently new and different way of looking at social systems. This is confirmed by Giddens's use of 'time-geography', which constructs models of people's day-to-day movements through time and space, and which he modifies towards sociological concerns. The detail of this, again, is less important than the overall intent, which is summed up most clearly by Stinchcombe:

> [W]hat has an institutional role is not the individual but the time–space unit, the situation of co-presence. What people know is not how to play a role, but how to respond to and learn the praxis of a situation. . . . The basic units of social structure for Giddens are not an individual's statuses and roles, as we have been taught to think, but situations with defined praxes, which we move into and out of and have our current behaviour shaped by. Institutional situations, with their moral and practical arrangements, create individuals' obligations and powers, create activities, so they and not the roles are causally significant. (in Clark *et al.*, 1990: 50)

It is easy to see how our implicit knowledge of how to go on, to continue in situations, 'supports' the social system conceived in this way. In his historical sociology, as well as arguing against evolutionary theory, Giddens argues that we are wrong to think about societies as somehow continuous with geographical borders; rather, he prefers to talk about systems which are more or less open and can cut across geographical boundaries.

THE REAPPEARANCE OF SOCIETY

The idea of society, or social structure imposing itself on individuals, reappears in a subtle way, and despite Giddens's intentions. In his theoretical work, he employs a number of concepts that at least sound as if they are appropriate to the sort of structural analysis one can find in Parsons or Marx: structural principles, sets and properties. The first two are the most important. A structural principle is a deeply embedded principle of organisation, and Giddens cites as an example the separation and interconnection of state and economy in capitalist society – whilst the economy is 'freed' from state control, there is a dramatic increase in the state's power over its citizenry. A 'structural set' is a set of transformations which are again central to a society. He draws directly from Marx here, citing the set of *private property : money : capital : labour : profit*. The reader might reasonably ask what this has to do with the notion of structure as rules, and I will be returning to this later.

The notion is there in his historical sociology as well. Perry Anderson notes it in connection with Giddens's apparent pessimism about the possibilities of nuclear war:

> Where Giddens's ontology evinces an unreasonable optimism of the agent, his history moves towards an unreasonable pessimism. (Anderson, 1990: 57)

Giddens insists all through his historical and theoretical writings on the openness of praxis, its undetermined nature. As I mentioned above, this leads to a critique of any sort of evolutionary theory, which, Giddens implies, involves the idea of a society moving through determinate stages; it seems to exclude, as well, any possibility of any sort of history that is not a fairly straightforward narrative history, telling the story of people's actions and their intended and unintended consequences. Nevertheless, as several critics have pointed out, some idea of evolution and of historical stages haunts his work.

It appears first of all in his classification of different types of society. Giddens classifies societies in terms of their range over time and space and the way in which they 'bind' time and space. He identifies three types. Tribal societies are based largely on face-to-face interaction, and social and system integration are the same thing. Class-divided societies see the separation of social and system integration, although the level of integration is comparatively low and there is what he calls a 'symbiotic' relationship between town and countryside. He also calls such societies 'civilisations', and they seem to include everything between tribal and industrial societies; he uses the term 'class-divided' to indicate that social classes existed in these societies but were not central. Finally, there are class societies, which are typified by a separation of social and system integration with a very high level of both, and where it is no longer meaningful to talk about a division between town and countryside; instead, they exist in a 'created environment'. The development of cities is important here, and he sometimes argues that urban sociology is at the centre of sociology.

Although Giddens is insistent that different types of society exist alongside each other and there is no inevitable progression from one to the other, and no – as it were – 'universal' history, he argues that we can identify 'historical episodes' – sequences of change:

> having a specifiable opening, trend of events and outcomes, which can be compared in some degree in abstraction from definable contexts. (Giddens, 1984: 274)

The episode with which he is most concerned is the transition to industrial society: from class-divided to class societies.

Now, despite his frequent insistence to the contrary, it is difficult not to conceive of Giddens's classification of types of society as a very loose evolutionary one. Erik Olin Wright makes this point in an interesting argument where he proposes that a loose evolutionary theory is actually quite helpful; if we add to this the fact that the transitions Giddens focuses on are those that usually concern evolutionary theory, it is difficult not to accept Wright's point. Despite Giddens's assertions, evolution creeps back in.

The sense, if not the theory or analysis, of a system with its own laws of development, however weak, is reinforced in Giddens's short book on *The Consequences of Modernity* (1990). Again his explicit arguments state the contrary, but there are a number of ways in which modernity as a system 'out of control' appears in the text. It appears quite explicitly when he is talking about what he calls the 'phenomenology' of modernity, the way it is perceived by those of us who live in it. It is there implicitly in the way in which – following through his arguments against evolutionary theory – he insists on the uniqueness of the modern world, its differences to anything that has gone before, and his rooting of these differences in what he calls a process of 'disembedding': this involves an 'emptying' of time and space, and carries the implication that in traditional societies both were bound up with the specific nature of social life, whereas now they are universal forms, the same for whatever activity we are engaged in, wherever we are. When he describes the development of modernity, one gets the sense of this as an inevitable process, and we are left with 'abstract systems' rather than concrete relationships and settings. Examples of abstract systems include 'symbolic tokens' – money is the clearest example – which enable exchanges independent of time and space, and 'expert systems' – referring to the way we are dependent on professionals who possess knowledge that we do not.

The inevitability is there as well in what he has to say about reflexivity and modernity: it becomes increasingly necessary to find rational justifications for everything; nothing can be taken at face value, or guaranteed by tradition, or faith.

I will return to these issues again in the chapter on postmodernism. What Giddens portrays is a world in which we are struggling in all sorts of ways to 're-embed' our relationships. Although this is necessary – no social system could work without face-to-face social relationships, even if they are mediated by telephones and computers – it leaves the sense of individuals fighting against something infinitely bigger than themselves – something indicated, perhaps, by his rather naive prescriptions for change: we must avoid ecological disaster, totalitarianism, economic depression and nuclear war. All very well, but it does not take us very far.

SOCIAL ONTOLOGY BUT NO SOCIAL THEORY

I should emphasise at this point that Giddens's work is much richer than the very bare outline I have presented; in the context of my main argument in this book, my concern has been with his particular conception of action and practice, and the way he moves from this to talk about social systems. My argument has been – in the last section, at any rate – that despite his assertions to the contrary, there is a sense in his work of social systems developing, with properties of their own. I now want to expand on this.

What strikes me most about structuration *theory* is that it has little to say, theoretically, about society. As a thoroughgoing action theory, Giddens surrenders from the start the possibility of explanations in terms of society. That, I believe, is why Giddens *has* to see his work in terms of a social ontology; it makes very general statements about the social world and what constitutes it, but does not point us directly towards anything. If we compare structuration theory to structural-functionalism, it is clear that it is possible to develop a range of research projects – a research programme – from the latter. This is not possible with structuration theory, as Ira Cohen (1989) – one of Giddens's most sympathetic exponents – points out. Instead, on various occasions, Giddens presents us with a series of pointers: we must look at the way in which action and systems bind time and space; at the reflexive knowledge that social actors possess; at the implicit knowledge they work with, and so on. When he discusses empirical studies, it tends to be a matter of translating them into the terms of structuration theory, and this generally adds little to our understanding of the specific topic.

There seems to be one point in the theory – as opposed to the historical sociology – where Giddens seems to me to imply the existence of social structures in the conventional sense. In fact, it emerges more clearly in the quotation from Stinchcombe. The structure consists of the time–space unit; when Giddens sets out his analyses of the time–space nature of interaction in *The Constitution of Society*, there is always an implicit vicious circle: the analysis of the social practice presupposes the system in which it creates. Smith and Turner (1986) comment on this; and if we think about what is involved in learning the praxis of a situation, it seems to me that it is a broader concept than learning a role, but not essentially different – it simply presupposes a time–space structure instead of a role structure.

I think this point makes sense of a range of criticisms of Giddens's conception of structure and the move to talking about systems. If we take 'structure' as referring to the rules that govern action, in particular the implicit rules of how to proceed, it is – as Thompson (in Held and Thompson, 1990) points out – difficult to see how this can lead us to structural principles about, for example, the relationship between the state and the economy, or 'structural sets' about the conversion of money into capital. 'Structure' in this latter sense seems to have more to do with the relatively autonomous development of societies or systems. Urry (1982) points to the fact that unless we can actually specify the mediations between structure in Giddens's sense and social systems, the way in which action produced by and reproducing structures also produces systems, the notion of structure remains a sort of essence which somehow magically produces systems.

Going back to my earlier comments on Parsons: we can find what I regard as the essential paradox of action theory. If we start from social action and build up a model of social systems from that starting point, and we then treat those social systems as if they were real, with emergent properties, we end with a theory that works with an 'oversocialised' conception of human action; if, on the other hand, we start with social action and see systems as the straightforward product of such action, then we cannot, as several critics (Archer, 1982;

Thompson in Held and Thompson, 1990) point out, comprehend the very real constraints that social structures and systems place on us. Yet the existence of such structures and systems, as constraining forces, has to be assumed.

FURTHER READING

Giddens's most important theoretical works are:

Giddens, A. (1976) *New Rules of Sociological Method*, Hutchinson, London.
Giddens, A. (1977) *Studies in Social and Political Theory*, Hutchinson, London.
Giddens, A. (1979) *Central Problems in Social Theory*, Macmillan, Basingstoke.
Giddens, A. (1984) *The Constitution of Society*, Polity Press, Oxford.
Giddens, A. (1987) *Social Theory and Modern Society*, Polity Press, Oxford.

and for his historical sociology and study of modernity:

Giddens, A. (1981) *A Contemporary Critique of Historical Materialism Vol. 1: Power, property and the state*, Macmillan, Basingstoke.
Giddens, A. (1985) *A Contemporary Critique of Historical Materialism Vol. 2: The nation state and violence*, Polity Press, Oxford.
Giddens, A. (1990) *The Consequences of Modernity*, Polity Press, Oxford.

Secondary works

Cohen is the most sympathetic, and perhaps the most difficult; Held and Thompson and Bryant and Jary are both useful collections, the latter with rather more intelligible exposition; Clark *et al.* is rather scrappy.

Bryant, C. G. A. and Jary, D. (eds) (1991) *Giddens' Theory of Structuration*, Routledge, London.
Clark, J., Modgil, C. and Modgil, F. (eds) (1990) *Anthony Giddens: Consensus and controversy*, Falmer Press, Sussex.
Cohen, I. (1989) *Structuration Theory: Anthony Giddens and the constitution of social life*, Macmillan, Basingstoke.
Craib, I. (1992) *Anthony Giddens*, Routledge, London.
Held, D. and Thompson, J. B. (eds) (1990) *Social Theory of Modern Societies: Anthony Giddens and his critics*, Cambridge University Press, Cambridge.

Critical articles mentioned in the text:

Archer, M. (1982) 'Morphogenesis vs. structuration', *British Journal of Sociology*, vol. 33, pp. 455–83.
Smith, J. W. and Turner, B. S. (1986) 'Constructing social theory & constituting society', *Theory, Culture & Society*, vol. 3, no. 2, pp. 125–33.
Urry, J. (1982) 'Duality of structure: Some critical issues', *Theory, Culture & Society*, vol. 1, no. 2, pp. 100–6.

Also mentioned:

Anderson, P. (1990) 'A culture in counterflow – 1', *New Left Review*, no. 180, pp. 41–78.
Goffman, E. (1974) *Frame Analysis*, Harper & Row, New York.

PART III

FROM ACTION TO STRUCTURE

INTRODUCTION

All the approaches dealt with in Part II were based on the same starting point: a model of human action that makes reference to people's intentions, the means available to carry them out, and the meanings in which they formulate their intentions and select what seem to be the appropriate means. It is recognised that people's surroundings limit their choices, and that these surroundings may be interpreted in different ways. Each approach works with an explicit or implicit idea of social structure as a system built up out of the actions and interactions of individuals. This is most explicit and worked out in structural-functionalism: indeed, it is so thoroughly worked out that we saw the emphasis of Parsons's work shift from consideration of interaction and choice to an analysis of the ways in which social systems limit and determine interaction and choice. I suggested that such a switch was built into his theory, given that there is no clear distinction between action and social structure or system. In effect they are the same – one is a congealed version of the other – and we can look at this same thing from one perspective or the other, from the point of view of the individual or the system, but not from both points of view at the same time. I also suggested that the various inadequacies in the structural-functionalist conception of social system can be traced to the view that the system is congealed action; most important, it could not distinguish between what David Lockwood called social integration and system integration. In other words, there is no conception of a social structure underlying people's actions and meanings, but separate from them.

127

The other approaches did not have such a thorough conception of the social system, and in this sense they can be considered as fragments of structural-functionalism – implicitly assuming some notion of structure and system that could be supplied by Parsons, and limited by not having an explicit conception of structure. The one exception to this – Giddens's structuration theory – is forced to remain at a very high level of abstraction and, as we have seen, is still haunted by a conception of a social structure or system over and above action.

I have argued that there are different types of object in the world, each requiring different types of theory to understand it. In the Introduction I concentrated on the distinction between action and agents on the one hand, and societies on the other. In the course of Part II, I have pointed to further distinctions on the agency side. I suggested, for example, that structural-functionalism might be an appropriate theory for looking at active organised groups in the process of establishing themselves. Such groups are halfway between individual interaction and established structure; they might contain aspects of both, yet be different from either. I also indicated that there might be different aspects to the analysis of action; generally, these approaches concentrate on the social processes of cognition, of how we come to know, at the expense of processes of emotion and unconscious levels of the person. Finally, in my criticism of ethnomethodology I suggested that there might be a level of 'general meanings': that the ideas which we share as members of society might make an object of study, with its own type of theory.

This leads on nicely to the general approach labelled 'structural-ism'. I want to discuss two aspects of approach. The first and most important is structuralism as a theory of social structures that exist independently of our knowledge and, in one sense, of our actions – the aspect of social life that is absent from all variations of action theory. I will look at this through the work of modern Marxist thinkers such as Louis Althusser and Nicos Poulantzas. Before I move on to this, however, I want to look at the other aspect: structuralism as a theory of general meanings. Here we find the notion that our ideas, the way we think, have an underlying structure which, in fact, determines what we think. As I write this book, it might seem to me that I am thinking creatively and freely; nobody is looking over my shoulder telling me what to write. A structuralist would argue that everything I write is predetermined by the ideas I start with. I want to deal with this aspect of structuralism for two reasons: first, it provides an introduction to a method employed by structural theorists of society and helps us to make more sense of them; secondly, this approach does seem to me to tell us important things about the world in its own right.

After dealing with structuralism as a theory of general meanings, and then as a theory of social structure, I will go on to look at the way this approach has fragmented. The process is the opposite one to that of action theory. Whereas the problem with action theory is that it tries to move directly from interaction to social structure, the problem with structuralism is that it tries to move directly from social structure to interaction: it sees our actions as determined by social structures rather than as affected by but different from social structures. As this problem has come to be seen as more acute, so structuralist theories of society have lost their distinctiveness. At this point, we meet again the other central theme of this book: the increasing difficulty of conceiving of society as a structured whole at all. This is illustrated most dramatically in the development of structuralism and post-structuralism.

Before moving on to structuralism, however, it is necessary to make some distinctions. The difficulty with words such as 'system', 'structure' and 'society' is that their meanings overlap without being exactly the same. So far, I have been careless in their use because the differences have not been all that important, but it is now time to try to use them more precisely. I will use *system* to refer to the structural-functionalist idea of social organisation as congealed patterns of interaction; approach should really, therefore, be called 'system-functionalism'. I will use *society* as I used it in Chapter 2, in the discussion of Bhaskar, to refer to an aspect of social reality which is distinct from agency and action and needs to be understood in a different way. Finally, I will use *structure* to refer to the underlying models of the world that structuralists seek to identify.

Chapter 8

THE WORLD AS A LOGICAL PATTERN: AN INTRODUCTION TO STRUCTURALISM

THE BACKGROUND

'Structuralism' is a form of theory which, during the 1960s and 1970s, became influential in a number of disciplines: philosophy, social theory, linguistics, literary criticism, cultural analysis, psychoanalysis, the history of ideas, the philosophy of science, anthropology, and others. It is difficult to provide an absolute definition, not least because for a while it achieved cult status. Originating in France, where intellectuals have generally played a greater part in public life than in Britain and America, and their work sometimes attracts a following amounting to a subculture, the movement also gained a following amongst young academics in Britain and America. Thus it took root in an intellectual climate very different to that of France. Traditionally, British (especially) and American universities have been suspicious of ideas originating from France and Germany; they are seen as vague and jargon-ridden speculations, and structuralism came under attack for precisely these reasons. The response of the disciples in these countries has been similar to the reactions I talked about in the Introduction: they retreated into their own world, made a virtue of jargon and complication, and tended towards dogmatism. As in the struggles over ethnomethodology, people lost their jobs.

As a school of thought, structuralism can trace several lines of descent. One line runs through British and French anthropology, and will be of comparatively little import for what I have to say here. Another runs through the central tradition of French sociology: Comte in the early nineteenth century, Durkheim around the beginning of this century, taking in particular the idea of society existing over and above the individual and 'social facts' as consisting of 'collective representations'. A third line is the philosophical tradition originating with Kant, whose crucial idea is that human beings possess rational faculties with which they impose order on the world. Yet another, and substantively the most important, is through the school of structural linguistics and the work of Ferdinand de Saussure and the Russian Formalist School of literary criticism. If there are many roots, I have already indicated that there are many branches, and the leading figures are still French: Claude Lévi-Strauss (anthropology), Louis Althusser (social theory and philosophy), Roland Barthes (literary criticism and cultural studies), Christian Metz (film criticism), Jacques Lacan (psychoanalysis), Michel Foucault (the history of ideas) and Jacques Derrida (philosophy).

Intellectual cults, like other modern cults, tend to pass quickly, and perhaps it was because of the intensity of the debate that the proponents of structuralism were the first to develop it in such a way as to undermine its own foundations. The names associated with what is now known as 'post-structuralism' are also associated with the original movement – Foucault and Derrida in particular. I will be following through one branch of this development in Chapter 10 – in relation to the structuralist Marxism of Althusser. For the moment, however, I want to focus on structuralism as a theory of general meanings rather than of societies.

A FIRST APPROXIMATION

The model I will take throughout this chapter is language. Structuralism regards all human products as forms of language, and this includes what I called 'general ideas'. My argument in relation to ethnomethodology was that when we talk to other people we use terms which already have a general meaning, and give them a specific, context-bound meaning. I suggested that these general meanings might be considered another realm of social reality, and I want now to suggest that structuralism contributes to our understanding of this area. We can take a set of general ideas, a particular theory, or perhaps what we call 'common sense', and look for an underlying structure, a rationale or a logic to them. Hence the title of this chapter – the world as a logical pattern. Just as we might look at all the different actions and choices of a friend and seek an underlying logic in order to understand her, so we might do the same for all the different statements that, say, a Christian makes.

This is not to say that I think structuralism is unreservedly a good thing. I would like to make a distinction between structuralism as a method and as a set of metaphysical assumptions. By method I mean a procedure, a way of looking at or thinking about the world which enables us to discover things that we did not initially know were there. This sometimes involves making certain assumptions about the world. For example, if I am making a journey by train or plane and I want to discover how long the journey will take, I assume that the transport will run on time, that I won't be struck down by lightning when I leave, and so on. The assumptions become metaphysical if I assume that they *really* are the case, that all trains *do* leave on time, that I shall *never* be struck by lightning, and so on. As a method, I think structuralism is useful; it can tell us things about the world that we could not find without it. As a set of metaphysical assumptions, I think it is a disaster and an absurdity. Paradoxically, the metaphysical assumptions have become most closely identified with and most clearly distinguish the school as a whole, and I want to begin by looking at them – this will give us a view of the carcase of the animal; then I will look at the method, trying to distinguish the edible parts and the points at which they are connected to the carcase. From the point of view of many structuralists I *will* be doing a butchering job, since the metaphysical assumptions are the most vital part of the approach.

THE METAPHYSICAL ASSUMPTIONS

By 'metaphysical assumptions', then, I mean statements about the nature of the world that cannot be proved and eventually have to be taken on faith, when in fact there are decisive arguments against taking them on faith.

The world as a product of ideas

I have mentioned several times the view that the world we see around us is a product of our ideas – this in turn has its roots in Kant's philosophy, or a distorted form of it. This is very much an assumption of structuralism, and in claiming to show the underlying structure or logic of general ideas, it is also claiming to show how we – or rather, our ideas – produce the world we see. Thus when Lévi-Strauss, for example, claims to have discovered the underlying structure of kinship systems in tribal society, he is claiming to have discovered the underlying structure of kinship terminology, the ideas with which these societies talk about kinship. Again I must repeat the same argument: there is a degree of truth in this view – people with different ideas do, to some extent, live in different worlds. But the world always offers resistance to these ideas, and then it becomes a matter of approximating one to the other. Structuralism in its extreme form does not consider this resistance: it does not matter to Lévi-Strauss that kinship behaviour is different from what the terminology would lead us to expect.

This assumption often takes the form of an attack on any attempt to prove theories by testing them; after all, if our theories produce the world, there is no point in testing them against the world. We will find only what we have put there in the first place. Any approach which sees some form of empirical testing as playing a role (such as the view I am arguing for) is dismissed as 'empiricist', one of the dirtiest words in the structuralist vocabulary.

The world as a logical pattern

The structuralist emphasis is always on the logical order or structure underlying general meanings. It is sometimes assumed that this 'structure' – which I will discuss in more detail shortly – matches the 'structures' of the world, sometimes on the grounds that since the mind is part of the world, the ideas it produces will have the same structure as the world. This is a sort of wager which we must make against our intuition – since the real world gives evidence of being illogical – and it leaves structuralism open to what, in the Introduction, I called the 'logical trap'. Any theory which is not entirely logical must be wrong, and since no theory is entirely logical, we fall into a bottomless pit.

'The death of the subject'

'The death of the subject' is the slogan most closely associated with structuralism. 'Subject' means what I have referred to as agency, action and persons. The idea being attacked is that people are the authors of their thoughts and actions. It is assumed instead that people are the puppets of their ideas, and their actions are not determined by choice and decision but are the outcome of the underlying structure of ideas, the logic of these ideas. If, for example, I am a Christian, I do not speak about Christianity; rather, Christianity speaks through me; some structuralists reach the extreme of saying that people do not speak; rather, they are spoken (by the underlying structure of the language)?; that they do not read books, but are 'read' by books. They do not create societies, but are created by societies.

Again I can offer a 'moderate' argument: it is true that we are always limited by our ideas, that they stop us saying certain things and perhaps force us to say things that we do not exactly mean. We are all engaged in a constant struggle with our ideas. But it does not follow that our ideas – or rather, their underlying structure – turn us into puppets. Choice, intention, goals and values still have a role to play and need to be understood; they are not entirely predetermined.

I will now turn to structuralism as a method, showing the origins of each of these metaphysical assumptions but also distinguishing the usefulness of the method. When we come to look at structuralist social theory in general in the next two chapters, these assumptions will appear again frequently, as they generate the tensions and difficulties that lead to the fragmentation of the approach.

STRUCTURALISM AS A METHOD

By 'method' here I mean that structuralism can act as a guide to the analysis of general meanings: it gives us some idea of what to look for and how to find it. I will begin with linguistics as a basic model and go on to look at how the model has been extended.

The linguistic model

Ferdinand de Saussure is often regarded as the founding father of modern linguistics. Putting it oversimply, before Saussure, linguistics had been concerned with how a language develops over time; Saussure argued, like Durkheim in sociology, that we do not know how something works by tracing its history. Just as we can understand a society only by looking at the relationships between the different parts, so we need to look at the relationships between the different parts of language. The attempt to understand something by looking at its history has been labelled 'historicist' – after 'empiricist' the second-dirtiest word in the structuralist vocabulary.

Speech and language

The function of language is to enable people to communicate, and we need to look at the way in which the different elements of a language contribute to communication through their relationships to each other. We cannot do that by looking at individual acts of speech; we need to look at the language as a whole, hence the distinction between speech and language. The individual speech act, what I say when I open my mouth, is always to some extent unique, and it cannot, therefore, be the object of a science. Language, on the other hand, is constant and possessed by everybody who speaks it; it is the raw material out of which we form our sentences. Each language is made up out of a finite number of sounds and rules about combining sounds, rather like the rules of grammar we learn at school. Speech refers to the apparently infinite numbers of sentences we may produce using these sounds and rules. Games provide helpful examples: the language of chess, for instance, consists of the board and the pieces and the rules of the game, and these are the same for every game; the speech act is the individual game, which is different from the other individual games.

The language, then, is the underlying structure or logic behind speech.

The sign

The elements of this structure or logic are 'signs'. In everyday life, we tend to use the word in different ways: a cross on a chain around my neck is a sign that I am a Christian; dark clouds are a sign of rain; a red light by the side of the road is a sign that traffic must stop. The American philosopher C. S. Peirce, one of the few non-European ancestors of structuralism, distinguished three types of sign: the *icon*, where the relationship is based on similarity the cross around my neck is similar to the cross on which Christ was crucified; the *index*, where the relationship is causal, such as that between clouds and rain; and the *symbol*, where the relationship is a matter of social convention or agreement. This is often called an *arbitrary* relationship, meaning that there is no necessary connection between, for example, the colour red and the instruction to traffic to stop. The colour could be blue, orange or purple; it just so happens that everyone agrees that red means stop or danger, and this is an external reality imposed on individual members of society. If I were to decide that, for me, red means go and green means stop, I would not remain a member of society for very long.

Signs, the basic units of language, are arbitrary. There is nothing intrinsic in the word 'dog' that means that it has to refer to some hairy four-legged creature; we might as well call such animals 'professors', but we don't. The sign has two aspects, a *signifier* and a *signified*; the relation between them is often likened to the one between two sides of a sheet of paper. The signifier is the 'material' element, the physical sound of 'dog', or the marks on a sheet of paper. This element is meaningless without the signified, which is the concept the sounds refer to. Both are necessary to each other: the concept cannot be articulated without the sound.

It is important to remember that the signified is the concept, not the object. We tend to assume that words are attached to objects like labels, but structural linguistics breaks this connection, insisting on the difference between the concept and the object. There are various pithy ways of pointing this out: the concept of a circle is not round; the concept of a dog does not bark. This is a first step along the road to the metaphysical assumption that the objects we see in the world are created by our language or ideas. It is, I think, a justified step, in that it is simply true that words do not 'grow out' of things naturally and are different from the things they denote.

Syntagm and paradigm

To say that the relationship between the sign and what it points to is arbitrary is only half the story. It is not a matter of agreeing the meaning of each sign in a language separately; rather, they are all agreed as a structure of a whole – the red of the traffic light is part of a structure that includes green; red means stop because green means go, and vice versa. *The meaning of a linguistic sign depends upon its relationship to other signs.* We know what 'three' means only because of its relationship to 'one', 'two', 'four', etc. If we regard a simple sound as a sign, in English the words 'dog' and 'god' are made up of the same signs, but they have different meanings because the sounds have different relationships to each other. Similarly, Althusser argues that the meaning of the word 'alienation' in Marx's later work is different from its meaning in his earlier work, because it is related to different concepts.

We find the significant elements of a language by a method of 'concomitant variation'. We take a sentence or a word, and in a sort of thought-experiment we vary each element, replacing one by another, and if there is a significant change in meaning, we have found a significant unit. If, taking the word dog, I substitute 'h' for 'd' and get hog, I have found a significant element. Structuralists often organise these elements as opposing pairs (binary oppositions) – d/h, for example. Lévi-Strauss would claim that the human mind is so constituted that it orders the whole world into such opposites. Whether this is true or not is less important than the fact that here already we are beginning to get to the rules which govern relationships between signs, and thus what meanings can be produced. They can be analysed on two levels, the *syntagm* and the *paradigm*, and the first is more clearly a matter of rules than the second.

The syntagmatic level refers to which sounds or signs can or cannot follow each other in the 'syntagmatic chain'. Thus in English we do not usually find the combination 'hd', though we might find 'dh'. Odd little rules at this level are sometimes taught at school as an aid to spelling: 'i before e except after c'. The rules of grammar are again the appropriate model. The syntagmatic level can be seen as a horizontal axis of language, the paradigmatic level is the vertical axis. The paradigm consists of the set of words connected with the word in question by rules of similarity of sound or meaning. In the same system as 'dog' we can find 'hog', 'bog', 'cur', 'bitch', 'golden retriever', and so on. Every time we use a word, we select from such a paradigm (see Figure 8.l).

This is as far as it is necessary to go with the linguistic model. We can see how the metaphysical assumptions are rooted in the method without following logically and necessarily from it. It seems to me justified to look at the language rather than speech, but it does not follow that speech is determined by language and that we must disregard the speaking subject. Similarly, it is reasonable to suggest that the meaning of a word or sign depends on its relationship to others, and that it stands for a concept rather than an object, but it

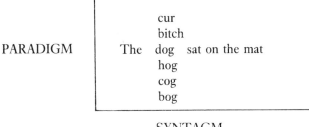

Figure 8.1 Sometimes the paradigm too may be described in terms of opposites (e.g. dog/cat, dog/bitch, etc.).

does not follow that it has no relation to an external object or that it creates that object. So far, I hope, I have demonstrated that structuralism seeks the underlying structure of a language – the basic elements and the rules which govern their relationships: the logic underlying a language.

The linguistic model extended: semiotics

'Semiotics' is the name given to the 'science of signs' (or general meanings) – not just of linguistic signs. I want to look at a couple of examples of structuralist analysis in this area – Roland Barthes on modern myths, and Will Wright's analysis of Westerns – to emphasise what I see to be the benefits of this type of analysis.

The extension of the linguistic model into a general theory or science of signs is not precise – linguistics is used more as an approximate analogy, as will become apparent when I look at the examples. It is based on the assumption that all human products are at some point a means of communication and can thus be analysed like language, with a similar distinction between language and speech. Thus Lévi-Strauss claims to reveal the basic unit or 'language' of kinship systems, in which the different kinship systems of each tribe are equivalent to speech acts. As we shall see in the next chapter, Louis Althusser identifies an underlying social structure or 'language' of capitalism, in which the individual capitalist societies are 'speech acts'. Semiotics proper deals with a more diffuse area of cultural products. Barthes, for example, talks about the language and speech of food. The elements or signs are the individual foods. At the syntagmatic level there are rules governing which food may or may not accompany other food. In Western societies we do not usually combine sweet and savoury items, pour custard over fried chicken or gravy over ice cream. If we eat such foods at the same meal, they must follow each other: savoury first, sweet after. The paradigmatic rules give us a choice of combinations: which meat with which vegetables. The individual meal, with its particular choices of food and methods of preparation, is the speech act, employing the elements and rules. The assumption is that, in principle, any human product may be analysed in this way.

Modern myths
In looking at the structure of modern myths, Barthes (1972) deploys the concepts of sign, signifier and signified, but tends to assume that the signifier may point not just to an idea but to a real object. He borrows from Lévi-Strauss's work on mythology in tribal societies, where it is seen as a means by which a society organises its world, comes to terms with its problems, maintains an image of itself and ensures that individuals embrace that image. As an example of Barthes's analysis, I will take a newspaper picture, not all that different from one of Barthes's own examples, some variant of which appears in the British press each year at the end of August. At that time, the Notting Hill Carnival takes place in London; Notting Hill is an area of racial tension and the Carnival is primarily a West Indian event, based on carnivals in the Caribbean, although all races take part. There are often minor or major incidents of rioting as the day draws on. The picture, however, shows a white policeman and a black person (of either sex) embracing and/or dancing together. Sometimes the black person is wearing the policeman's helmet.

We can see this picture as a sign, combining a signifier (the material element, the patterns of ink on the newspaper) and a signified (a policeman and a West Indian apparently enjoying themselves). This picture is also part of a myth; it has another meaning beyond the signifier which helps make it up. The picture as a complete sign is incorporated into another language as a signifier for another signified – a set of beliefs which are, to say the least, debatable and sometimes contradicted by other events on the same day. These mythical beliefs comprise the image the society has – or would like to have – of itself as a society in which people of different races coexist happily, where black customs contribute to the quality of white life, in which there is no mistrust between blacks and the white police, and the latter are sufficiently confident to surrender their sign of authority (the helmet) in order to enjoy themselves.

The alternative way of talking about this picture as a sign is to take it up as a *signified* into another language (a 'meta-language'); in other words, to analyse it rationally, which is what I have been trying to do. It is easy to see, in this example, how this modern myth obscures a possibly threatening reality. What this analysis shows is how the 'meaning' of the picture is produced on two different levels. It shows the machinery at work beyond what we might otherwise take for granted. There are plenty of mythical elements at work in our public life: the signs used by politicians to gain support – 'democracy', 'the silent majority', the 'evil of communism' – are all mythical signs that mean much more than they say. The structure of myth and meta-language can be represented diagrammatically, as shown in Figure 8.2, from Barthes (1972: 115).

The Western
Wright (1975) described the 'language' of the Western, its underlying structure or logic. In fact, he deals with four types, while I will

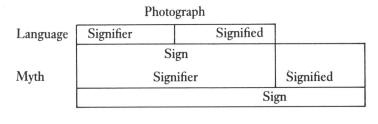

Figure 8.2 The structure of myth and meta-language.

discuss only two – the classical plot and the 'vengeance' variation, as shown in Table 8.1. The basic elements of the Western, the 'signs', can best be seen as the characters: the hero(es), society (sometimes different aspects of society, e.g. ranchers versus farmer) and the villain(s). Wright lists a set of 'narrative functions' for each type of plot, each function describing relationships between or qualities of the elements. The functions themselves can be considered as more complex signs. We arrive at these by the method of concomitant variation – if Wright's analysis is correct, then changing any one element will change the meaning of the plot. After you have read the next couple of pages, it might be useful to come back and experiment in this way.

As Wright presents them, the narrative functions are really a descriptive list, but we can rewrite them as rules, often simply by replacing 'is' with 'must be': 'the hero must be unknown to society', for example. They cover the succession of events, the syntagmatic level: each function enables the next to take place. In the classic plot, for example, nothing can happen until the hero arrives and is distinguished from the society, and then the conflict between the society and the villain may develop. Rewriting these as rules would provide a blueprint for a Western. All sorts of variation would be possible without affecting the basic plot – different types of fight, various sexual relationships, and so on.

Turning to the paradigmatic level, we again enter the realm of mythology. Wright arranges this level in terms of oppositions which present problems that the plot sets out to solve. He identifies four, the last being the least important: inside society/outside society, good/bad, strong/weak, and wilderness/civilisation. These are, first of all, oppositions which can be read off from the films themselves, qualities signified by the characters. According to Wright, they are also ways in which members of modern societies see their world – they divide it up into good and bad, strong and weak, what is inside and outside society. This creates a tension: how do we come to terms with a society divided in this way? The Western offers us a solution – not necessarily one we can practise in real life (although Wright suggests that it offers a model for individual action) but one which relieves the tension. It seems to me that what emerges from Wright's discussion is that the major opposition is not one of those listed above, but that of individual/society; the Western offers a model for the resolution of the tensions between the two, different types of

Table 8.1   Two types of Western

The classical Western*	The 'vengeance' variation†
1. The hero enters a social group	1. The hero is or was a member of society
2. The hero is unknown to the society	2. The villains do harm to the hero
3. The hero is revealed to have exceptional ability	3. The society is unable to punish the villains
4. The society recognises a difference between themselves and the hero; the hero is given a special status	4. The hero seeks vengeance
5. The society does not completely accept the hero	5. The hero goes outside society
6. There is a conflict of interests between the villain and the society	6. The hero is revealed to have a special ability
7. The villains are stronger than the society; the society is weak	7. The society recognises a difference between themselves and the hero; the hero is given a special status
8. There is a strong friendship or respect between the hero and a villain	8. A representative of the society asks the hero to give up his revenge
9. The villain threatens the society	9. The hero gives up his revenge
10. The hero avoids involvement in the conflict	10. The hero fights the villains
11. The villain endangers a friend of the hero	11. The hero gives up his special status
12. The hero fights the villain	12. The hero enters society
13. The hero defeats the villain	
14. The society is safe	
15. The society accepts the hero	
16. The hero loses or gives up his special status	

*Examples of the classic Western include *Cimarron* (1931); *Destry Rides Again* (1941); *Duel in the Sun* (1947); *Shane* (1953); and *Cat Ballou* (1965).
†Examples of the vengeance variation are: *Red River* (1949); *Apache* (1954); and *The Man from Laramie* (1955).

Western offering different types of solution. Structuralists often use the word 'code', less in a precise technical sense than with the implication of a hidden message: the Western is a code for these tensions and their resolution.

THE ADVANTAGES OF THE STRUCTURALIST METHOD

I want to use the Western as an example of what the structuralist method enables us to discover. First, the very idea of an underlying structure or logic enables us to organise and classify material in a way that would not be possible if we dealt with all aspects on the same level. We could watch Westerns until we went blind without finding any way of classifying them if we treated each incident and character equally. In one, the hero falls in love, in another, he doesn't; in one, the villains are killed, in another, they escape. There could be as many labels as there are types of film. Of course, structuralism does not offer a foolproof method of classification, but then neither does any other method: what it does do is guide us towards the core, the most important and central aspects of what we are studying, beneath the surface flux. The fact that it categorises not just the basic elements but also the relationships between them, or rather the rules governing them, means that the 'machinery' of the Western is laid open for inspection. We come to understand how the Western works. Particularly important here is the organisation of the paradigmatic level into oppositions which the 'syntagmatic chain' puts into motion and attempts to resolve. Structuralism takes the lid off the way in which cultural products work, the way they communicate.

It also presents us with a different and, I would argue, more useful conception of structure. Action theory possesses a concept of system, but that is seen in terms of the elements rather than the relationships between them; structuralism gives priority to the relationships. If we were to concentrate on the elements of Westerns, we would attempt to classify them by the roles of hero, villain, etc., and different roles would entail a different type of Western. We would examine the roles in terms of the qualities and actions of the individual(s) concerned, and these might not differ significantly from one type to the other. Wright shows that the elements might remain the same for each type, but the relationships between them give them a very different meaning.

This view of structure introduces the idea that there are different levels: a level which is more or less observable at first sight, and a level which is less observable and has to be sorted out. We can compare this to the functionalist notion of system, which deals with one level only (one level of reality, that is; functionalism deals with a number of levels of abstraction). Another way of putting this is that structuralism enables us to make the sort of distinction that David Lockwood was getting at in his differentiation between social and system integration; and it also suggests that the underlying level is more important, that it has some explanatory power when we look at the surface level.

THE DRAWBACKS OF THE METHOD

Reductionism

All the drawbacks of the method are associated in some way with the metaphysical assumptions that have come to characterise structuralism; they represent the method's tendency to lead towards the assumptions. Thus the ability to distinguish an underlying structure or logic which has an explanatory importance can tempt the theorist to reduce the world to this level, and so to lose dimensions of meaning that exist at the surface level. For example, the various surface-level incidents of the Western might add dimensions that do not change the underlying meaning but none the less add to the complexity and richness of the film. These incidents might have to do with sexual or racial relations, with historical events or situations, and so on.

The tendency to reductionism, to losing secondary but none the less significant aspects of what we study, is built into the separation of language and speech, since these aspects occur at the level of speech. The reduction can go much further than the underlying structure. It would be possible, for example, to describe the relationship between the syntagmatic chain and the paradigmatic oppositions as an algebraic equation; this could be done for each type of Western, and we could then develop a higher-level equation to describe the rules of transformation between the different types. I am not, you will be glad to hear, going to attempt this, but it can be done. Lévi-Strauss sometimes comes close to it. In the process, *all* meaning seems to be lost and we end up with a formal equation that is of no use to anybody. I should point out that Wright does not engage in this exercise and in fact moves in the opposite direction that I am implicitly recommending: towards the complexity of the surface level.

The problem of change

The problem of change stems from the criticism of historical development that I mentioned at the beginning and the tendency to regard the 'subject' as determined by underlying structures. Structural analysis is intended to replace historical accounts, and the structure revealed is static – a set of relationships between elements. Wright, for example, is able to identify a classic plot and three variations, but at the level of structural analysis he cannot show why the variations develop and the classical plot changes. To do this properly he looks at social developments outside the film itself which, in this context, is a return to the subject, to speech. Many structural linguists have argued that change in language can be understood only by reference to speech and the subject; structuralists at the heart of the modern movement, however, rule out this possibility and they are left to talk about 'transformations' as rather magical events with no real cause. Wright's explanation of the development of different types of Western also presupposes a world existing outside the structure of ideas encoded by the Western, a world which effects this structure. This again would not be allowable to the strict structuralist, who would have to assume that the external world is completely defined by the structure of ideas.

FROM GENERAL MEANING TO
SOCIAL STRUCTURES

In this chapter, I have looked at structuralism as a way of identifying the underlying structures or logic of general meanings; we all have to live in and work by such structures even if they cannot be seen as determining precisely what we think or do. I have dealt with it only as a fragment of social theory, however, concerned with just one area of the social world. I now want to move on to structuralism as a general social theory, attempting to embrace the whole; in other words, moving back to the realm of Grand Theory and Parsons, although the Grand Theory is of a very different type. The metaphysical assumptions of structuralism will play a much greater role here, since I think that the fragmentation of the approach owes much to their existence.

FURTHER READING

There are now numerous introductions to structuralism; Hawkes is probably the most accessible, although my personal favourite is Jameson – this is the most difficult, but employs some useful images and sensible criticisms. Kurzwell provides the best general survey of individual writers.

Blonsky, M. (ed.) (1979) *The Essential Semiotics Reader*, Basil Blackwell, Oxford.
Clarke, S. (1981) *The Foundations of Structuralism*, Harvester, Sussex.
Culler, J. (1976) *Saussure*, Fontana, London.
Ehrmann, J. (ed.) (1970) *Structuralism*, Doubleday Anchor, New York.
Gardner, H. (1982) *The Quest for Mind*, Quartet, London.
Hawkes, T. (1977) *Structuralism and Semiotics*, Methuen, London.
Jameson, F. (1972) *The Prison House of Language*, Princeton University Press, Princeton, NJ.
Kurzwell, E. (1980) *The Age of Structuralism*, Columbia University Press, New York.
Lane, M. (ed.) (1970) *Structuralism: A reader*, Jonathan Cape, London.
Robey, D. (ed.) (1973) *Structuralism: An introduction*, Oxford University Press, Oxford.

Of structuralist works relevant to the ideas of this chapter, Barthes's *Mythologies* is probably the best to start with, although all the works listed are worth reading. And, of course, there is Wright.

Barthes, R. (1967) *Elements of Semiology*, Jonathan Cape, London.
Barthes, R. (1972) *Mythologies*, Jonathan Cape, London.
Barthes, R. (1975), *S/Z*, Jonathan Cape, London.
Barthes, R. (1977) *Image – Music – Text*, Fontana, London.
Wright, W. (1975) *Six Guns and Society: A structural study of the Western*, University of California Press, Berkeley.

If you are interested in literary structuralism, see also

Lodge, D. (1981), *Working with Structuralism*, Routledge & Kegan Paul, London.

Most examinations of the relationship between structuralism and sociology are not very helpful; of the following Badcock is the best, though it has little to do with the material dealt with in this chapter:

Badcock, C. (1973) *Lévi-Strauss: Structuralism and sociological theory*, Hutchinson, London.
Bottomore, T. B. and Nisbet, R. (1978) 'Structuralism', in Bottomore, T. B. and Nisbet, R. (eds), *A History of Sociological Theory*, Heinemann, London, pp. 557–98.
Goddard, A. (1976) 'On structuralism and sociology', *American Sociologist*, vol. 11, pp. 133–9.
Runciman, W. G. (1979) 'What is structuralism?', *British Journal of Sociology*, vol. 20, pp. 253–65.

Chapter 9

STRUCTURALIST MARXISM:
THE WORLD AS A PUPPET THEATRE

INTRODUCTION

It is almost ten years since I first wrote this chapter, and since then the real world has changed dramatically, in ways which would have been beyond belief then; in fact, they would have been beyond belief even four years ago. And the changes are such that it is now very difficult to write about Marxism, especially about anything which approaches orthodox Marxism. It seems that any regime that calls itself communist is now discredited; communism is no longer a major political force anywhere in Western Europe, and increasingly unimportant in Eastern Europe. What will happen to socialism as a form of politics, and Marxism as a form of social science, is difficult to predict. At times, it seems they might have vanished altogether, but I have my doubts about that. In personal lives, it is perhaps when people think they are changing most dramatically that they are in fact simply affirming what they have always been – only to discover this, to their chagrin, at a later date. Current changes in the world are, I suspect, more profound, but just as many of the ideals of Marxism and socialism seem to me to be important to hold on to, so the contributions of Marxist theory to social science seem considerable, and not to be relinquished.

In discussing the work of Althusser and Poulantzas, this problem is compounded first by the rapidly changing intellectual fashions of radical thought during the late 1960s and 1970s – a process which has, I think, slowed down a little over the last decade, although it has continued – which left structuralist Marxism disappearing well within a decade of its appearance. Secondly, it is difficult to look at the development of the thought apart from the tragic history of the thinkers. Althusser himself, a manic depressive for most of his life, spent his last ten years in obscurity, largely in a mental hospital, after killing his wife; Poulantzas committed suicide. It seems to me that these facts should be noted with a great deal of sadness; they should not be used to detract from the powerful intellectual contribution of their work.

All this is leading me towards saying that I am much more sympathetic to structuralist Marxism than I was when I first wrote this chapter; I will leave my statement of why this is so until the end.

THE TARGETS OF STRUCTURALIST MARXISM

For structuralist Marxism, the 'death of the subject' became an overriding priority: the theory's claim is that the experience we have of being the authors of our actions is, in some sense, mistaken or 'ideological'; what really happens is that underlying social structures determine our actions, work through them, and our actions serve to reproduce and maintain these structures, or, on occasion, to transform them through revolution. Human beings become the puppets of social structure, which in turn becomes a sort of machine in permanent motion, and I want to argue that despite the usefulness of its analysis of social structures, the theory begins to break down when it approaches social action, when it describes the strings which work the puppets.

This is the first chapter to deal with a theory in which the cognitive aspects, concerned with knowing the world, are intimately and often explicitly bound up with the political aspect, the attempt to change the world. There is already a tension here: if we are the puppets of social structures, how can we change those structures? This tension will reappear regularly. For the moment, I want to look at the practical, political context of structuralist Marxism: it is perhaps too easy for those of us who live in the West, especially now, to think of Marxism as a monolithic entity in both theory and practice, a totalitarian regime matched by a dogmatic set of assertions about the world more akin to religion than to science. Given what has happened in Eastern Europe over the last three years (or, indeed, the last seventy years), there seems to be a great deal of truth in this: the theory and the regimes that deployed it had become so ossified that renewal from within became impossible. However, there have always been debates within Marxism, and in the West these became intensified when the mass Communist Parties in Europe began to search for electoral support – which, by and large, they never achieved to the extent that they desired.

The emergence of 'Eurocommunism' was only one result of a long and painful debate amongst European communists. The arguments sparked off by tactical debates about political survival were also carried on in terms of theory – about how Marxism can tell us about the world and, indeed, about the nature of the world (i.e. modern capitalism) itself.

Like structuralism, structuralist Marxism originated in France, and in this chapter I will look at the work of Louis Althusser, the most prominent figure, and, in less detail, that of Nicos Poulantzas. In the context of modern socialism, Althusser and Poulantzas are representatives of a more orthodox and traditional form of Marxism, which they see as a science, giving us scientific knowledge of the world that can be employed in developing a political strategy for bringing the working class to power. The representative of the working class is the Communist Party, the bearer of knowledge and decider of tactics. We find in their work the same tendencies to dogmatism (we are right) and authoritarianism (the Party knows best) that have unfortunately become the hallmarks of traditional Marxism. At the same time, they have produced a remarkably sophisticated and stimulating interpretation of Marxism that has been, in different ways, influential on both sides of the Atlantic. In Britain it has led to increased sophistication and some original work in the philosophy of science in particular: Bhaskar's work, discussed in the Introduction, owes much to the debates stimulated by Althusser. In the USA it has helped to generate a rich empirical investigation of class structure through the work of Erik Olin Wright.

Their sophisticated form of orthodox Marxism was developed against two targets, usually graced with the labels 'voluntarism' and 'economism'. Economism is a crude form of orthodox Marxism. It entails the assumption that everything originates at the economic level of society: that a particular form of economic organisation determines the nature of the rest of society, its political organisation, its ideas of itself, and so on. There is also an assumption that the progress of history is determined by this same economic organisation, that the development from capitalism to socialism has something inevitable about it. 'Voluntarism', on the other hand, works with the assumption that people, not economic organisations, determine what happens; that human beings are free agents who have lost their freedom to a particular type of social organisation – capitalism. Socialism will come when people realise this and seize back their freedom. This point of view owes much to Marx's earlier works – in particular, the *1844 Manuscripts* – and it became very important after 1960 amongst French Marxists arguing for radical changes in Communist tactics and organisation. Althusser was thus trying to separate himself from the orthodox Marxism and at the same time to defend it – another manifestation of the tension I mentioned at the beginning.

I ought to note two points before continuing. The first is that Althusser always denied that he had been influenced by structuralism, which he called an 'ideology'. I suspect that this denial is itself of a political nature, but in any case the influence should be apparent in my account of his ideas. Secondly, in the early 1970s he published a short book, *Essays in Self-Criticism*, in which he makes a number of modifications to the framework of ideas he built up during the 1960s. I will barely refer to this at all: it seems to me that the most important modifications lose the originality of his theory and leave him with little new to say. The important and instructive criticisms have come from those who have tried to develop and employ his work.

THE NATURE OF THEORY

In this chapter I shall proceed through as straightforward an exposition of the ideas as possible, beginning by looking at Althusser's conception of theory itself, which reveals some of the tensions which have led to the fragmentation of the approach. It is worth bearing in mind throughout that with structuralist Marxism we are back in the world of generalising theory *à la* Parsons, attempting to develop concepts that will grasp both societies and agency. Parsons starts with agency, the structuralist Marxists with society: both founder when they try to move from one to the other. Like Parsons, Althusser is an obscure and difficult writer: in some of his work the aim of communication has been given up for the empty aim of being precise over what is by nature imprecise. But Althusser, unlike

Parsons, can bring to his theory a real passion and concern which are all too often lost by his followers.

One reason for Althusser's obscurity might be that in all his work there is a tension between two different views of theory: between, on the one hand, the need to find some way of testing a theory against 'facts', even if the theory talks about things we cannot see; and, on the other, the view that our ideas about the social world actually create the facts we see in it. This latter view is similar to the structuralist view discussed in the previous chapter. Althusser seems to argue on occasion that the world we see is in some way 'created' by the structure (or 'problematic') of the theory we employ. Each scientific theory creates its own world of 'theoretical objects', and he argues that one of the defining features of a science is that it produces a world of theoretical objects – different from the world we see in everyday life, but a world seen by the scientist in her scientific work. The problem with this approach is that each theory creates its own world; we cannot discover a 'real world' outside theory against which we can test our theories. In other words, we cannot judge between theories: each belongs in its own world and is, presumably, right for that particular world. This poses an evident problem for a Marxist trying to establish that Marxism is *the* science of society, *the* theory; Parsons, after all, introduces 'theoretical objects', such as the general systems of action and its various subsystems. How do we choose between them?

The other view of theory in Althusser's work is an answer, at least in part, to this problem. Despite the fact that a theory creates its own world of 'theoretical objects', these nevertheless have some relationship to real objects which have an independent existence in the world – independent both of the theory and of whether we can actually see them. This view comes very close to the one I have been arguing for since the beginning of this book: theory identifies real but unobservable social structures, the nature of which explains what we can observe. It still leaves the problem of how we know that our theory is right, or at least better than others; how do we know that we have identified real underlying structures – or, in Althusser's terms, 'appropriated' them? Since a theory creates its own theoretical objects which are 'appropriations' of unobservable structures, we cannot test the theory directly against what we can see, so what do we do?

For Althusser, this is tied up with the problem of how we identify a science, of what is scientific and what is not. A science does not present us with a once-and-for-all 'truth', but goes through stages of development or 'revolutions', the first of which marks its foundation as a science, the moment when it creates its 'theoretical objects'. Beyond this, he suggests two criteria by means of which we can distinguish a science or show that one theory is more scientific than others. One of these criteria is, I think, not very helpful, the other helpful but partial, and the partiality contributes eventually to the undermining of his theory. The first he refers to as the 'openness' of the theory's 'problematic' – the body of concepts which make it up. If a theory is a body of concepts which help us to understand the world, it functions by enabling us to ask questions about the world in terms of these concepts – it enables us to pose problems; hence 'problematic'. According to Althusser, a closed (non-scientific or 'ideological') problematic asks questions but presupposes the answer. If we take Christianity as an example, it leads us to ask questions such as: 'If God is good, what is the meaning of suffering?'; the answer is presupposed, because if we are not to challenge the whole belief system, we must find some answer that preserves the idea that God is good. Now it seems to me that this is true of any theory, scientific or not. For example, Marxist theory leads us to ask why there has been no revolution in the advanced capitalist countries; an answer in terms of the functional equilibrium of different subsystems would challenge the basis of the theory, which assumes quite clearly that capitalism is subject to regular crises. The answer must involve instead reference to the development of the capitalist mode of production, class struggle, and so on – it must involve the conceptual tools of the theory and uphold the more basic propositions to which those tools lead us.

Althusser's second criterion has to do with what he calls the 'order of exposition' of the concepts in a theory. You might – correctly – find this ambiguous; as far as I can understand it, he is arguing that the more 'logically' or 'rationally' related the theory's concepts are to each other, the more each depends upon and can be derived from the others in some particular order, the more scientific is the theory. I have already argued that logical or rational coherence is one of the means by which we can judge a theory but that there are other, equally useful ways. These can include the scope of the explanation it offers – how much it can cover – and the extent to which it can be directly or indirectly confirmed by our observation. All these play a part, and it is never a matter of simply accepting or rejecting a theory on the basis of any or all of them. I have also argued that the problem with this – apart from what we may mean by 'logical' or 'rational' coherence – is that the world itself is not necessarily a logical and coherent place, and it is doubtful whether a fully coherent theory could be produced; it would be like the seamless web with no beginning and no end. It is in the search for such a theoretical web that his followers, particularly his English followers, began to fragment the theory; Althusser himself left them little else to go by.

For Althusser, then, theory creates its own theoretical objects which none the less 'appropriate' real but unobservable objects (i.e. underlying social structures). A scientific theory is rationally and logically coherent in its production of theoretical objects. I should emphasise that Althusser is talking about the theory, not the theorist, who is as much the puppet of the theoretical structure as we all are of social structures. He tries to show that in the course of Marx's work we find the theoretical revolution (the 'epistemological break') which founded a science of society, and that the conceptual structure of this science can be found in his later work, especially *Capital*. This is a vital part of his case against humanism: the earlier works on which it is based are not scientific. He does not claim, like other modern Marxists, to be developing or interpreting Marx, but rather to be presenting what Marx really said. This gives much Althusserian work the air of biblical exegesis, the attempt to discover revealed truth. To some extent Althusserian social theory rests its claim to validity on the grounds that 'this is what Marx really said', but there is no reason to take this too seriously. We can regard Althusser as a developer and interpreter of the Marxist tradition, and thereby get more out of his work than we could by engaging in arguments about sacred texts.

ALTHUSSERIAN SOCIAL THEORY: BASIC CONCEPTS

Practices and structures

We can now turn to the basic concepts – or, less charitably, jargon – of Althusser's social theory, trying as far as possible to avoid the less attractive aspects of his style. These are the concepts that make up Marx's scientific problematic, and I will proceed by looking at the most general ideas first, setting out a 'map' of the social machine that works the human puppets. I will begin with the ideas of 'practice' and 'structure', and then move on to the ways in which these are brought together in Althusser's model of social organisation, or the 'social formation'. I will then look in more detail at the basic level of the social formation, the economic structure, and the way in which this enables us to distinguish between different types of society.

'Practice' is the term used to refer to human action, and in Althusser's theory it plays the important role of removing from the beginning the aspects of agency which I have argued are important, such as intention and choice. A practice consists of three elements, and the model for all practices is economic practice, the act of producing something out of something else. There is the raw material, the means of production – including labour-power and available tools – and there is the finished product. The determining element in a practice is seen as the combination of labour-power and means of production, the former acting as a sort of fuel for the latter; agency is simply the power which moves material things. There is certainly a sense in which Althusser produces a metaphorical description of many work processes: people do become dominated by their tools, they become the energy that keeps the machine going; for many industrial workers there is no question of choice or intention. There is, however, a difference between a metaphorical description of the work process, which may also be used as a basis for criticising capitalist society, and a basis for social theory.

Be that as it may, human action is seen as a number of practices, analytically distinguishable from each other but modelled on economic practice. *Political* practice works on the raw material of social relations, by means, presumably, of political organisation; *ideological* practice works on the way people see themselves and their world; *theoretical* practice works on ideology by means of the theory's problematic in order to produce knowledge, the scientist providing the 'thinking power'. The analogy with economic practice is not always entirely clear, because, I would suggest, agency is much more important at the political and ideological levels. I will return to this later; for the moment I will stay with theoretical practice because it underscores a significant difference between theory as conceived by Althusser and theory as conceived by exponents of action theory. For the latter, theory is an elaboration of common-sense knowledge, a matter of making explicit what people know already. For Althusser, theory is a transformation of the common-sense or ideological world; the finished product is radically different from the raw material. If we are going to produce a theory of social structures as opposed to agency, then it should be apparent from what I have said before that Althusser's conception is closer to the one we need.

There is no *a priori* reason why the list of practices should not extend indefinitely; Althusser himself has added artistic practice to the list. However, three are particularly important because they provide the basis of the analysis of society: economic, political and ideological. Each of these practices takes place in structures, sets of relationships constructed around the basic elements of the practice: raw material, means of production, and finished product. The structures in which these three practices are placed comprise the basic levels (or 'instances') of society – the economic, political and ideological levels. All societies can be seen as comprising these three levels: they make up the 'social formation', a structure of structures. The basis for arguing that there are three levels is that Marx said so. I do not want to dispute this; it seems to me quite a useful way of looking at the world, with a pay-off which will emerge shortly. For the moment it is worth pointing out that the words 'political' and 'ideological' should be given a wider meaning than we give them in everyday life. Most organisations can be treated as political and ideological, and the latter refers to all our ways of seeing ourselves and the world. Such a division of society into three levels covers most of what we would want to talk about in social theory.

Structural causality and overdetermination

One important difference between Althusser and the more orthodox structuralists is that he does work with an idea of causality, as opposed to 'rules of transformation'. There is, however, the same emphasis on the importance of relationships, and the 'causes' about which Althusser writes lie not in distinct things (or the elements of the structure), nor, of course, in people's intentions, but in the relationships between the elements. My discussion of causality in Chapter 2 owes much to Althusser, with the difference that I maintained that the teleological notion is essential for understanding agency, whilst Althusser takes the opposite view.

Now I argued above that Althusser was fighting on two political and theoretical fronts: he was arguing both against the crude forms of orthodox Marxism and against humanist Marxism. For the moment I want to deal with the first argument, against crude Marxism. The idea of structural causality is already something of an advance, since Marxists have always had a tendency to write as if the economy were a thing with a simple linear causal influence on everything else – as if it were the billiard cue and the political and ideological levels were the billiard balls it sets in motion. Althusser thus draws attention to the fact that these three levels *are* structures, that they have different elements and relationships between them, and that we must take care to analyse them. They are not simple. He also goes on to argue that the political and ideological levels are not produced as the simple effects of the economic level. Each has its own real existence and is related to the others in various ways ('complex' is a favourite word).

There is a useful architectural analogy here, which comes original-ly from Marx and takes us some of the way to understanding Althusser's view. We can look at the relationship between the floors of a multi-storey building: it would be nonsense to say that the first and second floors are caused by the ground floor, even though they rest upon it, have some sort of dependent relationship to it. Each is separate from the floor above and below it, and what goes on on each floor is not determined by what goes on below it. The first floor might be a shop, the second floor offices, and the third floor living quarters. Althusser's term for describing this relationship, where there is a causal connection but not complete dependence, is 'relative autonomy'. The political and ideological levels are neither completely dependent on the economic nor completely independent of it. If we take this building as a single enterprise, the office work which goes on on the second floor obviously depends upon the sort of trading that goes on in the shop, but there are various ways in which it might be organised, and the work relationships there may develop in ways that are not influenced by the economic activity going on below. Similarly, if the owners live on the third floor, their standard of living and way of life have limits set by the nature of the business they run, but there are choices within these limits, and the development of a marriage and family life has its own dynamics.

Althusser's next step away from crude Marxism is to argue that the causal processes are two-way: the political and ideological levels affect the economic. Returning to our example: decisions based on administrative criteria in the offices may have an effect on the trading in the shop – a 'streamlining of the management structure', for example, might lead to increased turnover. Similarly, if the business is jointly owned and the marriage fails, the settlement between the partners might have an important effect on the nature of the business. This, however, is as far as we can take this analogy; to follow Althusser's argument further, we need to return to a more abstract level.

Marxists have always seen the economic level and its development as determined by a contradiction – usually identified as the contradiction between the forces and relations of production. It is not necessary to know the technical details of the arguments, but the basic idea is that the productive forces of capitalism, its ability to produce wealth, are immense and continue to grow; on the other hand, the relations of production, the fact that wealth is privately owned and appropriated, restrict their growth. This sets up a dynamic in the system which, amongst other things, leads to a recurrent crisis – the system produces too much, so production falls and unemployment rises. The contradiction, which is a matter of the *relations* of production, is then the causal factor. Now Althusser argues that the causal factors at the other levels can also be seen as contradictions, and what happens in the day-to-day life of a society is a result of the way in which the contradictions in the underlying 'structure of structures' come together. This he calls *overdetermination*; in one sense this is another word for 'a lot going on out there', but sometimes it means something more – when it is used to refer to the way in which the contradictions at the different levels come together to reinforce each other or to inhibit each other's development. In the first case, the result is revolution and the emergence of a different form of society; in the second, it is stagnation and decay. Russia and India respectively are often given as examples.

The Russian Revolution is a particularly good example of 'overdetermination'. It is especially useful for Althusser because he can draw on the 'sacred texts' of Lenin, although perhaps a better and clearer account can be found in the first chapter of Trotsky's *History of the Russian Revolution* (1967). Oversimplifying, the argument is that we can identify first the contradiction at the economic level: in the still small but rapidly growing Russian capitalism, the contradiction between the forces and relations of production led, as always, to a class conflict between workers and owners. Coupled with this, in the much larger sector of feudal agriculture, a different economic contradiction produced a conflict between peasants and landlords.

Based on this were other contradictions and conflicts: between Russian capitalists and Russian landlords, the latter threatened by the growth of capitalism; and between Western financiers who were backing Russian capitalism and some sections of Russian capitalism who desired to control their own industries, as well as the more traditional Russian feudal aristocracy. All these can be considered as primary and secondary economic contradictions.

At the political level there was a conflict between the defenders of the old regime under the Tsar, authoritarian and hierarchical, and those who wanted to move towards some form of political democracy. This conflict was based on the economic level in that feudal regimes are authoritarian and hierarchical, whilst the development of capitalism often – but not always – tends to encourage political democracy; but it also had its own developmental logic of conflict and compromise. On the ideological level, the conflict was between those influenced by modern Western scientific ideas and those who supported the traditional religious beliefs of Russian feudalism. This conflict, too, was related to the economic conflict, but had its own logic of development. These separate logics of development would mean that, for example, people whom one might expect to be on one side because of their economic position would take the opposite political or ideological standpoint. Russian society was riven by contradictions in a way that was by no means simple. The factor that brought these contradictions to breaking point, causing a fragmentation out of which the Russian Revolution emerged, was the Russian defeat by the Germans in World War I.

'Determination in the last instance' and 'structure in dominance'

In order to understand the meaning of these rather daunting phrases, we have to remember the other side of Althusser's political battle. Despite attacking the cruder forms of traditional Marxism, he was still defending a Marxist orthodoxy against humanist revisions which tended towards abandoning the view that the economic level had any priority at all. He still needed to argue that despite the comparative independence and causal effect of the ideological and political levels, the economic level has some priority in determining what goes on (and consequently in understanding what goes on). His way round this dilemma is summed up in the phrase 'the economic is determinant in the last instance', a phrase from Engels, which Althusser immediately qualifies by pointing out that 'the last instance never comes'. This seems to amount to saying that the economic contradiction is the most important but it is never found in its pure form, it is always overlaid by other contradictions. I hope the next few pages will establish that in trying to understand the general shape and development of different types of society, this is quite a useful approach; however, it sets up a number of tensions that I have already mentioned – between the 'dependence' and 'independence' of the different levels – which, if one is demanding logical consistency, have a destructive effect.

One way in which Althusser both distances himself from crude Marxism and maintains the idea of the causal importance of the economic level is through arguing that different types of society are distinguished by the 'dominance' of different structural levels. By this he means that in the day-to-day internal development of a society, one particular level – or levels – is most important. In feudal societies this role is shared by the political/ideological levels; in early-capitalist societies it is the economic; and some would argue that in late-capitalist societies the political level is dominant. However, it is the structure of the economic level which determines which level, including the economic, is dominant. It is as if the economic level hands over its power to one of the other levels, or keeps it to itself, for the duration of that type of society. Clarifying this entails looking at Althusser's analysis of the 'mode of production', or the economic level; this, remember, is the most basic of society's underlying structures.

The mode of production[1]

A lot of what I have to say here comes less from Althusser's own work than from that of Etienne Balibar, one of the co-authors, with Althusser, of *Reading Capital* (1970), a central source of structuralist Marxist theory. We have already seen that economic practice involves a raw material, a means of production – including labour-power – and a finished product. In the analysis of the economic level these elements are grouped together as one element, the means of production, to which two other 'elements' are added: the 'labourer' and the 'non-labourer'. The term 'labourer' refers to the person (or people) who transform the raw material into the finished product, who work directly upon the goods produced. The term 'non-labourer' refers to those who do not work directly on the product, even though they might work – in effect, it refers in most societies to the owner of the means of production. These are sometimes called 'positions' to emphasise that while the personal characteristics of those who occupy them are not important, the positions they occupy are. Thus a society in which there is a high degree of social mobility, in which people can move from 'labourer' to 'non-labourer' with relative ease, is still capitalist, since it is the existence of the positions that defines it as such.

This is, of course, a misleading way of putting it, because what defines a society as capitalist or otherwise is not the simple existence of the positions or elements (they are present in all types of society) but the relationships between them. There are two important relationships between these elements. The first is that of ownership – the 'labourer' or 'non-labourer' may own the means of production. The second is, in effect, the relationship of 'control' – referring to which position, labourer or non-labourer, has the power to work the means of production. This should become clearer as I work through some examples of different types of society, since variations in the way in which the three elements are joined together by these two relationships enable us to distinguish between different types of society. Four types of society can be distinguished immediately:

1. *Feudalism* The non-labourer is the feudal lord, the labourer is the peasant. The lord effectively owns the land (although he cannot dispose of it at will – in theory, it is held in trust from the king, who in turn holds it in trust from God). The peasant family, on the other hand, control their piece of land in the sense that they choose when to work it, what to grow, etc. This is no big deal, since we are talking about a subsistence economy with few crops which have to be worked during all daylight hours.
2. *Capitalism* The non-labourer is the factory owner, the labourer is the worker. The non-labourer owns and controls the means of production – it is the owner who decides what to produce, when it will be produced, and so on.
3. A *transitional* mode of production between capitalism and feudalism, often referred to as a period of 'cottage industry'. This was the form taken by the textile industry during the Industrial Revolution in Britain. The worker and family still control and

work a piece of land, but their income is supplemented by producing goods on machinery (a loom, for example) which they own and keep in their cottage. The worker, or labourer, therefore owns the means of production. The non-labourer is usually a merchant who buys the raw material, farms it out to his workers and takes the finished product; in this sense the non-labourer controls the use of the means of production. When the machines are moved into one place, factory production and capitalism proper emerge.

4. *Socialism* The labourer owns and controls the means of production through an extended form of participant democracy.

I want to make three points about this conception of the underlying economic structure before moving on to look at its relationship to other structures. The first is pedantic: Althusser argues that one reason why this theory cannot be regarded as structuralist is that the elements themselves change with the relationships. The means of production under feudalism is land; under capitalism it is machines. For orthodox structuralism the elements are constant – 'd', 'g' and 'o' remain the same in 'dog' and 'god'. This might be true, but seems to me unimportant in the face of the shared feature of giving priority to the relationships rather than the elements. Althusser would certainly argue that it is the change in the relationships that leads to the development of the elements, since the opposite would lead him back to crude economic determinism.

The second point is that the model as it stands can distinguish between only four modes of production, and these by no means cover all societies we know about. Something that Marx called the 'Asiatic mode of production' is a particularly thorny problem – like feudal society it is pre-capitalist, but the state appears to play a very important role. Those followers of Althusser who demand complete logical consistency have tried to argue that there are societies without modes of production, on the basis that the theory cannot describe them; I do not think this is very helpful. The proper theoretical alternative is to look for other elements – or, more important, relationships that might help us to distinguish other types. Nicos Poulantzas, for example, has distinguished between 'juridical' and 'real' ownership – ownership as defined in law and in practice. In Eastern European societies, until recently, juridical ownership was in the hands of the labourers while real ownership was in the hands of the state bureaucracy, who control and reap the benefits of the means of production. Such a system might be called 'state socialism' or 'state capitalism', depending on how sympathetic you are to the regime in question.

The third point is the classic structuralist problem of change. These models are the static models of different types of society; if the argument was that these models identified mechanisms which led the society to change, then it would take us back to crude economic determinism. Althusser cannot resort to agency to explain change, since he is arguing precisely against such a position. As a result, it seems to me to remain unexplained on a theoretical level, although it can be described – just as I was describing the Russian Revolution above. Why these contradictions should come together in such a way at such a time is explained by the Russian defeat, not in terms of some theoretically identified mechanism. The 'transitional mode' is an attempt to come to grips with the problem, but it succeeds in producing another intermediate static model. Here we come back to another form of the basic tension which contributes to undermining the theory as a whole.

We can now move on to look at the causal mechanism framed by these economic relations and the way in which it affects the relationship between the economic, political and ideological levels. The best comparison is provided by feudalism and capitalism, and the assumption is that in both systems an economic surplus is produced (i.e. more than is strictly necessary to keep all or most members of that society in existence). In class societies, which include all but socialist societies, this surplus is appropriated by the non-labourer. The causal mechanism we are looking for is the mechanism of appropriation, the means by which the non-labourer takes the surplus.

In feudalism the non-labourer owns the land, but the labourer controls it. The labourer may produce sufficient to keep the family in existence, but since he controls the land, it does not follow automatically that a surplus is produced and handed over to the lord. In practice this is ensured in various ways: the peasant might have to pay an annual tax to the lord, or work on the lord's land or in the lord's household for so many days in the year; so the peasant has to be persuaded that this is the right thing to do, a moral obligation or duty, or he has to be forced to do it under threat of judicial punishment. The theoretical explanation of this is that the relations of production are such that the non-labourer must assure appropriation of a surplus through political and ideological structures. Hence the nature of the economic level places the political and ideological levels in dominance.

We can compare this to capitalism, in which the non-labourer owns *and* controls the means of production. When the worker goes to work, she must produce goods of sufficient value for her own keep (her wages) and a surplus at the same time – she cannot decide to go to work to produce just enough for herself; the employer would fire her or, if everybody did it, go out of business. The worker cannot use the factory for her own purposes, only for the employer's. She has to work the length of time the employer stipulates, or she leads an impoverished existence amongst the unemployed. If the worker works, she produces a surplus which is automatically appropriated by the employer, since he controls the product. The mechanism of appropriation thus operates at the economic level, and the economic level, as well as remaining determinant in the last instance, is also dominant. The economic structure is the most important cause of developments in the day-to-day life of the social formation.

It seems to me that what we have here is as good a theory as is available for distinguishing in general terms *between* different types of society, and for delineating the *internal* relations of the 'structure of structures', of the social formation. I have already indicated some of its problems – enough, I think, to show that it is not a perfect theory. It is open to further development and some problems, such as that of change, might remain beyond its scope. *As far as it goes*, however, it is useful, and that is perhaps as much as we can ask from any theory at the moment.

IDEOLOGY AND POLITICS: PUSHING THE THEORY BEYOND ITS LIMITS

I will now look at the structuralist approach to the other levels, the political and the ideological, the parts of the machine that are engaging most directly in working the puppets. This will lead directly on to Althusser's view of ideology – the puppet's strings.

It has always seemed to me that the logical way to develop the theoretical basis – the fruitful logical way, that is – would be to attempt to analyse the underlying structures of the political and ideological levels, with their respective causal mechanisms, and identify the way in which they in turn act upon the economic level. This has not happened; when they turn to the other levels, Althusser and his followers deal not with underlying structures but with surface institutions. I can suggest a reason for this: to identify underlying structures at these levels that do not originate at the economic level would involve granting some independent structure to agency, since in politics and ideology the problem of agency is posed most clearly: the material world of nature and machines can exercise some control over human beings; in thinking and political action, human beings attempt to control the material world. To recognise independent structures at these levels would be to grant too much to the humanists, so they resort to a form of economic determinism in which the underlying economic structure produces surface political and ideological institutions. It is not a straightforward economic determinism – some peculiar contradictions are involved.

In this section I want to explore this by looking at Poulantzas's work on social classes, and the work of Poulantzas and Althusser on the state and the 'ideological state apparatuses'. Returning to the metaphor of the puppet theatre: we are moving close to the puppets, now reaching the second level of the machinery that works them, the first being the mode of production.

Social classes

The analysis of class structure is one area where Althusserian theory has made positive contributions, although not as radical as it claims. Nicos Poulantzas has undoubtedly contributed most. Certainly the analysis of class structure is more sophisticated than that offered by cruder forms of Marxist analysis, without breaking down into the kaleidoscope of distinctions offered by theorists such as Dahrendorf. The basis of the argument is that social classes are determined not just by the economic structure but by political and ideological structures as well. The advances, however, seem to me to have been in understanding class determined by the economic level, and this is what I will look at first.

The extreme version of crude Marxism would hold that capitalism produces two classes, owners and non-owners, bourgeoisie and proletariat, with a third class – the petty bourgeoisie, small-scale producers – gradually squeezed out. The first contribution of structuralist Marxism is to point out that modes of production can coexist in the same social formation, and the problem of the way in which they are 'articulated' has received considerable attention. This means that different social classes belonging to different modes of production can exist in the same society. Poulantzas talks about 'petty commodity production', which seems to be a modified transitional mode continuing into capitalism, in order to explain the continued existence of the petty bourgeoisie. Beyond this, however, he suggests that we can identify 'class fragments' determined by secondary economic criteria. Amongst the non-labourers we can distinguish owners of land, of industrial capital and finance capital who, at different times, might have conflicting political and ideological interests as well as conflicting economic interests. He goes on to suggest a difference between a 'reigning class' who hold political office and a 'hegemonic' or ruling class as that class in whose interests political decisions are taken. In Britain for the last part of the nineteenth century, for example, the landed aristocracy held political office but exercised it in the interests of the industrial capitalists. On the side of the labourers, we can distinguish between skilled and unskilled workers, conflicts between whom have been important in the development of the British trade-union movement. Poulantzas's debate with the English Marxist Ralph Miliband (in Blackburn, 1972) illustrates the difference between this type of analysis and conventional Marxism, and – if you can cut through the jargon – the increased sophistication.

So far, so good: we have a relatively complex model of the class structure. When Poulantzas turns to the political and ideological determinations of the class structure, however, he seems to end up back at the economic, and I have already suggested a reason why. He discusses at some length the 'new petty bourgeoisie'. These people have a different economic position to the 'traditional petty bourgeoisie': they are not owners of family enterprises but workers in such areas as advertising, non-productive workers. Yet they can be categorised as petty bourgeoisie because ideologically they have much the same beliefs as the traditional section of that class. When we look at why they have these beliefs, however, it seems that they stem from an economic position – a different economic position none the less causes the same set of political attitudes. Poulantzas also talks about 'social categories' which are determined by their position in political institutions, such as state bureaucrats and intellectuals and the military. In certain situations, he argues, these social categories can play a crucial role: they are particularly important, for example, in fascist regimes. However, he also argues that in times of crisis they tend to divide along the lines of their class of origin, the social class from which they came. Thus again economic determination takes on major importance. I will not go into these arguments in any detail: what I hope I have shown is that we can, using structuralist Marxism, gain a more complex and useful model of class structure than we can from cruder forms of Marxism and from conflict theory; but that despite itself, despite the intentions of the theory, an economic determinism emerges. This is not necessarily mistaken – structuralist Marxism still gives us a sort of skeletal analysis of the class structure; but by itself it cannot explain the complexity of political groupings that we find in modern society, which conflict theory can at least describe. To go further, we would need a more detailed theoretical analysis of underlying structures at the political and economic level.

The state and ideological state apparatuses

More conventional Marxists, crude or otherwise, would trace political conflicts from classes defined by economic structures, but most would acknowledge that all sorts of other factors must be taken into account before we can fully understand the political life of a society. For the structuralists this issue seems to have become a touchstone by which one can judge the 'crudity' of a theory – in such a way, eventually, that any attempt to relate political conflict to economically defined classes is dismissed as crude or deterministic. This is so despite the paradoxical fact that they have produced a comparatively complex and useful model of the class structure based on economic definitions, and seem unable to get away from it. There are some even odder paradoxes.

The state has become a key area for investigation, largely under the influence of structuralist writings. It will soon become apparent that the term 'the state' means much more in this context than it does in everyday language. This is clearest in Althusser's (1971) paper on ideology and ideological state apparatuses. I recounted above the argument that what is distinctive about capitalism is that the 'mechanism of appropriation' is guaranteed by economic relations. Althusser argues that though this is true, there are many other features required by those relations which are not guaranteed at the economic level itself. For example, labourers require to be fed and housed from day to day if they are to continue 'in working order'; they need to be trained in the requisite skills in general terms – they need a certain level of ability in reading and writing, for example – and in more specific skills; their children must be reared and trained to provide future labourers; they need to know their place, so that they do not become discontented or paralysed by hopeless ambitions or by resentment at being told what to do. All these things are necessary; they are the 'conditions of existence' of the continuation of capitalist relations of production.

For Althusser (and Poulantzas) the role of ensuring these conditions is fulfilled by the state; the state comes to be seen as the centre of the social formation and the continued existence of capitalist relations of production. The state fulfils its role in two ways – in extremes it uses force: the army, the police, the 'repressive state apparatuses'. Most of the time this is not necessary, because of the more or less efficient working of the 'ideological state apparatuses' which ensure that people do what the underlying structure demands they do. These apparatuses are all institutions which ensure that the conditions of existence I listed above are actually met, and they include – as well as obvious 'state institutions' such as the education system – many institutions we would normally regard as private: the media, the Church, the family, and even trade unions. All these work to ensure the continuation of capitalism.

One line of criticism is that this argument blurs very important distinctions between state and private institutions, but more telling is the argument that Althusser's explanation is functionalist and, in fact, not an explanation of much at all. To say that the economic level requires a number of conditions to be met is not an explanation of how they are met; they need not be met at all, and they may be met in several ways: witness the different education systems in North America and various European countries. To state the need for something is not to explain that it is met or how it is met – this is as true for societies as for individuals. I need a vast sum of money, but I do not get it. Lurking behind this explanation is an economic determinism; the implicit assumption – which cannot be made explicit, since it is precisely what Althusser is arguing against – is that the existence of these institutions is determined by the economic level.

A further problem for both Althusser and Poulantzas is that

Marxists have always argued that the conflict between social classes is carried on in many of the state institutions they discuss; if this is so – and both would like to maintain that it is – where does such conflict originate? It cannot come from the ideological and political apparatuses themselves, since they exist to ensure the smooth running of the system, and they would not be doing that if they generated conflict; and it cannot come from economically determined classes – that would be to grant too much to crude Marxism. 'Class struggle' is produced from nowhere. The tension this creates in the theory leads Poulantzas in particular in two directions: one is to a more orthodox, though by no means crude, Marxism, influenced by the Italian theorist Gramsci; the other is towards some of the ideas of post-structuralism, on which I shall touch in the next chapter.

The subject: the puppet's invisible strings

Althusser's discussion of the ideological apparatuses leads us on finally to the stage presentation of structuralism's puppet theatre. His discussion of the 'ideological state apparatuses' is a step on the way to his discussion of the subject and subjectivity – or, more appropriately, the death of the subject. In dealing with this in the last chapter, I discussed the idea that our experience of being the authors of our own actions is in some way mistaken or misleading. Althusser wants to explain how such an experience occurs, and why it is misleading – why we are really puppets: why my belief that I am writing this book (when it is really social theory writing itself through me) is mistaken. In fact he develops a subtle argument around this issue, claiming that the experience is both necessary and misleading: in doing so, he makes the core of what we mean by 'ideology' this experience of being the authors of our actions. He terms the experience 'imaginary', borrowing a term given a technical meaning by the French psychoanalytic structuralist Jacques Lacan.

Lacan sees this experience as a precondition for calling ourselves human; the gaining of the experience of being a subject marks our entry into society and culture. It occurs during the first years of childhood, which he calls the 'mirror stage' – a stage which runs conjointly with the stages of development that Freud described. The idea is that the new-born child experiences itself as a bundle of conflicting and very strong drives pulling it in opposite directions. Most psychoanalysts would agree with this, seeing the process of growing up as learning to control and channel these drives. For Lacan, the process is one of gaining the experience of being a subject. It happens through the infant seeing a mirror-image – not necessarily in the mirror, but perhaps through the parent, in the way that G.H. Mead saw the 'Me' as being produced. For Lacan it is the 'I' that is produced: in the image the child sees a being not torn apart by powerful drives, but in control of itself. Anyone who makes a habit of looking in a mirror will understand that sometimes the image seems to possess everything the viewer lacks. The infant, argues Lacan, tries to become like this image; it tries to become this subject, which is 'imaginary', whilst underneath, the contradictory drives continue to exist in some form. Most of us go through periods of stress when they come to the surface.

Lacan is concerned with the structure of the unconscious, which underlies this imaginary experience of being a subject. All I want to say here is that it would certainly give us a more sophisticated conception of agency than we met amongst action theorists. This, however, is not Althusser's concern: his argument is that this imaginary sense of being a subject comes from the ideological apparatuses. They exist before the person is born and they map out our lives for us – we are born into a role already waiting for us in the family, in the school, at work and so on. This idea, in fact, is very much like that of Parsons's 'status role'. Our sense of being a subject and many other aspects of our ideas stem from the actions (or practices) which await us and which we are compelled into performing. Althusser quotes the Jansenist theologian Pascal to the effect that one does not believe in God and then kneel to pray; one prays and, through praying, comes to believe in God. Through acting in the prescribed way in the roles in which I am placed, I come to believe that I am the author of my actions.

WHY THE THEATRE MACHINERY IS INTERESTING

Here we have the puppet theatre in full view: the strings originate at the economic level, the mode of production; they pass through the state and the ideological state apparatuses, a second level of machinery that services the mode of production, keeping it in operation. And they finally work the puppets through an imaginary sense of being free, of choosing, of acting. There is a fatal flaw in this argument, which I will postpone to the next chapter; for the moment I want to recapitulate on the usefulness of the machinery:

1. It gives us a model of society that enables us to make distinctions which, for example, Parsons cannot make, and does adequately separate society and agency, even if problems arise when we reach the latter.
2. It provides a way of looking at different types of society, and at how two or more modes of production might conjoin in one society.
3. It provides a more complex model of class and political structure than crude Marxism, without giving way to the flux of events, as conflict theory does.
4. It at least enables us to start thinking about processes of reciprocal determinations between the economic, political and ideological levels; and there is a way forward here if it were to prove possible to identify underlying structures at the political and ideological levels, together with the relevant causal mechanisms.
5. Despite the fatal flaw in its conception of the subject, it can hint at a more profound conception of agency than we have met so far through its reference, via Lacan, to the unconscious.

On the other hand, tensions have emerged at the very heart of Althusser's conception of Marxism, originating in the tensions of his political battles. These can be summed up in the theme of this book as a whole: the tension between the analysis of social structure and the analysis of social action. Althusser's sophisticated structural determinism leaves us with a number of problems in explaining change conflicts which do not appear to be related to the economic contradictions, and also in explaining human action itself. These are in addition to the specific theoretical tensions and problems I discussed in the section on the nature of theory. In the next chapter I will look at the way in which these problems have led to the fragmentation of the approach.

TEN YEARS AFTER: A POSTSCRIPT

I now want to return to the theme of my opening remarks. What are we to make of all this in the light of the apparent collapse of communism as a serious political movement? I have tried to set

Althusser in a political context, but his development was much more
intimately bound up with the development of communism and the
history of Marxism–Leninism than I have actually indicated. Hegel
remarked that 'The owl of Minerva flies at dusk' – a suitably obscure
reference to the fact that it is only towards the end of a historical
period that it becomes possible to grasp what has been happening. It
seems to me that Althusser developed and articulated as coherent a
form of orthodox Marxism as is possible, and that this very
achievement became possible only as orthodoxy became untenable.
His influence has been immense – even though perhaps very few of
those whom he affected have remained working in the framework he
set out. The development of Bhaskar's philosophical realism clearly
owes much to Althusser's epistemology, but there have been many
more concrete investigations based on it – a number of the most
important are listed under Further Reading.

However, Althusser and the tradition of structuralist Marxism
seem important to me not for historical reasons, and perhaps only
secondarily for their influence on the philosophy of social science.
The 'good side' for which I argued ten years ago now seems more
important than ever: Althusser's framework offers the most sophisticated conception of social structure available in the social sciences. It
seems to me that the major alternative is Parsons's systems theory or
some variant of it, and it is worth spending a while comparing the
two. Althusser's work offers a conception of an *underlying* social
structure. The notion of positions is actually 'deeper' than that of
roles: a position is something I am in whether or not I know about it,
and whilst it clearly does not have the essentially deterministic role
that Althusser gives it, it is something that determines, in the sense of
limiting, my actions, and it is something I cannot change – by myself,
or perhaps even collectively. Paradoxically, since Marxism is often
accused of offering single-cause explanations, Althusser offers the
possibility of complex, multi-causal explanations, with an ordering of
priorities amongst the causal processes that goes beyond the description of what happens. Parsons's explanations, with the exception of
the notion of a cybernetic hierarchy, seem to me not to offer this
possibility.

It is also a paradox that a philosopher who was concerned to renew
and develop an orthodox Marxist tradition of thought should in fact
have opened a path for the development of postmodernist theories
which reject, in a radical way, the sorts of analyses that come from

Marxism. The fact that Althusser's work should have been so easily taken up and swept away in a form of thinking that seems to me highly ideological is another good reason for holding on to it. Whatever might be wrong with his epistemology, Althusser at least holds on to a commitment to knowledge, and the use of that knowledge to bring about beneficial political change. I still think that is important.

NOTES

1. This term is often used to refer to all three levels rather than just the economic level (which is the sense in which I am using it here), and 'social formation' is used to refer to combinations of modes of production. Such a usage goes further in avoiding simple economic determinism.

FURTHER READING

The structuralist Marxist tradition

All work in this tradition is difficult; from Althusser the best starting points are the essays 'Contradiction and overdetermination' and 'On the materialist dialectic' in *For Marx*; the ideology essay is in *Lenin and Philosophy*; the *New Left Review* article is probably the best starting point for Poulantzas.

Althusser, L. (1969) *For Marx*, Allen Lane, The Penguin Press, London.
Althusser, L. (1971) *Lenin and Philosophy*, New Left Books, London.
Althusser, L. (1976) *Essays in Self-Criticism*, New Left Books, London.
Althusser, L. and Balibar, E. (1970) *Reading Capital*, New Left Books, London.
Poulantzas, N. (1973a) 'On social classes', *New Left Review*, no. 78, pp. 27–54.
Poulantzas, N. (1973b) *Political Power and Social Classes*, New Left Books, London.
Poulantzas, N. (1974) *Fascism and Dictatorship*, New Left Books, London.
Poulantzas, N. (1975) *Classes in Contemporary Capitalism*, New Left Books, London.
Poulantzas, N. (1976) *The Crisis of the Dictatorships*, New Left Books, London.

Poulantzas, N. (1978) *State, Power, Socialism*, New Left Books, London.

For the differences between structuralist and more orthodox Marxism, see the debate with Ralph Miliband in

Blackburn, R. (ed.) (1972) *Ideology in Social Science*, Fontana, London.
Poulantzas, N. (1976) 'The capitalist state: A reply to Miliband and Laclau', *New Left Review*, no. 95, pp. 63–83.

Other works influenced by the tradition

Balibar, E. (1977) *On the Dictatorship of the Proletariat*, New Left Books, London.
Bois, G. (1984) *The Crisis of Feudalism*, Cambridge University Press, Cambridge.
Castell, M. (1977) *The Urban Question: A Marxist approach*, Edward Arnold, London.
Godelier, M. (1977) *Perspectives in Marxist Anthropology*, Cambridge University Press, Cambridge.
Jessop, B. (1982) *The Capitalist State: Marxist theories and methods*, Martin Robertson, Oxford.
Jessop, B. (1985) *Nicos Poulantzas: Marxist theory and political strategy*, Macmillan, Basingstoke.
Macherey, P. (1978) *The Theory of Literary Production*, Routledge & Kegan Paul, London.
Terray, E. (1972) *Marxism and 'Primitive' Societies*, Monthly Review Press, New York.
Wright, E. O. (1978) *Class Crisis and State*, New Left Books, London.

Useful introductions

Benton provides an especially good critical discussion, Elliott fills in the detail of the political background and surveys the range of Althusserian influence.

Benton, T. (1984) *The Rise and Fall of Structural Marxism*, Macmillan, Basingstoke.
Callinicos, A. (1976) *Althusser's Marxism*, Pluto Press, London.
Elliott, G. (1987) *Althusser: The detour of theory*, Verso, London.
Geras, N. (1977) 'Althusser's Marxism: An assessment', in *Western Marxism: A critical reader*, New Left Books, London, pp. 232–72.
Smith, S. B. (1984) *Reading Althusser*, Cornell University Press, Ithaca, NY.

A selection of more recent assessments can be found in:

Appignanesi, L. (ed.) (1989) *Ideas from France: The legacy of French theory*, Free Association Books, London.

Also referred to in the text:

Marx, K. (1964) *The Economic and Philosophical Manuscripts of 1844*, International Publishers, New York.
Marx, K. (1967) *Capital*, Lawrence & Wishart, London.
Trotsky, L. (1967) *History of the Russian Revolution*, 3 vols, Sphere Books, London.

Chapter 10

POST-STRUCTURALISM AND POST-MODERNISM: THE WORLD GONE MAD

INTRODUCTION

In the last chapter I argued that despite certain advantages in the way that structuralist Marxism conceptualised societies, problems begin to arise when the structuralist form of analysis attempts to deal with agency, with human action. I tried to demonstrate this in relation to the political and ideological levels where, I suggested, the alternatives were to grant some form of autonomy to agency, or to resort to a deterministic model based on the economic level. I suggested that both Althusser and Poulantzas take the second option, producing a sort of economic functionalism rather than a system functionalism – whereas Parsons attempts to explain institutions in terms of their function for the whole system, Althusser does so in terms of their function for the economic level. I likened Althusser's system to a puppet theatre with various levels of machinery, working a set of invisible strings which give the appearance that the actors work of their own volition. Finally, I suggested that there was a crucial flaw in his explanation of the working of these invisible strings.

In this chapter, I will begin by tracing the fragmentation of structuralist Marxism, but it is a particularly interesting form of fragmentation, because we end up with something that is almost the complete opposite to what we started with. The puppet theatre collapses, and we are left with no hidden machinery, nothing pulling the strings, and in one sense no puppets – and, beyond that, no people. In fact it is difficult to say exactly what we are left with – but it is definitely something, and something else at the same time.

177

The critique of structuralist Marxism is closely connected to what has become known as 'postmodernism'. A regular complaint in the literature is that it is difficult to define the term itself, or the terms in which we discuss it, but it will become apparent that this difficulty is inherent in its nature. Postmodernism is an artistic movement, perhaps most evident in architecture but spreading throughout the arts, and this will be the area I concentrate on least. It embraces a range of developments in modern philosophy which follows on directly from what has become known as the 'linguistic turn'. In sociology, the idea of postmodernism carries the implication that the social world has undergone a major and dramatic change. In this sense, it is not all that new an idea – Toynbee's writings in the early 1950s are often referred to as an origin, and it has certain affinities with Daniel Bell's notion of a post-industrial society. Postmodernism is often juxtaposed to something called 'modernism', although the exact relationship between the two is open to debate.

However, perhaps this is a good way to start. Modernism is associated with the Enlightenment, 'the project of the Enlightenment', involving the idea of universal rationality – a search for a knowledge that is more or less certain, and for a control over the natural and social world. In contrast to this, postmodernism denies the existence of a universal rationality or the possibility of knowledge in the way we might conventionally think of it. One thing that follows from this is the argument that Enlightenment thought is concerned with establishing hierarchies – for example, between rational and irrational, knowledge and non-knowledge, but also good and bad literature, good and bad art. This argument is often taken further: there is a link between establishing hierarchies of knowledge and social hierarchies: Enlightenment rationality is really white, male rationality, and is another aspect of the oppression of women and ethnic groups. Postmodernism thus has its radical political associations. It will become apparent that the linguistic model is paramount, but in a way that denies the existence of any underlying linguistic or social structure. There is only what goes on on the surface, and what goes on on the surface, for many, is talk.

To begin with, I will approach postmodernist sociology through looking at critiques of structuralist Marxism and post-structuralism; then I will return to a sociology of postmodernism in an attempt to make sense of why these ideas should be appearing.

THE FAULT LINES OF STRUCTURALIST MARXISM

One feature of postmodernism is, perhaps, the speed with which ideas appear and disappear; in a series of arguments that now seem rather dated, two British sociologists, Barry Hindess and Paul Hirst, played a major role in introducing Althusser's work to a British audience and – all within a period of ten years – dismantling it.

The most prominent fault lines, and the ones they seized upon, have to do with the attempt to force a theory of societies on to other inappropriate areas of social reality. The most important of these is that of agency, the problem being that the subject never quite manages to give up the ghost; beyond this, however, the area I referred to as that of 'general meanings' proves troublesome as the metaphysical assumptions of structuralism reassert themselves. The specific political factors at work in this British development had to do with the attempt to explain conflicts that have arisen around race, sex and nationality, since it proves very difficult, if not impossible, to make sense of these issues using traditional Marxist, or Althusserian Marxist, economic categories. This prepares the ground for collapsing the idea of a social formation with the economic level 'determinant in the last instance'. We are left with only a multiplicity of free-floating political and ideological phenomena which are seen not as results of causal processes in the social formation, but as constituted in and by discourse. Perhaps the best way of describing this fragmentation is as a slide from a theory of societies to a descriptive theory of the interplay of general meanings.

First, the 'fatal flaw' in Althusser's argument about the subject and subjectivity. To summarise his argument again: the 'ideological state apparatuses' arise to fulfil certain needs at the economic level; they involve 'material practices', courses of action carried out by individuals placed in them – born into them, in the case of the family. Through engaging in these institutional practices, already mapped out before the person takes up position, the agent comes to see herself reflected as the author of her actions, and experiences herself as such. This experience is real but imaginary, and hides the deeper reality that she is the bearer of underlying structures. Now the flaw in this argument is that neither Althusser nor Lacan is proposing a view of the unsocialised individual as a *tabula rasa* – a blank slate upon which society writes whatever it desires. We are not the *simple* product or 'effect' of underlying social structures. Both argue that the experience of subjectivity, of being the author of one's actions, comes from recognising an image of oneself – in a mirror, to use Lacan's metaphor, or in a 'material practice' – and then identifying with that image. Now this presupposes that the individual already possesses certain characteristics of subjectivity; she must be able to recognise an image and identify with it, and if she is the author of these actions, there is no *a priori* reason why she should not be the author of others. If Althusser's theory is intended to explain why – as he puts it – people 'work by themselves', it seems to presuppose what it is trying to demonstrate. The explanation holds only if individuals already possess that quality. The subject refuses to lie down.

This point is argued with considerable subtlety by Paul Hirst (1976). The conclusion I would draw from it is that we need to maintain some notion of the subject as the author of actions, even if it is modified – or 'de-centred', to use another favourite structuralist term. However, this is not Hirst's conclusion; he is firmly committed to abandoning such a notion. His way out will emerge shortly but I want to leave this argument for a while. For the moment it is sufficient to note that the gap between society and agency proves unbridgeable.

I now want to turn to other tensions in Althusser's theory that encourage the process of fragmentation. These lead in one way or another to examples of what I called, in the Introduction, the 'logic trap': the idea that one can know what the world is like through logical theoretical argument alone. In the criticism of Althusser's theory, this takes the form of posing either/or questions and coming down on one side or the other. The important point is that the logical criticisms we will be looking at arise around the different areas of social reality that the theory attempts to embrace, in particular social structures and general meanings.

The first such criticism focuses on what I have already identified as a tension in Althusser's view of theory. This involves a combination of the structuralist metaphysical assumption that a theory (or language) creates its own objects, its own world, and that theory none the less 'appropriates' a real external object, in this case underlying social structures. The criticism, as simply as I can put it, is this: if the theory creates its own objects, and if we can judge a theory only by its rational or logical coherence, we have to make the implicit assumption that the world is logically coherent if we are to maintain a realist position. This assumption involves the view that our theory and the external world should be of the same structure – we can match one against the other – and are therefore (God forbid) empiricist. This sort of argument can lead to an attack of vertigo unless you take it slowly. In effect, the critics are saying: *either* a theory creates its own objects, *or* it somehow describes objects in the external world. The latter has already been ruled out of court, therefore the former must be true. We are left with the fairly simple view that the world is a product of our ideas; in other words, we are left only with general meanings.

Now it seems to me quite reasonable to suggest that a theory does not refer necessarily to observable objects in the world, but it does not follow that it does not refer to any external and independent object. We cannot *see* a mode of production, but it is reasonable to suggest that it exists as an underlying structure. Althusser is trying to grasp and master a subtle problem, and he does so by introducing a tension in his explanation. Logically, this tension may be called a contradiction and resolved on one side or the other, but such a resolution does not help us to understand the world any better. The Hindess/Hirst resolution ignores the fact that the world often refuses to be as our theory says it should. It also removes any possibility of judging between theories, except perhaps on arbitrary political grounds. From saying that a theory creates its own world, it is only a step to saying that it creates its own rationality or logic. Each theory, then, is logical in its own terms. This introduces a particular absurdity into the position. The argument that there is no way of judging between theories is disagreeing with an argument that says that we can judge between theories – it is therefore implying that it is a better theory. The very act of arguing that we cannot judge between theories contradicts itself by its very existence. This is the sort of spiral into which the logic trap leads us.

Two further logical hatchet blows have been dealt to Althusserian theory. The conception of 'relative autonomy' is one target. It is argued that *either* the political and ideological levels are autonomous, *or* they are dependent upon and in some way 'caused' by the economic level. The latter would be crude economic determinism, which doesn't work, so the former must be true. I discussed the alternative to this in the last chapter: a closer analysis of the underlying structures and causal mechanisms at work at each level. However, the either/or argument removes any possibility of a causal relationship between the levels and, in effect, collapses the idea of the social formation, making any distinction pointless. We are left with a mixture of politics and ideology, and led back to the level of general meanings.

The next step is to remove any idea of causality altogether. In the Introduction I suggested that some notion of teleological causality was necessary to understand human action: it involves notions such as intention and project. The logical criticism here argues, first, that any relationship between cause and effect is teleological, since the effect must somehow be present in the cause, just as my intention is present at the beginning of the action to which it leads. If we accept Althusser's argument against teleological causality, which is part of his general attack on traditional ideas of the subject, then any idea of causality is outlawed, and it is argued that the most we can do is talk about 'conditions of existence'. We can say, for example, that parliamentary democracy has certain conditions of existence, and other things must exist if parliamentary democracy is to come into being, but we cannot say that it is caused by these conditions. Again, sensitive – albeit, sometimes, ambiguous – distinctions are dismissed in favour of logical clarity. Logical clarity leaves us with no way of distinguishing levels or 'regions' of the social world, no means of identifying causal relationships, and no way of choosing between different theories; in other words, it leaves us in a mess – *all* we can say is that there is a lot going on.

It is not quite as bad as this, however: we are left with just one level of social reality, that of 'general meanings', and when I talked about Paul Hirst's discussion of the theory of the subject, I indicated that he took a different course to the one I took. In fact he suggests that we must look at the 'constitution' of the subject, the creation of the subject at the level of general meanings, in what he calls 'signifying practices' or 'discourses'. This is not the same as talking about the 'constitution of the subject' by underlying structures of language; rather, it is the use of language that constitutes subjectivity.

I will elaborate on this shortly; for the moment, I want to take a detour through the political background to post-structuralism. From 1968 onwards there had been a steady disillusion with the French Communist Party and a growth of organisations further to the Left. On a theoretical level, this led eventually to a wide-ranging criticism of Marxism itself. It was argued that the conservative and authoritarian nature of Western European Communist Parties was itself a reflection of the conservative and authoritarian regimes in Eastern Europe, and both were the product of Marxism, an authoritarian and conservative theory. Now part of Althusser's appeal had been the return to the original works of Marx, and the implication of this was that Stalinism and all that it entailed could be explained as some form of deviation. Given the 'relative autonomy' of the ideological and political levels, for example, it might be argued that the transformation of the economic level in Stalin's Russia had not yet led to the revolutions in the political and ideological levels that would be necessary for the establishment of socialism. The return to Marx was a way of bypassing Stalin and associated evils. However, the Communist Party's inability to maintain its radicalism, and in some places, such as Italy, its tendency to enter into alliance with conservative opposition parties, together with its failure to change its own internal organisation, led some people to conclude that the return to Marx made no difference. In the graphic words of Foucault reviewing a book by André Glücksmann: 'Those who hoped to save themselves by opposing Marx's real beard to Stalin's false nose are wasting their time' (quoted in Callinicos, 1982, p. 108).

André Glücksmann's own development is interesting. He produced the first systematic critique of Althusser's work (see Further Reading), a very difficult piece aimed mainly at *Reading Capital* (1970). The points he made were telling – so telling, in fact, that there was no direct reply, and when the second edition was published (this was the one to be translated into English) sections that Glücksmann had particularly savaged were simply omitted. Glücksmann himself later became associated with a group known as the *nouveaux philosophes* who adopted what is basically a traditional right-wing criticism of Marxism – that any attempt to create socialism automatically leads to dictatorship and concentration camps, this being built into Marxist theory itself.

However, this right-wing critique is not the one I shall trace. There is a leftist, radical version, best represented by Foucault himself, which leads to a pessimistic anarchism. Partly a criticism of Marxism, and partly an alternative, it abandons the classical Marxist view that revolution involves the seizure of the state, and thus of power, on the grounds that power itself is not centralised in the state. Instead, the social world is seen as a kaleidoscope of power struggles which can never be transcended. All that can be done is to encourage the resistance that arises wherever power arises. In place of a revolution we are confronted with an endless series of power struggles which cannot be resolved because power is a necessary and inherent part of any relationship. This, in fact, is the way the 1968 rebellions appeared in France – as a series of localised power struggles in colleges, factories and offices – and many recent political conflicts in Western Europe generally may be seen in the same way. In the approach that has become known as 'post-structuralism', fragmentation becomes explicit, both politically and theoretically.

THE THEMES OF POSTMODERNIST SOCIOLOGY

Hirst's criticisms of Althusser lead on to Foucault, post-structuralism, and postmodernism in general. There is an absence of causal explanations which involves a rejection of the notion of ontological depth, and a concentration on appearances, representations, and a rejection of historical explanation – at least in so far as it is an *explanation* (a result of the criticism of teleological explanation). The philosophical roots of postmodernism are rather firmer than Hirst's criticisms might suggest. It certainly owes much to the German philosopher Nietzsche, who was writing at the end of the last century and whose philosophy has variously been described as nihilistic, anarchistic and existentialist. In his work we find themes that have reappeared in post-structuralism: the relationship between knowledge and power, the relativism of knowledge and the death of God. But these have been developed through the filter of structuralism and postmodernism in the arts.

We have already met the idea that a language creates its own objects, and this idea has developed – particularly in the work of Derrida – into a theory of meaning. The starting point is that meaning does not come in any way through a relationship to something outside language; there is absolutely nothing to which we can look to guarantee meaning, to assure us that we are right. Another way of putting it is that there is nothing playing the role of God, there is no 'transcendental signified'. Yet another formulation of the same idea is that meaning is never *present*, it is always somewhere else. On the simplest level, we have learnt from structuralism that the meaning of a word depends upon its relationship to other words – meaning lies between words rather than in the relationship between word and object. We know the meaning of 'dog' only because of its relationship to other words in the relevant paradigm and syntagm, not because of any inherent quality of the word itself. Meaning, then, always lies elsewhere and it is not guaranteed by anything outside itself; and of course, the world we see is created in and by meanings. There are only meanings.

The concept of sign implies that there is something signified, and the concept of 'structure' that there is something firm and ordered. Post-structuralism abandons these ideas: there is only one level, a surface level. There are no hidden depths in the world, and in its primitive form the surface level is chaotic and meaningless – a kaleidoscope. A variety of puzzling metaphors are employed to describe this ('the body without organs' is my personal favourite, since it leaves me completely mystified), but the idea of life itself as a meaningless chaos upon which we must impose some order has a long history in European philosophy.

Any order that exists is seen as coming from a process of differentiation within the chaos – remember that meaning lies in the relationships between words, the differences between words. The 'process of signification' is the drawing of these differences. When we make a statement, we bring a momentary order to the world – we define something according to its relationship with something else. A statement is often described as an 'event', and the term 'discourse' is usually employed to refer to a collection of related statements or events. The argument to which Paul Hirst is moving in his criticisms of Althusser's philosophy is that 'subjects' are created or 'constituted' by 'signifying practices', by the production of statements in discourses – discourses being what bring a general order to chaotic experience. No statement or discourse has a fixed meaning – its meaning always depends upon its relationship to other statements or discourses. As a result, there is a constant movement or slippage: when we ask the meaning of one discourse we are referred to another, and so on. This has a resonance with the insights of ethnomethodology, but it is much more radical in the sense that it undermines any sense of order in the world – hence the anarchistic colouring of much post-structuralist writing. A multiplicity of possible interpretations becomes a sort of aesthetic standard in the arts, and in literary criticism the interpretation itself has come to be regarded as a creative act of equal value to the work being interpreted.

For some writers, however, there are sources of order, or at least fixity -- points at which meaning becomes comparatively stable. Lacan uses the analogy of the points at which a loose chair-covering is fixed to the upholstery, and for him the fixed points in the sea of discourse come through the production of male sexual identity. Some of his ideas have been taken up critically by feminist theorists. Of more immediate relevance to the concerns of this book, however, is the work of Foucault: his points of fixation have to do with power.

Foucault does talk about an external world, an 'extra-discursive' order, the institutional structure out of which discourses develop and which embodies discourse; this distances him somewhat from other post-structuralists. Discourses and institutions are both 'fixed' by the power relations inherent in them. Following Nietzsche, he inverts the common-sense view of the relation between power and knowledge: whereas we might normally regard knowledge as providing us with the power to do things that, without it, we could not do, Foucault argues that knowledge is a power over others, the power to define others. Knowledge ceases to be a liberation and becomes enslavement. Thus, in his *History of Sexuality* (1979–86) he argues not only that the Victorian period was the opposite of what we suppose it to have been – a period when talk about sexuality was repressed – but also that the popular modern view that talking about sex is a form of liberation is wrong. The Victorian period was one in which a number of disciplines, such as medicine and psychiatry, developed their investigations into sexuality, and this process of bringing sexuality under control, of developing classifications and treatments and techniques, has continued to grow ever since. A discourse embodies knowledge (or, rather, what it defines as knowledge) and therefore embodies power. There are rules within a discourse concerning who can make statements and in what context, and these rules exclude some and include others. Those who have knowledge have the power to fix the flow of meaning and define others. The world is thus made up of a myriad of power relations, and each power generates a resistance; therefore, the world is a myriad of power struggles – something that is illustrated precisely by the 1968 uprisings in France.

This rather rarefied philosophical atmosphere in which the world is seen as created by language might seem strange; in fact, we have already met the idea in a different way in ethnomethodology. As far as Foucault's work is concerned there is, I think, a striking resemblance to conflict theory in the nature of his approach. As with conflict theory, we have only a few real theoretical statements – about discourse and meaning and power – but at a much higher level of abstraction, that of philosophical metaphysics. Also as with conflict theory, these statements point to the variegated, kaleidoscopic nature of the social world. The next step is to describe that social world, and the most interesting of Foucault's work comprises studies of the knowledge/power relations in the growth of different sciences – in psychiatric medicine, in criminal law, and in theories of sexuality. His methodological works can be seen as developing rules for studying the world in the light of the metaphysical-theoretical statements, just as conflict theorists produce a series of hypotheses and rules for studying role conflict. There is, I think, rather more to be gleaned from post-structuralism than there is from conflict theory, and I will return to this shortly.

The development of postmodernist thought has been in the direction of disorder – or, more accurately, towards emphasising the multiplicity of orders, the kaleidoscope. In Foucault, this seems to be a desired end, a result of radical politics, but in other writers it seems to be a description of what is actually happening. Jean-François Lyotard, for example (in *The Postmodern Condition*, 1984), draws on the Wittgensteinian notion of a language game, which we have already come across in the discussion of ethnomethodology. His concern is to establish that there is no such thing as a meta-language game, a game which enables us to bring all the others together and judge between them. The basic argument seems to me very much like that presented by Peter Winch in *The Idea of Social Science* over thirty years ago, but in terms of style, it is as different as *Twin Peaks* is from *The Lone Ranger*. Lyotard argues that all knowledge is presented in the form of a narrative, a story – even scientific knowledge, which apparently points directly to things in the outside world, must call on a story if we are to understand it. Postmodernism doubts the existence of any 'meta-narrative', whether of Science, Reason, Marxism, or whatever, which claims to guarantee Truth, any aesthetic narrative which offers standards of Beauty, any moral narrative which offers standards of The Good. Instead of such a meta-narrative holding everything together, we are left with a complex network of different language games, between which we move, and our grasp of the rules of these games and our ability to move from one to the other keep everything together. At this point, we are closer to Giddens.

Within much postmodernist social theory there is often an embryonic and sometimes rather crude sociology of postmodernism. In Lyotard this takes the form of referring to the information revolution, the 'computerisation' of knowledge. In an argument which is perhaps not as far from Parsons's systems theory as many would like it to be, he suggests – as I understand it – that meta-narrative is undermined, or even destroyed, by the packaging of knowledge. Knowledge can be seen no longer as a value, but as something which has a use; and knowledge which cannot be so packaged will disappear. Anyone who is aware of what has been and is happening in universities in Western societies will recognise that he has a point; whether it is as dramatic as he claims is something to which I will return later.

Jean Baudrillard (whom David Harvey describes as 'never afraid to exaggerate') takes the dramatic nature of his claims much further; my own reaction to his work fluctuates between turning away in bewildered incomprehension and laughing at what often feels like a pleasant craziness. Modern society has progressed from copying the real object (the Renaissance) to reproducing it (consumer capitalism) to copying the processes of copying (the 'hyperreal', the postmodern). It is as if we have left any contact with the real world far, far behind, and our punishment lies in wait in eco-disaster, AIDS, and practically anything else he doesn't like. He calls this 'fatal theory', and it is expressed in increasingly obscure terms. His exaggeration, it seems to me, serves to obscure a very real point: that there is a sense in which some of us who live in the modern world are bound up with signs, with copies of copies of copies, in a way that does break our contact with something outside. The fact is that I make a major part of my living thinking, talking and writing about others' ideas, copying other people's copies of others' copies.

Jameson (1991) suggests two metaphors that capture postmodernism: the first is pastiche (copies of copies of copies) and the second, more interesting one is schizophrenia in Lacan's sense, where it can be seen as a breakdown in meaning. The points where meaning is fixed become loosened or disappear and we are left not with a 'chain of signification' but with a collection of unrelated signifiers, moving from one to the other in no particular order. It is this that makes postmodernist sociology difficult to understand, and it calls for a sociology of postmodernism. The *sociological* question is: why should people start thinking this way now?

THE SOCIOLOGY OF POSTMODERNISM

To talk about the sociology of postmodernism is, of course, to step outside postmodernist sociology, and implies a return to something like a causal explanation, even if the causal processes are obscure and undefined. I am going to look here at three 'explanations' of the phenomenon which vary in the way in which they see it, but do enable us to get a grasp on it, and beyond this to demonstrate some of the points I want to make about social theory as a whole. In fact these explanations are to some degree explanations of the developments in social theory over the past twenty years which I have noted in earlier chapters. It is not just the breakdown of structuralism that leads us in the direction of postmodernism, but also the disappearance from functionalism of its causal explanations and its 'opening up' in the work of Alexander; the development of symbolic interactionism, with all its relativist implications; the development and establishment of ethnomethodology – all are part of this process, and in intellectual terms there are links and common sources, particularly between interactionism, ethnomethodology and postmodernism.

To begin with, I want to go back to structuration theory, and in particular to Giddens's approach to modernism and postmodernism. Part of his emphasis on reflexivity is an analysis of the reflexivity of modernism; his emphasis on the uniqueness of the modern world centres on the way in which increasing areas of social life are no longer justified by tradition but have to be justified on rational grounds. This rational questioning increasingly turns in on itself; there is a constant process of undermining the grounds for knowledge, or at least for certain knowledge – in Lyotard's terms, we might talk about meta-narratives undermining themselves; the result is rather like what happens when one constantly questions oneself about one's own motives.

Beyond this, Giddens sees modernity in terms of time–space transformation: the standardisation of time and space and the 'disembedding' of our relationships from the specific features of time and space and our various attempts to 're-embed' them. I do not want to go any further into this at the moment, but I will be returning to these issues shortly; for the moment, I think I have said enough to show that Giddens sees postmodernism as a product of modernism itself – modernism, as it were, taken to its extreme, its latest stage. He argues that a 'true' postmodernism would involve a break from these processes. As a result, he rejects much of what postmodernism has to say, particularly its emphasis on relativism in all fields.

Scott Lash's *The Sociology of Post-Modernism* (1990) is much more sympathetic to the approach, and much of it is inspired by the work of the French sociologist Pierre Bourdieu. Lash sees postmodernism as involving a reverse of the modernist development of differentiation and the increasing autonomy of the different areas of social life, a process generated by two 'motors'. The first is the development of new social classes:

> the development of the post-industrial middle classes, the cultural-capital based fraction of the bourgeoisie. In contemporary times, the cultural field of these symbol-producing middle classes undergoes such expansion, such 'mass-ification', that it begins to engulf or implode into the more general social field itself. The cultural field expands thus to such a point that it bursts through the barriers that had previously contained it as only a delimited field (Lash, 1990: 263)

The second is the development of a new type of avant-garde that actually promotes orthodoxy – he cites architects such as Ventura here. We can find the same tendencies in post-structuralist theories. Lash points to Foucault's de-differentiation of different discourses, and perhaps we could argue that Lyotard's conception of language games illustrates the emphasis on the conventional, if not the orthodox.

Lash, unlike Giddens, seems to regard these processes as representing a real social change rather than the continuation of modernism's drive to a new level. The third approach I want to look at, David Harvey's *The Condition of Postmodernity* (1989), is a Marxist approach which combines elements of both and seems to me to take the analysis much further, in that it maintains a notion of an underlying system or structure. Thus Harvey sees postmodernity as a real change at one level of the social formation, generated by developments, at a deeper level, of the same system. The following is a crude reconstruction of a comparatively subtle argument.

Harvey locates both economic and cultural changes as a response to the classic capitalist crisis – an overproduction – or, as he calls it, overaccumulation crisis – which, in Marxist theory, is seen as a result of the contradiction between the forces and relations of production. This response is seen in terms of a change in the structure of capital – finance capital, more flexible than industrial capital, taking over a controlling function, and a move from what has become known as 'Fordism' to 'post-Fordism'. This involves a number of aspects, but the crux is a changing organisation of the labour force, away from the routinised, highly organised and controlled model based on the innovations of Henry Ford. The new form of organisation involves more small-scale production, a flexibility of skills and location in the workforce, where workers carry out multiple tasks; and, at the level of the state, de-regulation and some degree of privatisation. There is much more to it, of course, and Harvey – rightly, I think – sees 'post-Fordism' not as a total change but as a process which might vary in extent and dominance. He calls the whole process a change to 'flexible accumulation', and it is bound up with the rapid development of new technology.

Harvey then goes on to talk about the effect of all this on our experience of space and time, and it becomes clear that there is more going on here than Giddens deals with. Harvey argues that the change to flexible accumulation has led to 'an intense phase of space–time compression'. Flexible accumulation involves small-batch production, rapid turnover time, the speeding up of the labour process, the rapid change of styles in mass fashion markets, the movement from consumer goods to consumer services which are 'spent' immediately, and so on. All this leaves us in a world where things change quickly and appear ephemeral; at the same time, modern communication systems have broken down spatial barriers and, according to Harvey, it has therefore become important for *places*, actual geographical locations, to differentiate themselves in order to make themselves more attractive to investment:

> The result has been the production of fragmentation, insecurity and ephemeral uneven development within a highly unified global space economy of capital flows. (Harvey, 1989: 296)

In addition, Harvey comments on the increasingly ghostly nature of money itself. This began to develop when money was no longer coined in precious metals, but it has accelerated rapidly over the last twenty years. I see only a very small proportion of my salary as actual cash; most of it passes through my hands not as money but as cheques and, increasingly, plastic; or as bits of paper I signed many years ago – when, for example, I took out my mortgage. I could, if I wanted to, move chunks of it around by telephone or computer. The process goes beyond this – money's devaluation through inflation means that it can no longer be trusted to store value: putting money in a bank can be a sure way to see its value deteriorate.

Harvey talks about this as a crisis in representation, money's ability to represent value. This has clear links to the explicit themes of postmodernist theory, as do fragmentation, etc. But it seems to me also to represent the *form* of postmodernist theory – which, especially in a writer like Baudrillard, is chaotic, fragmented – and the speed with which concepts and fashionable theorists can appear and disappear. Harvey's book, on the other hand, presents an interesting and useful contrast: it takes the change it discusses as real and significant, and it is clear that Harvey understands what we might call the postmodernist consciousness; at the same time the change is understood as a change at a deeper level, the understanding of which draws on theories rejected or surpassed by postmodernism, and his analysis lays claim to be knowledge, rather than accepting our experience of knowledge as impossible. This leads me on to the conclusion of this chapter.

WHAT'S THE POINT OF IT ALL?

It is – to coin a phrase – a sign of the times that ten years ago I was able to conclude this chapter by juxtaposing structuralist Marxism and post-structuralism to E. P. Thompson's argument in *The Poverty of Theory* (1978), a straightforward attack on theoretical work and an appeal for a return to the real world. There is a current in modern culture, and modern sociology, which is now so generally accepted that to talk of a 'real world' is difficult, and to talk about it in the simple terms of Thompson's argument almost impossible. Many sociologists get on with their work as if that world were still there, but any excursus into theory has to take account of the phenomena I have been discussing – whether we regard them as the result of a fundamentally new type of society, of our old society – as it were, living out its fate – or of yet another crisis of capitalism.

The advantage of Harvey's analysis is that we can take postmodernism seriously and at the same time maintain a theoretical analysis in a more traditional sense – of looking for underlying structures and causal mechanisms. Postmodernism, both as theory and in its artistic manifestations, tells us what it is like for a large number of people –

going, I suspect, beyond Lash's new classes – to live in modern Western society, where arguably, at least occasionally, and perhaps frequently, we perceive the world as going mad: change is too fast, nothing is reliable. This has perhaps been the experience of every generation since industrialisation and perhaps even before, but the speed of change certainly seems to be accelerating.

However, postmodernism tells us more than what it is like to live. There is a very real sense in which it tells us about what the world is like – despite itself, we can see it as a theory in the traditional sense. To begin with, it is now impossible not to consider seriously the 'means of representation', language, the various languages in which we express ourselves and which determine what we express. We do not have to elevate this level of analysis to the status of the only reality to understand that we are, in part, the product of our language; that meanings are not fixed once and for all, but are engaged in perpetually changing relationships with each other. In a similar way, in epistemological terms, we can no longer hold on to an idea of 'firm knowledge' established through rigorous scientific means, but it does not follow that we have to give up the search for knowledge, or that we cannot judge between better and worse knowledge.

Postmodernism also tells more about agency. I argued that structuralism fragments over the issue of agency, and that we cannot actually avoid some conception of agency. At the same time, however, postmodernism suggests a deeper understanding of subjectivity than does action theory. All the approaches we looked at in Part II assumed a comparatively simple notion of the subject as the author of choice and action. From the development of structuralism into post-structuralism we can learn of the individual as driven and torn by unconscious desires and conflicting ways of making sense of the world, as placed amongst 'discourses' which are independent of her. We can use this 'de-centred' view of the subject, but within this de-centring there is still choice and action. The subject, and the experience of subjectivity, can be seen as a sort of flux. We are constantly buffeted and torn apart by forces beyond our control; they limit us and sometimes push us in directions we do not want to go. But at the same time we are constantly striving to control them; perhaps the best we can hope for is to ride them without falling off and being trampled underfoot.

FURTHER READING

General background

Sarup offers a basic, good introduction; Callinicos a committed political account; Jameson is rather difficult, but interesting; Dews offers a good discussion of Foucault.

Callinicos, A. (1982) *Is There a Future for Marxism?*, Macmillan, Basingstoke.
Descombes, V. (1980) *Modern French Philosophy*, Cambridge University Press, Cambridge.
Dews, P. (1987) *Logics of Disintegration: Post-structuralist thought and the claims of critical theory*, Verso, London.
Jameson, F. (1991) *Postmodernism or, The Cultural Logic of Late Capitalism*, Verso, London.
Poster, M. (1989) *Critical Theory and Post-Structuralism: In search of a context*, Cornell University Press, Ithaca, NY.
Sarup, M. (1988) *An Introductory Guide to Post-Structuralism and Post-Modernism*, Harvester Wheatsheaf, Hemel Hempstead.

Critics of Althusser

None of the criticisms moving towards post-structuralism is simple, though the work of Hindess and Hirst is reducible to the logical either/or trap.

Burchell, G. (1977) 'Review of Hindess and Hirst', *Radical Philosophy*, no. 18, pp. 22–30.
Centre for Contemporary Culture Studies (1978) *On Ideology*, Hutchinson, London.
Glücksmann, A. (1972) 'A ventriloquist structuralism', *New Left Review*, no. 72, pp. 68–92.
Hindess, B. and Hirst, P. (1975) *Pre-Capitalist Modes of Production*, Routledge & Kegan Paul, London.
Hindess, B. and Hirst, P. (1977) *Mode of Production and Social Formation: An auto-critique of pre-capitalist modes of production*, Macmillan, Basingstoke.
Hirst, P. (1976) 'Althusser and the theory of ideology', *Economy and Society*, vol. 5, no. 4, pp. 385–412.

For an excellent discussion of these arguments, see:

Benton, T. (1984) *The Rise and Fall of Structural Marxism*, Macmillan, Basingstoke.

Woodiwiss, A. (1990) *Social Theory after Post-Modernism*, Pluto Press, London.

E. P. Thompson's attack:

Thompson, E. P. (1978) *The Poverty of Theory*, The Merlin Press, London.

Post-structuralism

Foucault's most important works:

Foucault, M. (1967) *Madness and Civilisation*, Tavistock, London.
Foucault, M. (1970) *The Order of Things*, Tavistock, London.
Foucault, M. (1972) *The Archaeology of Knowledge*, Tavistock, London.
Foucault, M. (1973) *The Birth of the Clinic*, Tavistock, London.
Foucault, M. (1977) *Discipline and Punish*, Allen Lane, London.
Foucault, M. (1979–86) *The History of Sexuality* (3 vols), Allen Lane, London.
Gordon, C. (ed.) (1980) *Power/Knowledge*, Pantheon, New York.
Rabinow, P. (ed.) (1985) *The Foucault Reader*, Pantheon, New York.

Useful introductions to Foucault; Smart is the best start:

Cousins, M. and Hussain, A. (1984) *Michel Foucault*, Macmillan, Basingstoke.
Dreyfus, H. and Rabinow, P. (1983) *Michel Foucault: Beyond structuralism & hermeneutics*, Routledge & Kegan Paul, London.
Gane, M. (1986) *Towards a Critique of Foucault*, Routledge & Kegan Paul, London.
Hoy, D. (1986) *Foucault: A critical reader*, Basil Blackwell, Oxford.
Poster, M. (1984) *Foucault, Marxism & History*, Polity Press, Cambridge.
Smart, B. (1983) *Foucault, Marxism & Critique*, Routledge & Kegan Paul, London.
Smart, B. (1985) *Michel Foucault*, Ellis Horwood & Tavistock, London.

Works by and on Baudrillard and Lyotard:

Baudrillard, J. (1975) *The Mirror of Production*, Telos Press, St Louis, MO.
Baudrillard, J. (1981) *For a Critique of the Political Economy of the Sign*, Telos Press, St Louis, MO.
Baudrillard, J. (1983) *Simulations*, Semiotext(e) Foreign Agent Press, New York.
Baudrillard, J. (1988a) *Selected Writings*, Polity Press, Cambridge.

Baudrillard, J. (1988b) *The Ecstasy of Communication*, Semiotext(e) Foreign Agent Press, New York.

Baudrillard, J. (1988c) *America*, Semiotext(e) Foreign Agent Press, New York.

Gane, M. (1990) 'Ironies of postmodernism: The fate of Baudrillard's fatalism', *Economy and Society*, vol. 19, no. 3, pp. 314–33.

Kellner, D. (1989) *Jean Baudrillard: From Marxism to postmodernism and beyond*, Polity Press, Cambridge.

Lyotard, J.-F. (1984) *The Postmodern Condition: A report on knowledge*, University of Minnesota Press, Minneapolis.

Lyotard, J.-F. (1888) *The Differend: Phrases in dispute*, University of Minnesota Press, Minneapolis.

On the sociology of postmodernism:

Featherstone, M. (1991) *Consumer Culture & Postmodernism*, Sage, London.

Giddens, A. (1990) *The Consequences of Modernity*, Polity Press, Cambridge.

Harvey, D. (1989) *The Condition of Postmodernity*, Basil Blackwell, Oxford.

Lash, S. (1990) *The Sociology of Post-Modernism*, Routledge, London.

PART IV

FROM STRUCTURE *OR* ACTION TO STRUCTURE *AND* ACTION

INTRODUCTION

In Part III, I portrayed a process opposite to that of Part II. What began as a theory of social structures ended by breaking apart when it tried to encompass social action and agency within the same theoretical framework. The first problems arise in attempting to identify the relationship between the economic level and the political and ideological levels, and I suggested that Althusserian Marxism is unable to define this relationship clearly, as it would mean granting some sort of autonomous reality to structures of action, which is precisely what it is trying to avoid. The clearest difficulty is the failure to show how our experience of being a subject is determined – the subject will not lie down and enjoy being determined. The various overlogical criticisms emphasise these difficulties and result in collapsing the model of the social formation to one level, abolishing any idea of causal relations and portraying an essentially kaleidoscopic social world. A third area of social reality – of what I called 'general meanings' – also became evident, and I suggested that if structuralism could be stripped of its metaphysical assumptions it could provide a useful method of analysing this level. Both structuralism and structuralist Marxism were subject to similar processes of fragmentation, caused not only by the theoretical difficulties on which I concentrated but also by political developments and conflicts.

Now both action and structuralist theory attempt to reduce the social world to one of its parts. There is a third approach which goes some way to avoiding this, recognising the independence of both structure and action, although not in the way for which I have been arguing. Its proponents often use the word 'dialectical', which has an elaborate philosophical meaning that need not concern us here; often it is used to mean 'There are two contradictory things going on here, and I don't know how to sort them out.' The idea of two contradictory tendencies is obviously appropriate. The name most commonly given to this approach is 'critical theory', and it, too, originated in the work of Marx – but in his early work, which Althusser dismissed as 'unscientific'. If it has one clear origin, it is in Marx's theory of alienation. I do not want to discuss this theory in detail, but a summary of its essentials will be useful.

Marx's theory of alienation presupposes certain features of human life which distinguish it from other animal life. The basic feature is that human beings are able to transform their environment; they have continuously and systematically transformed the face of the earth, whereas kangaroos, for example, follow much the same daily round from one century to the next, and have had no such impact. This process of transformation is a collective effort; it involves humans working in groups, and as they transform the environment, so they transform themselves. As people change their social environment, so they must change themselves; industrial society is populated by a different kind of person to pre-industrial society; driving a car develops a different set of qualities to riding a horse. Put crudely: people produce societies and societies produce people. Now the most general way of defining alienation is to say that it occurs when the social environment, the social structures established by human beings, come to dominate those who produce them. Marx identified a number of aspects of this which are appropriate to capitalism – people are separated from what they produce, they have no control over the result of their labour; they are separated from each other, and the collective nature of work becomes obscured; and they are divorced from their own capacities to work and make decisions – rather, it seems as if they are forced to work by other people and, in fact, this is often the case. In fact, alienation is a matter of people becoming the puppets of social systems they produce.

The term 'critical theory' is built into this schema. It is based on the idea that there is something which is essentially human, the ability to work together to transform our environment. This provides us with a measuring stick, a means by which we can judge and criticise existing societies. Societies which fragment our social relationships – which in one way or another prevent us from working co-operatively, which take away our ability to make choices and decisions in co-operation with each other – can be subjected to a systematic criticism: they are oppressive, unfree societies. There is a further related basis for social criticism to be found in critical theory, stemming from Marx's philosophical forebear, Hegel. Hegel was, *par excellence*, the philosopher of consciousness and rationality. Part of what enables human beings to transform their environment is the fact that they possess a rational awareness of the world, which for Hegel meant that each of us comes to know the world as a whole; we are each capable of achieving an 'absolute knowledge'. In fact he saw history as a long process through which this rational knowledge developed. 'Rationality' is a sticky word; it means different things to different people. The point here, however, is that whatever we mean by 'rational', the possession of rational faculties is also a defining feature of being human. Thus, any society which prohibits people from developing and employing those faculties can be criticised – it is, in fact, an irrational society.

In this respect, critical theory is significantly different from either action theory or structuralism, which are primarily concerned with cognition, with establishing what is or is not the case, even if they then go on to derive some form of political practice from the theory. Critical theory is also concerned with cognition, but insists on an intimate link between the way the world is and the way it ought to be. This is often taken to the extent of arguing that we cannot understand what the world is until we have some idea about what it ought to be – that a value judgement about the ideal society underlies any social theory. Thus it might be possible to make a case (although there is no space to do so) that action theory is based on the implicit judgement that a liberal capitalist democracy is an ideal society, and structuralist Marxism is based on the view that a technocratic, bureaucratic society is the ideal form. Proponents of these approaches would certainly disagree, but the main point is that critical theory emphasises the value judgements or the moral drive behind social theory, and at least this encourages us to look at other approaches with some suspicion.

Now if critical theory combines both a form of action theory and a form of structuralist theory, you might well ask whether it does not provide a solution to the problems of the other approaches: we could work in the other areas of the social world that we have come across in the argument, and there's the answer. Unfortunately, it is not quite so simple. Although critical theory attempts a combination of the two approaches, it does not view each as dealing with an *ontologically* distinct area of social reality, as separate 'materials' different from each other. At root, it sees social structures, however alienated and independent they might become, as having their origins in human action; this is so despite the fact that the relationship is seen as more complex than it is in Parsons's action theory. The differences will become apparent in the following chapters; for the moment it is sufficient to say that it sees structures in the sense in which they were discussed in Part III rather than as systems of roles.

We find in critical theory an oscillation rather than a fragmentation. It is possible to emphasise one side of the dialectic or the other – the creative ability of human action to shape the social world, or the oppressive and deterministic nature of alienated social structures. I will look first at the origins of some of these ideas in their early optimistic form in the work of Lukács, but I will be primarily concerned with those theorists who most commonly fall under the label 'critical' and who congregated around the Frankfurt Institute for Social Research in the late 1920s and early 1930s – the 'Frankfurt School', where the term 'critical theory' originated. These writers, by and large, represent the pessimistic pole. They are primarily philosophers rather than social theorists, although the distinction becomes blurred; they are not, however, systematic theorists like Parsons, Althusser and Poulantzas, and I will be concerned with drawing out the main themes of their work rather than attempting brief and systematic expositions. Then, in Chapter 12, I will look at the work of a contemporary descendant of the Frankfurt School, Jürgen Habermas, who tries to break out of the circle by attempting a more systematic social analysis, and in so doing produces an analytic system somewhat similar in principle to that of Parsons. Habermas, however, engages in and with the 'linguistic turn' in philosophy, but does so in a way that enables him to hold on to the idea of social structures as separate from social action, and to defend the Enlightenment project that postmodernism abandons.

Chapter 11

THE FRANKFURT SCHOOL: THERE
MUST BE SOME WAY OUT OF HERE

THE BACKGROUND:
LUKÁCS AND HEGELIAN MARXISM

In the first edition of this book, I included a chapter on the Hungarian Marxist Georg Lukács; its exclusion from this edition is a further sign of the times: Lukács's earlier work represents a stream of revolutionary optimism that has not only faded but, in the present political climate, seems incredible. None the less, he worked out many of the more important themes of Marxism, and many of the ideas that were built on and expanded by the approach that has become known as 'critical theory'. I am, therefore, rescuing my account of these ideas, but dropping the wider account of Lukács. Lukács takes theses from Hegel and Marx and develops them further. The notion of 'totality' – that human society and life form a coherent whole – is important (and has been a major target and casualty of postmodernism), and the assumption of much action theory – that human beings create society – becomes not something we assume about the present but an ideal that can be realised in a future, socialist society. In Lukács's work, theory is bound up with history: it is both a product and a motor of historical development – an idea that has been lost in structuralism and postmodernism.

Totality

All the views of theory we have met so far have tended towards one or the other of two opposite poles. Either theory is seen as producing

203

knowledge which, until disproved, is valid everywhere and for everybody, so that, for example, $2 \times 2 = 4$ for the President of the USA, a Vietnamese peasant and the person whose car I can hear in the distance; or it is always relative, depending upon a particular person's point of view on a particular situation. Lukács attempts to produce a rather difficult combination of both views: on the one hand he argues that our knowledge depends upon our historical (rather than individual) situation: different societies at different historical stages of development will produce different forms of knowledge. On the other hand, it is not true that any one form of knowledge is as good as any other. We can choose between different theories and say that one is better than the other. Oversimplifying, the basic criterion for choice is comprehensiveness – one theory is more inclusive than others.

This presupposes that adequate knowledge is a knowledge of a whole rather than of different parts. It is not possible to say that I know what a room looks like by knowing what the different parts look like. I can have a good idea of the chairs and the table, the colour of the carpet and walls, and so on, but I know the room only if I know the ways in which all these parts are related in the whole (again, note the importance placed on relationships rather than the elements related). Thus, knowledge of society should take the form of knowledge of society as a whole rather than knowledge of different parts of it. I cannot know the nature of the family until I understand its relationship to the economy, the state, the education system, and so on; and I cannot discover these relationships by looking at the family and the economy and the state separately – I have to take them as a whole. At one point Lukács says that the concept of totality is the most important concept of Marxist theory. The development of capitalism makes it possible for us to gain a knowledge of society as a whole, because capitalism is itself a 'totalising' system – it possesses a self-expanding mechanism which eventually embraces all societies (otherwise known as imperialism, colonialism or neo-colonialism).

Our knowledge changes as it becomes integrated into a larger system of knowledge. This means we cannot say that our knowledge is true or false in any absolute sense; it always has aspects that are true and aspects that are false. If we move from the grandiose level of the development of world history to the more modest level of our own lives, then perhaps the point becomes easier to understand. If we are lucky, we find out more about ourselves as our life progresses, but this does not necessarily invalidate what we previously knew; rather, its meaning is changed. When I was fifteen, I knew I was ugly; now I know I am not ugly (however, only occasionally do I go as far as saying that I am the most beautiful person in the world). On the face of it, these pieces of knowledge are contradictory – my looks might have changed, but not that dramatically. But there is a sense in which both are true and both false. At fifteen I *was* ugly – I still think so when I look at my photographs – but it was not, as I then thought, some judgement placed on me at birth. Perhaps it was my fear of my own growing sexuality which made me make myself ugly, emphasise the least attractive aspects of my appearance. Now I think I am more attractive, but I still have the same ugly features – rather more so, in fact, since I have become distinctly flabby in places; nevertheless, I have more attractive features, which I can emphasise. Thus my knowledge of myself as ugly was not wrong, it was partial, and my history has enabled me to see that partiality, and at the same time recognise other features of myself.

Returning to society: the link between historical social development and our knowledge is *praxis*, another difficult concept the meaning of which can slide from one use to another. At its most general it would include all forms of activity – long-term projects, the practical actions taken to realise those projects, thinking, conducting relationships with others. Any form of action in the world gives us an experience of what the world is like, and knowledge, theory, is the articulation and working out of this experience. I want to emphasise an important difference between this approach and action theory, which lies in what we mean by action. For all the approaches dealt with in Part II, 'action' was seen primarily as something to do with meanings, and social systems were congealed meanings. 'Praxis' embraces not just meanings but our practical physical relationship to nature (i.e. it embraces labour), and this enables critical theory to develop a view of material economic structures closer to those considered by structuralist Marxism than to the status role systems of action theory.

Commodity fetishism

Lukács takes most of the Marxist structural analysis with which I dealt in Part III for granted, at least in general terms – the structure of the economic level in particular, although he discusses it in very different terms to Althusser. He is most interested in the relationship between the economic, ideological and political levels of social structure. To approach this, he starts with the theory of commodity fetishism that Marx outlines in the first chapters of the first volume of *Capital* (1967). Very briefly, Marx starts from the fact that dissimilar goods can be exchanged for each other (usually via money). We can say, for example, that two books equal five beers. We make this equation all the time if we live on a finite income: buying one thing means forgoing another – something economists call 'opportunity costs'. Conventional economists would explain each equation in terms of supply and demand – how much of a good is available and how many people want it. These two forces determine price, and that enables us to equate dissimilar goods.

Marx's analysis is rather different. Price is seen as a – not necessarily accurate – reflection of the *value* of a good. He distinguished between use value, which is entirely subjective – I hate getting drunk but I enjoy a good book, whereas my friend takes the opposite view – and exchange value, which is the value of one good measured in terms of another: one book equals two-and-a-half beers. Now, he argues, if we can equate different goods, they must have something in common. What they have in common is the amount of labour expended on them – this is the much-argued-about labour theory of value. Of course, it is not as simple as that. If it were, the labour I have expended in producing this book would give it sufficient value to keep me in reasonable comfort for several years; as it is, I'll be lucky if I get a short family holiday from it.

Marx makes various qualifications and distinctions to overcome the obvious difficulties which do not concern us here. The main point, as far as commodity fetishism is concerned, is that the amount of labour expended in producing different goods, thus determining the values at which they exchange for each other, is part and parcel of a complex of social relationships. The division of labour in a society, the way the society allocates its labour force to different tasks, is a network of relationships between people. The market system of capitalism turns this into a network of exchange relationships between things – the comparative values of different goods reflect a network of relationships between people. Now the word 'fetishism' can be used in two contexts: a fetish is an inanimate object that is worshipped by a society, an object often believed to be inhabited by a spirit; and it is an inappropriate object of sexual desire – a shoe fetishist is turned on by shoes. Both uses are relevant. In the same way that human sexuality is essentially social, concerned with another human being, so is the process of production; just as the social activity of sex becomes diverted to an object, so does the activity of production become diverted in exchange relationships between objects. We talk about 'the market' as if it were a living thing which determines what we do – it becomes a power which dominates us. Here again we have the idea of levels of society: an underlying level of social relationships and a surface level of market relationships, relationships of exchange value, which hides and dominates social relationships.

Reification

Lukács develops these ideas in several ways, all united by the term 'reification'. Perhaps the best definition is 'thingification': the way in which human qualities come to be regarded as things and take on a mysterious non-human life of their own. This produces a powerful moral criticism of capitalism, which is seen as turning people into things that can be bought and sold. In marriage – a favourite example – I buy the sexual and other services of a woman in return for keeping her, usually somewhat above subsistence level but not by any means in luxury. It can be argued that her value depends on her physical attractiveness, her submissiveness, her ability to cook or the money she will inherit from her father. Similarly, I sell myself as a commodity to my employer.

Lukács, however, is more interested in other aspects of reification. He is particularly concerned with looking at its effects on theory and knowledge. We have seen that the social world comes to appear as a world of objects – like the natural world. Society becomes a 'second nature'; it seems to be as independent of human action as the laws and phenomena of nature, and it comes to seem that we could no more change society than we could stop the sun shining. This is not only an 'appearance'; the processes involved in commodity fetishism and reification do create external social structures of which human beings become puppets.

There is more to it than this, however. Social life and social relationships are matters of process: they develop and change, giving rise to what we call history. Reification hides that process from us. Instead of seeing everything in movement, we see only static objects in fixed relationships to each other. Thus the social sciences model themselves on the natural sciences, looking for regular relationships between different phenomena which can then be seen as laws of society. We might claim, for example, that in the same way as a metal expands when heated, so a society with full employment will suffer inflation. Beyond this there is a further tendency to break a social whole into its separate parts and develop different sciences for each: sociology, psychology, economics, history, geography, etc. The hidden reality of the social world is that all these different parts make up a whole in a constant process of development. Reification prevents us from grasping this. It has more concrete effects where social activities are concerned: thus legal institutions are separated from welfare institutions, or have only limited connections, or medical services are separated from industrial production despite the prevalence of industry-based diseases. This process of fragmentation has real effects on social organisations as well as knowledge. The world is split into separate parts.

THE FRANKFURT SCHOOL

The themes of Lukács's work sit easily beside much non-Marxist work of the nineteenth and early twentieth centuries, often lumped together under the label 'Romanticism'. Much of this work is not just anti-capitalist, but anti-modern society. People in modern industrial societies are seen as isolated individuals or as a conglomerate mass, but either way, everything that is good about individuality has disappeared. The modern world is seen as a spiritual desert; any meaning attached to life is disappearing, and people are empty and lost souls in a world they cannot understand. These themes appear in different ways in the work of the founding figures of sociology – in Marx as alienation, in Durkheim as anomie, and in Weber as disenchantment. In the work of the Frankfurt School, this bleak landscape has turned into a nightmare: the social world has become an electronic monster feeding off its own members, manipulating and absorbing any resistance that may be offered. We can make sense of this, at least in part, by looking at the world in which the main writers developed.

The Frankfurt Institute for Social Research was founded as a centre for socialist research in 1923, the year in which Lukács's

History and Class Consciousness was first published. Already the revolutionary tide that had followed World War I was abating. Subsequent years saw, first, the rise of Stalin and the decline of the principles behind the Russian Revolution, ending in horrors that need not be recounted here. Ten years later the rise of Hitler led to further horrors, driving the members of the School into exile (in the USA) and causing the death of one of its more marginal but now increasingly popular members, the literary critic Walter Benjamin. After World War II the horrors abated in their more extreme forms, but as a social system capitalism seemed to become firmly established and unchallengeable, supplying material goods but systematically destroying centuries of culture. It seemed as though the possibility of radical social change had been smashed between the twin cudgels of concentration camps and television for the masses.

A range of intellectual stars were associated with the School: amongst those whom I will not discuss here, but you may come across elsewhere, are Walter Benjamin, Leo Löwenthal, a sociologist of literature, Erich Fromm, a psychoanalyst, and Karl Wittfogel, an expert on China. The three main figures, however, were Theodor Adorno, Max Horkheimer and Herbert Marcuse. All three are now dead, and whilst there are differences between them, there are also common themes. Perhaps the most evident difference is that after World War II, Adorno and Horkheimer returned to Germany whilst Marcuse remained in the USA. These three are major thinkers who have written more in their lifetime than many of us could hope to read: to deal with them in one chapter is even more absurd than previous discussions of other thinkers. Nevertheless, I shall be absurd.

DOMINATION

I said of Lukács that whilst he took a Marxist analysis of social structure for granted, his own contribution to Marxism did not enable him to engage in any original structural analysis. The same is true of the critical theory of the Frankfurt School, with the difference that they do not take Marxist structural analysis for granted. Rather, they argue that the early forms of capitalism that were analysed by Marx and taken for granted by Lukács have disappeared, but they do not provide an alternative structural *analysis*: they do discuss general trends and perhaps the general functions of different social institutions, but no more. In later years Marcuse contributed more to the structural backcloth of critical theory than the others. He argued that the contradiction between the forces and relations of production was no longer a contradiction. The productive forces now produced such immense wealth that rather than come into conflict with private ownership, they could be employed to reinforce it; the wealth was employed to produce waste products and false needs – of which more later. The growth of monopolies and large-scale state intervention on a national and international level has led to people's lives being controlled in ever more sophisticated and successful ways.

Despite this, Marcuse remained the most optimistic of the three thinkers: he thought that the contradiction between people's real lives and the lives made possible by the available wealth might provide a focus for discontent. In the period in which he was writing it would have been possible, for example, for all the Western governments to provide well-equipped free health services, yet wealth was spent rather on armaments, or on producing twenty-three different brands of similar washing powder where one would suffice. Health services remained non-existent or set about with restrictions. He also argued that even if the working class could no longer initiate social change – since it had been bought or manipulated into the system – certain other groups, not so well integrated, could provide the spark which would awaken others: intellectuals, students, minority groups, Third World nations. It is easy to see why Marcuse was to become popular during the 1960s – the Vietnam War, the Civil Rights Movement and the student revolt all spoke for his theory.

However, the bulk even of Marcuse's work belongs to the pessimistic side of the oscillation. Whereas Lukács was concerned with the spread of reification *and* the working class's ability to halt and break the trap it set around them, the Frankfurt School catalogued the victory of reification, arguing that the theory needed to be extended and developed to account for modern conditions. The one consistent and uniting theme is *domination*. For reasons that will become clear shortly, they do not offer any precise definition of domination. Perhaps the best meaning is its common-sense one: if somebody dominates me, they are in some way able to make me do what they want me to do. If I dominate my wife, she does as I desire; her personality and her freedom of action are subordinated to my life. If there were no domination, she might lead a very different life. The

Frankfurt theorists are concerned with the way the system dominates: with the ways in which it forces, manipulates, blinds or fools people into ensuring its reproduction and continuation. I want to look at three areas of domination dealt with by all three thinkers: the way of looking at the world which justifies people's domination over each other and the system over the people: instrumental reason; the way in which modern popular culture integrates people into the system; and the sort of personality structure which not only accepts but actually seeks domination.

Instrumental reason

'Instrumental reason' is explored in a series of books, the most important being Adorno and Horkheimer's *Dialectic of Enlightenment* (1972), Horkheimer's *Eclipse of Reason* (1974) and Marcuse's *One-Dimensional Man* (1964). Instrumental reason is a logic of thought and a way of looking at the world. We have already seen how, for Lukács, the economic level of capitalist society is such that human relations come to appear as relations between things; that people come to see themselves and others as objects, and the social world comes to seem a 'second nature' as unchangeable and independent of our actions as nature itself. This is the heart of the Frankfurt School's conception of instrumental reason, but its implications are explored in greater depth, and it is seen as having a significantly different history from that assumed by Lukács.

The term 'instrumental' carries two dimensions: it is a way of looking at the world and a way of looking at theoretical knowledge. To see the world as an instrument is to see its elements as tools, instruments by means of which we can achieve our ends. I do not see this tree for its beauty and the enjoyment it brings me; I see it as timber, which can be processed into paper on which to print the book I am writing. I do not see my students as people engaged upon learning but as people who, if I impress them sufficiently, might be useful in furthering my career; I do not see my ability to understand other people as something to be placed at their service but as a means by which I can persuade them to do what I want to do. I will return to this dimension of instrumental reason when I look at its history.

We can also look at knowledge as an instrument, a means to an end. This, perhaps, is a more difficult idea because it so imbues our culture that an alternative might seem inconceivable. I will try to illustrate the distinction by looking at alternative views of philosophy. Most people do not think very much about philosophy in the normal course of events, but those who do often see it as a way of thinking that enables us to try to divine the meaning of our lives, of life in general and our place in the world. It is a way of living, a way of becoming reconciled to life and nature. It holds out the possibility of a harmonious world of Truth with a capital 'T'. Truth is the ultimate value, rather as God and His will is the ultimate value for Christians. For the Frankfurt theorists, such a view of philosophy would not be mistaken: it is a way of living. If a person holding such a view went to university, however, this is not likely to be the sort of philosophy she would find being taught there. Instead of philosophy as a way of life, she would find philosophy as an instrument. The most common view of philosophy is as an 'underlabourer' to science: science produces knowledge; philosophy can help sort out problems that science runs into – conceptual problems: that is, difficulties with its theory. Philosophy is a sort of mechanic for the engine of science; the idea of Truth as a way of living is nowhere to be seen.

Instrumental reason, then, is concerned solely with practical purposes. Another way of putting this, which takes us further, is that instrumental reason separates fact and value: it is concerned with discovering how to do things, not with what should be done. Science can provide us with the knowledge to produce electric prods; it does not matter to science whether they are used for controlling cattle or torturing people. It is often argued, particularly in the Western democracies, that science can find us the most efficient means to reach an end, but the end must be decided by others, by the democratically elected representatives of the people. If these representatives decide that inflation damages social organisation, it is then up to the science of economics to find the most efficient means of halting inflation. If we follow this argument through, it can be seen that this instrumental, 'value-free' view of science actually reduces the area open to democratic debate. Economic science might tell us that the most efficient means of cutting inflation is by drastic reductions in public spending; but reductions in public spending can lead to very high levels of unemployment, increasing poverty and everything that goes with it. Some people might argue that a certain level of inflation is an acceptable alternative to the strains and misery of unemployment and poverty. The most efficient means, then, is open to dispute on the grounds of value judgements – a less efficient means of producing inflation might be preferable.

There are various types of instrumental reason, but the Frankfurt theorists tend to lump them together under the heading 'positivism'. This can be misleading, since positivism is also a precise technical philosophical label, but it does have some justification. The man who coined the term 'positive science', Auguste Comte, also regarded as the first sociologist, was writing in the period of social conflict following the French Revolution. He thought that a science of society would tell us what society really is like, and thus put an end to all the debates about what it should be like. This is precisely the attitude to which the Frankfurt theorists object. It leads to a passive attitude to the social world; it is seen not as a human product but as an external reality governed by laws as fixed as the laws of nature. We can deploy our knowledge in a technical way, to alter this or that, but we cannot bring about any fundamental change. By and large, we have to adjust to things as they are.

Instrumental reason is seen as the dominant way of thinking in the modern world, governing both natural and social sciences. When Lukács described the effects of reification on thought, he was evidently getting at much the same thing. For the Frankfurt School, however, the roots of instrumental reason go much further back than the development of capitalism. Rather as Max Weber traced the origins of the Spirit of Capitalism back through Christianity to Judaic beliefs, so Adorno and Horkheimer find the origins of instrumental reason in Judaism. It came into its own in the period we call 'the Enlightenment', the period during which the revolutions in thought that founded the natural sciences took place. Over this period, the 'instrumentalisation' of nature occurred. Whereas previously people had seen nature as God's creation, entrusted to humanity to care for and preserve, they now came to see it as an instrument, a raw material, to be developed and exploited for God's greater glory. This view evolved over the following centuries, up to the present day – to cover first society and social organisation, where the change is from seeing the social world as a source of support and security to seeing it as a basis for individual exploitation and advancement; and then individual human beings, who are no longer seen as beings with their own integrity, rights and duties, but as possessors of qualities and skills to be exploited for some purpose outside themselves. I do not judge my colleagues on the basis of qualities such as warmth, sense of humour, depth of knowledge or intelligence, but on the basis of the number of books and articles they have published, their efficiency in disposing of teaching and administration, their use to me in my search for promotion. People get jobs on the basis not of their integrity but of the successful completion of tasks.

In this account, instrumental reason seems to be something that establishes itself throughout our history, coming to dominate one area after another. Adorno and Horkheimer (but not Marcuse) seem closer to saying that capitalism is a product of instrumental reason rather than that instrumental reason is a product of capitalism. Once Marxism loses its concern with praxis – as began to happen immediately after the publication of *History and Class Consciousness* – the positivist aspects to Marx's work begin to stand out. In later years the Frankfurt theorists became increasingly critical of Marx, seeing him as accepting the instrumentality of the natural sciences and – especially in his later work – extending it to society. The regimes of Eastern Europe can be seen as the fruition of instrumental reason as much as the capitalist societies. According to this view, Althusser's Marxism is clearly a form of instrumental reason. Society is portrayed as the opposite of a human product; rather, it is the producer of human beings. Revolution and socialism seem to have nothing to do with human freedom; rather, they are an updating of the machine, a new model.

There are, however, evident similarities between the view of the Frankfurt School and post-structuralism. For the former, knowledge – at least in the form of instrumental reason – is equated with power and domination, and there is a similar desire to undermine this domination in the very style of writing adopted by both schools. Both are often deliberately vague and elliptical, refusing to present definite statements about the world or even about their own approach to it. The difference seems to be that the Frankfurt theorists juxtapose another form of knowledge of reason to instrumental reason – critical theory. Each writer has his own variant, but the differences between them do not concern us here. Critical theory is critical in the way I described in the introduction – it is able to show how existing society is irrational or oppressive in that it takes away or destroys basic features of human life: the ability to transform our own environment and to make collective rational choices about our lives. It also claims to show how in the past we have actually created this society, how it is really a human product even if it can no longer be recognised as such. In other words, it puts our present society and views back into their historical context, showing that they are not fixed for all time but part of a long and difficult process in which we are still engaged.

The way in which this can be shown, however, differs from period to period, and here we come to the roots of the particular difficulties of the style of the Frankfurt writers. We saw how, for Lukács, 'totality' was a central idea, referring to the possibility of a unified humanity and world and a rational knowledge of that world. For the Frankfurt theorists, present-day societies, both East and West, are already 'totalities' in the bad sense of totalitarian: they are unified entities which absorb and remove all real opposition. The idea of totality is no longer associated with liberation but with oppression; the attempt to gain a total knowledge is precisely the aim of a totalitarian society. Against this frightening prospect, it does no good to oppose another total system of knowledge – that is, to play the other side at its own game. Rather, we must undermine that system wherever we can, adopt a negative attitude towards it, revealing its holes and contradictions. *Negative Dialectics* (1973) is the title of one of Adorno's most important books. The outcome of all this is that Frankfurt theory frequently takes the form not of long and systematic arguments but rather of short paradoxical pieces which emphasise ambiguity and contradiction. The most accessible work of this kind is again Adorno's *Minima Moralia* (1974), and in the introduction he suggests that the only place we might now find truth is not in the whole, the totality, but in the more obscure parts of individual experience which escape the totality. At times it seems as if any direct statement about the world is a concession to instrumental rationality. This emphasises his affinities with postmodernist theory, and I will return to this issue later.

One-dimensional culture

When it comes to more direct social analysis, the historical perspective I have just outlined gives the Frankfurt theorists a distinctly nostalgic air. They often seem to be looking back to a golden past that is no longer and can never be again. Paradoxically, this golden past often seems to be the early period of capitalism, which is seen as a time of real individualism to be contrasted with the modern denial of the individual. This emerges in the School's analysis of culture.

It is not surprising that so much of the Frankfurt School's work has concentrated on culture: given that its members see society as no longer riven by economic and structural contradictions, the successful integration of individuals becomes the major problem, and culture in the sense of the ways in which societies and individuals formulate their views of the world becomes the major way in which integration is achieved. Perhaps the clearest statement of the arguments can be found in Marcuse's *One-Dimensional Man* (1964), but there is also an analysis of the culture industry in *Dialectic of Enlightenment* (1972), and Adorno in particular has produced a vast amount of work on literature, music and popular culture. The analysis covers all forms of culture, from highbrow to lowbrow, and the central theme is already familiar: human beings have certain capabilities and potentialities which are taken away from them in modern societies. It seems to be generally agreed that the highest forms of culture, art, literature and music, can be a product of our human abilities and a criticism of our present society, although the way this works changes from historical period to historical period. The Frankfurt theorists do not offer an economically based explanation of works of art but concentrate instead on their form. Whilst a crude Marxist might say that a Jane Austen novel, for example, is just a product and reflection of British middle-class life in the nineteenth century, they would concentrate on the way in which it is put together, the relationships between characters and plot. The structural analysis of Westerns (see pp. 141–4) was an analysis of form, but not quite the same as that found in Frankfurt work.

The period of 'early capitalism' is hard to pin down, but generally seems to cover anything from the end of the seventeenth to the end of the nineteenth century. During this period, it is argued, a work of art could, through the perfection and balance of its form, offer a vision of an alternative to existing reality. The works of Mozart or Beethoven, for example, hold out the possibility of a harmonious and ordered world, which can be contrasted with the existing disorder and misery on which they throw a critical light. With the development of modern totalitarian societies, such a function of art is being squeezed out. Modern societies insist that they are already harmonious. Mozart is played to cows to keep up their milk yield; Beethoven's Ninth Symphony is the anthem of the European Economic Community and was that of white Rhodesia. Now the critical function of art lies in anything that challenges this supposed harmony, makes us think, is difficult to understand: the music of Schoenberg, for example. More and more, this type of art has become marginal, avant-garde, of interest to fewer and fewer, and the 'culture industry' has become dominant.

Marcuse talks about the way in which the culture industry produces and satisfies 'false needs'. The idea of a false need is a difficult one, because it means that we should question an individual's assessment of her needs and in effect claim 'we know better than you what it is you need'. You might like the Beatles, but you ought to listen to Schoenberg. At the very best it can lead to cultural elitism, even snobbery. At the same time, the possibility of people experiencing false needs is built into critical theory. A 'true' need is a need that can be defined as deriving from or expressing the creative and rational powers that make me a human being; it is a need which, if satisfied, will enable me to extend control over my life in conjunction with others, and to deepen and enrich my relationships with others. False needs can be seen as a perversion of true needs. The following examples are my own.

One clear example is the way in which part of the impetus of the feminist movement has been diverted. Feminism is a social movement: a campaign on a number of different levels by people who have been excluded from large areas of public and social life, and social responsibility. Its message is one of social equality and freedom, of deeper and different relationships between women themselves (sisterhood) and between men and women. The way in which this movement has been or is being absorbed (not necessarily successfully) into the dominant culture is by the transformation of these real needs into false needs. The demand for equality becomes transformed into a demand for the right to pursue a career as men pursue their careers; women, too, must become competitive, surrender their more intimate satisfactions and human qualities for the sake of success. That this involves not deepening and different relationships but more shallow and exploitative relationships; and that instead of encouraging real collective control over our lives it encourages individual competition – these aspects go unnoticed. The modern woman of the advertising industry is as shallow, as plastic, a figure as the modern man. The success of a book by Colette Dowling entitled *The Cinderella Complex: Women's hidden fear of independence* (1982) reflects the reality of such a distortion.

A second example is the current concern in Western nations about

218 Modern Social Theory

health, manifesting itself in preoccupations with health food, jogging, self-righteous 'thank you for not smoking' notices, and so on. It is evident that health is not a false need, but it is a collective need. There is a great deal of evidence available about the links between social conditions and ill-health, and to change these social conditions requires a collective effort. The popular concern for health, however, is individualised, and for that very reason its real effectiveness is questionable. If lead pollution of the atmosphere remains high, jogging will mean that I absorb more lead. If I am a coal-miner, no amount of wholemeal bread will give me the same life expectancy as a university professor. The further removed we are from real collective control over the major threats to our lives, the more enthusiastically we try to control the minor threats: I can do nothing about the possibility of a nuclear war, but I can stop smoking. In similar ways, the true need for freedom of choice becomes a need to choose between twenty-three brands of similar washing powder, and the need for freedom of speech becomes a need for a few rich combines to publish empty and ignorant daily papers.

The analysis goes further. Adorno suggests that the system still generates an economic insecurity – he was writing during the 1950s and 1960s – and we could also make the argument that any social system which denies basic human abilities creates insecurity. The feeling that we have a power we cannot employ is a frightening feeling. In any case, popular culture is geared to produce a substitute, false security that is none the less effective. It does so in two ways: first through the standardisation of its products. All aspects of popular culture – from television soap operas to pop records to sporting events – attempt, in their various ways, to emphasise the familiar and the secure. At the basic level, plots, lyrics, rhythms, the order of play, are the same and interchangeable with each other. If this were not the case, we could not have identified the basic plot-types of Westerns discussed in Chapter 7. At the same time these basically standardised products are given a gloss of false individuality, leaving the impression of a freedom of choice and an individuality of meaning. We can argue endlessly about which pop song is the better, which football team is the better and all the time we are arguing about superficial differences and gaining a false security from the underlying similarities.

In a brilliant article, 'The stars down to earth' (1975), Adorno shows how this effect is achieved through the immensely popular press horoscopes. To begin with, astrology presents itself as a sort of science; it can lay claim to a (largely spurious) expertise which by itself represents a reassurance. There is more to it than that, though, as we can see without using Adorno's examples. My own horoscope in the London *Sunday Express* of 3 October 1982 makes the point equally well: 'Monday is an especially good day for trying out new ideas or dealing with officialdom. The week ends in fine style too.' I evidently have something to look forward to. I am a creative person, I 'deal with' officialdom, and the week is going to end well. The reassurance is obvious, and the least important part. Most important is, first, the fact that the horoscope reassures me not only that everything will be OK, but that it is me who makes it OK despite the fact that it is written in the stars. After all, I am creative, I have new ideas, and I possess a certain degree of power, since I 'deal with' officialdom. 'Deal with' is an especially nice touch, since it can mean one of two opposite possibilities. If I storm into the tax office, point out numerous mistakes in my assessment, and come away having received abject apologies and a large cheque, I have 'dealt with' officialdom. If, on the other hand, I sit there through a series of embarrassing and humiliating questions and come away feeling acutely depressed, I have still 'dealt with' officialdom. I would suggest that most people's experience approximates to the latter, but the phrase 'deal with' adds a gloss to it – we can hope, or even pretend, that the former meaning is appropriate. What the horoscope leaves at the end is an empty affirmation of my humanity by a pseudo-expert, empty because it has no tangible effect outside my own more ephemeral and less-well-understood feelings.

The need for domination

Domination is not simply built into the culture industry, it requires a particular character structure, one that is not only receptive to domination but actually seeks it. This is the third major theme of the Frankfurt School: the way in which domination enters into the very heart of the individual. Much use is made of psychoanalytic theory, and Freud is frequently interpreted in a more orthodox way than Marx. I will try, however, to present an outline of this theme without assuming a detailed knowledge of Freud – my aim, once again, is to get across the general idea rather than the detail of the arguments. The best-known works in the area are very different from each other. I will deal first with Marcuse's *Eros and Civilisation* (1966), a work of speculative theory and philosophy, very influential during the 1960s, and close to the theme of the last section. I will then look – again in very general terms – at *The Authoritarian Personality* (1969) by Adorno *et al.* This is a large-scale study using a variety of empirical methods to investigate the claim that there is a correlation between personality structure and political and social attitudes. It was carried out in the USA at the end of World War II and was one of five 'studies in prejudice' supervised by Horkheimer.

Turning first to Marcuse: we find the most general levels of Freud's work employed to develop a theory of sexuality in modern society. There is space here to deal with only the most basic of his arguments, which has to do with the degree of repression necessary for society to operate. Freud's view was that civilisation depends upon repression, and thus necessarily involves misery. If we tried to gratify all our desires, sexual or otherwise, as and when they arose, society, civilisation and culture would vanish overnight: life would be a chaos in which we used each other only as objects of gratification, an immense non-stop orgy, ending in destruction. For some sort of ordered life to exist, we need to restrain ourselves, to repress our desires and direct the energy elsewhere, into socially useful activities. Freud seemed to see the level of repression as constant for all societies. Marcuse suggests that it can be different for different societies. In the earlier stages of capitalism, a high degree of repression is necessary to ensure that people spend most of their energy working, that profits are reinvested rather than enjoyed. Very few desires are allowed to emerge into consciousness, and the pleasure-giving areas of the body are confined to the genitals. Freud can be seen as describing the process by which this confinement takes place.

The growth of the productive forces in late capitalism means that such a high degree of repression is no longer necessary; a 'surplus repression' appears, over and above that necessary for modern society to remain in existence, and the tension this causes is seen as a possible force leading to social change, a 'de-instrumentalising' of the world, so that we begin to see things for the pleasure they give us rather than their practical uses. The whole body becomes eroticised.

However, the system is also capable of manipulating this tendency to maintain itself, through what Marcuse calls 'repressive de-sublimation'. Sublimation involves the repression of a desire and the direction of the energy elsewhere: instead of being promiscuous, I write a book on social theory. De-sublimation allows the desire to come into consciousness: I become aware of wanting to be promiscuous. Repressive de-sublimation persuades us to satisfy that desire in ways that are useful to the system. Commodities become associated with sex – naked women are draped over everything from new cars to typewriter correction fluid as a way of selling them and at the same time providing a vicarious sexual pleasure (this is almost certainly true for new cars, although I'm not so sure about the correction fluid). Books and films become more explicitly erotic, not to say pornographic – a new 'opium of the masses'. There is a growth in non-dangerous forms of sexual activity – open marriages, 'swinging', and so on. A potentially dangerous development in human needs is again turned to the benefit of the system.

The fundamental theory behind *The Authoritarian Personality* is much less speculative and more down to earth, although it too is concerned with the social manipulation of our inner drives. This time the contrast with the early period of capitalism is clearer. The period of early capitalism is seen as one of individualism, where men developed strong personalities, took decisions for themselves, and adopted critical attitudes to the world. The strong private personality is in effect the second dimension to culture that Marcuse sees as being lost in modern society – one way of summing up the whole process is as the absorption into the public area of the private world and the consequent stripping away of an independent basis for judgement.

Such strong and independent personalities are seen as produced through the processes described by Freud. Their production requires a strong and independent father whom the son may use as a role model, as someone to identify with and to fight in his own development. The most basic conflict is the Oedipal conflict, where the father and the young boy first clash over possession of the mother. Simply because the father is adult and more powerful, he wins; the conflict is repeated in different ways throughout adolescence. The combination of identifying with and fighting the father produces a son who is equally strong and independent in his turn.

For the pattern to continue, the requirement is for a strong father, a patriarchal figure in charge of the household and with some power in the world.

As capitalism develops into corporate enterprises with a strong centralised state, so both the role of the family and the internal and external power of the father diminish. The decline in the role of the family is well documented: the state takes over an increasing number of functions, primarily through the education system; the family loses its productive function as factory production takes over, and so on. The father becomes an adjunct to the machine, separated from home and family for most of the working day; as a consequence, his power diminishes and he becomes unable to exercise an independent judgement even in those areas where it still remains possible – the decreasing sphere of the family. This is reinforced by the son finding other bases for identification at school, and his earlier economic independence. He soon comes to realise the weakness of the father, and the battles through which his personality developed either no longer take place or take place in a weakened form. Late capitalism produces a weak 'narcissistic' personality, ridden with anxiety and seeking strong models with which to identify. Since the model can no longer be found within the home, it must be sought in the outside world. It might be a pop star or a sporting personality, but in a more sinister way it might be a strong political leader – a Hitler or a Stalin – or a strong political party. Since the personality is weaker, the unconscious drives are nearer the surface and more open to manipulation by such forces. *The Authoritarian Personality* was particularly concerned with investigating the relationship between personality structure and the support likely to be given to the mass irrational movements of fascism.

The first question that half of its readership might ask is 'What about women?' The answer, in the work of the Frankfurt School, is 'Not a lot.' Implicit in their arguments seems to be the idea that we need to return to proper patriarchal family relations. It sometimes seems as if the mother might offer a more gentle model for the child, but the mother is also stripped of her own rather different powers by late capitalism. There seems to be considerable difficulty in envisaging an alternative, and in the most powerful book taking up these arguments, Christopher Lasch's *Culture of Narcissism*, the absence of an alternative to the more traditional family form is very clear. The implication is that we must put the historical clock back, not forward.

PROBLEMS AND CONTRIBUTIONS

The fortunes of critical theory have fluctuated since the end of World War II; after being of marginal – and largely philosophical – interest for many years, it became surprisingly popular during the 1960s and much of the 1970s, providing not just a way of thinking for political activists in the student movement but also a means by which radical academics could a find a basis for their own work. Looking back – and in particular looking at a recent collection of work in the area – what is surprising is how little of interest emerged from it, before it was left behind in the wave of structuralist and postmodernist philosophies that attracted philosophically interested sociologists. I suspect that this was because it does operate on such a high level of abstraction and, in sociological terms, generality.

Indeed, Frankfurt School work came under attack from two main directions: from those they label as 'positivist' social scientists, and from Marxists. The basic criticism from both sides was the same, although it was expressed in different terminology: critical theory is empty speculation. From the point of view of more conventional social scientists, critical theory has no foundation in the real world – it cannot be tested and confirmed or refuted against any external measurement; it is often put in deliberately obscure terms which indicate not so much profundity of thought or the complexity of the problem under examination as the self-indulgence of the authors; much of it is logically meaningless, even when we can translate it into intelligible terms. The Marxist version is only slightly less dismissive: critical theory represents a return to classical idealist German philosophy; as such, it cannot provide us with knowledge about the world or an analysis of real social structures. Its generalisations are abstract and speculative, though they might be interesting as representing the attitudes of a particular group of disenchanted intellectuals. It is usually emphasised that critical theory is connected to 'high culture', is university-based, and has no connection with practical politics.

All these points seem to me to have some validity, but also to miss something important. I have already suggested that the Frankfurt School can be seen as the pessimistic swing of the pendulum in the battle between alienated and reified social structures and human action. We can, of course, find discussions of social structure; they are ever-present in the work of all three thinkers; but they are generalisations rather than the careful analysis of relationships that we can find in Parsons and Poulantzas, and if the presupposition behind my argument is correct, then a proper structural analysis would involve the recognition that social structures are not a product of human action separated from their origin. In the case of the Frankfurt School, however, it is not that they cannot or do not engage in structural analysis; rather, it often seems that they *will* not. It is as if they think that to engage in a structural analysis is to surrender to instrumental reason. Adorno sums it up when he points out that economics is no joke: to understand it, one has to make oneself an economist. This does leave their social analysis with the quality of overgeneralisation. It is possible, without any great trouble, to point to the difficulties. Family structures, for example, vary from social class to social class, and what these theorists seem to consider as the original family structure of early capitalism was arguably confined to the industrial and commercial bourgeoisie, the social classes whose members were Freud's patients. The 'private area' that provided a base for independent judgement was also arguably confined to the same classes, and – perhaps more important – a similar function might be played at present by the working-class community or the ethnic community. The failure in the USA to integrate different national communities into a common 'melting pot', despite the use of all the instruments of the culture industry, is strong evidence that the process of domination is not quite as complete as much Frankfurt theory would lead us to think. Of the three thinkers considered here, Marcuse is most aware of this.

At the same time as it fails to engage in structural analysis, the Frankfurt approach does not allow the development of criticism in any practical direction. The conception of human action, or praxis, remains very general. A closer and more detailed analysis of both structure and action is necessary to bring the two together in a way that can lead to the 'practical criticism' of bringing about social change, or even to a full understanding of the present situation. Taking the culture industry as an example, we would need, on the one hand, to identify the significant institutions and their relationships to each other, and we would require some way of identifying the most and least important; we would also need to look at the internal structure of these institutions and understand the relationship of all of them to other levels of society. On the other hand, we would need to know the objectives, the intentions and the choices of the people who work in these institutions, the way they make sense of the world and see their place in it. For this we have to turn to the empirical sociology that is an anathema to most Frankfurt thinkers.

However, there is more to their work; that it can and does make sense of our experience indicates that the analysis identifies real trends in the outside world. We do not have to accept that the social world is in its entirety a human product to acknowledge the possibility of a greater degree of human freedom and control than we have at present. It is certainly true that the work of the Frankfurt School articulates the feelings of many who recognise that possibility. In this sense it is a useful corrective both to structuralism and to action theory. In relation to structuralism, it affirms that human beings are not simply the puppets of the social machine, whilst at the same time it recognises that for most of our history this social machine has dominated us and forced us along paths we might not desire. In relation to action theory it emphasises – especially in the work of Lukács, and residually in that of the Frankfurt theorists – that human action is a collective, not just an individual, matter, and that the social relationships produced by human action can take on a dynamic of their own. Beyond this, it can provide us with what empirical sociologists might call 'working hypotheses' – ways of looking at the world which we might find useful in explaining some, but not all, of the things we want to study. I hope some of my examples in this chapter have indicated a few of the more useful practical applications.

If we look at the Frankfurt School's work at what I consider its most valuable and most abstract level, in the light of the themes of postmodernism, interesting features and a new value emerge. This level is that of the nature of knowledge itself, of ideals, and the relationship between these and history. There is a sense in which Adorno in particular could be considered a forerunner of postmodernism. The critique of Enlightenment thought points to those features criticised by postmodernism: its intimate connection with domination and exclusion. The link between totality and totalitarianism also finds an echo in the criticisms that the *nouveaux philosophes* directed against Marxism, which are implicit in the work of Foucault and others. And Adorno's very style, as well as his explicit arguments, in such works as *Negative Dialectics* and *Minima Moralia*, seem to herald the fragmentary themes of postmodernism.

The subtlety of Adorno's work, however, seems to take it well beyond what postmodernist theory has to offer – an argument also put forward, in a rather obscure way, by Fredric Jameson. Jameson makes the point that Adorno's use of the concept of totality, a frequent target of postmodernist thought, is central, and it is precisely this that gives his work its critical edge. 'Totality' means 'society', 'social structure', and it cannot be avoided without masking what is going on in our world. The paradox is that the free play of postmodernist art and theory appears at a time when the 'totality' has reached a new, higher level of administration and domination. Jameson argues that the collapse of the Communist states heralds a new stage in the advance of the organising, all-powerful totality, and to talk of free play in this context is to hide the reality of the extent to which we are dominated. This view sees postmodernism as an ideology in the classical Marxist sense of something partial which is elevated to the status of the whole.

More important from the point of view of my arguments here, it provides an ethical and critical standpoint and an alternative notion of rationality. Throughout Adorno's more abstract philosophical work lies the problem at the centre of structuralism and post-structuralism: that of the relationship between the concept, the language, and the thing, and he tries to hold together two opposite ends of the continuum. If we identify the concept and the thing, the object, we are caught up in the instrumental drive of Enlightenment rationality, and we lose – damage – the complexity of our individual experience; yet if we give ourselves over to that experience in all its complexity and variability, then we are unable to use ideas to stand back from what is happening to us and gain some sort of critical understanding of what is going on, and begin to think in terms of change.

If we try to hold on to both ends at the same time, thought becomes a constant movement from the concept to the experience and back again. The answer to the title of this chapter is that there is *no* way out of here – we keep going round in circles, but necessary and, in effect, unavoidable circles. We could indeed think of history as a very complex form of such a movement. It is certainly possible to think of our own individual histories in this way: we think, try to distance ourselves and understand, and at the same time we experience, lose our understanding, and fluctuate, if we are working well, between giving priority to one or the other. And there is the hope, which we will never actually realise, that one day the two might come together: but that hope is necessary for the enterprise to be undertaken at all – even if we know we cannot realise it. In Adorno's philosophy, the hope is of the eventual, but impossible, reconciliation of humanity and society. However speculative and difficult this type of philosophy, we can find in it a reason for theorising. It is, if you like, a tragic philosophy of history, but not necessarily a pessimistic one.

There are, of course, other reactions to postmodernism, and the next chapter will look at the work of the second-generation member of the Frankfurt School Jürgen Habermas who, in the face of modern developments in philosophy, has returned to a defence of the Enlightenment project.

FURTHER READING

On Hegelian Marxism

By far the clearest, and pitched at an introductory level:

Agger, B. (1979) *Western Marxism: An introduction*, Goodyear, Santa Monica, CA.

Lukács

His most important, and very difficult, work is:

Lukács, G. (1971) *History and Class Consciousness*, Merlin, London.

Secondary works

Jameson is good but difficult; Lowey is excellent in bringing together Lukács's life and theory; Lichtheim and Parkinson are both reasonable introductions; and I am very fond of my own paper. Stedman-Jones's is the central critical article of recent years.

Arato, A. and Breines, P. (1979) *The Young Lukács*, Pluto Press, London.
Craib, I. (1977) 'Lukács and the Marxist critique of sociology', *Radical Philosophy*, vol. 17, pp. 26–37.

Jameson, F. (1971) *Marxism and Form*, Princeton University Press, Princeton, NJ (ch. 3).

Lichtheim, G. (1970) *Georg Lukács*, Fontana, London.

Lowey, M. (1977) 'Lukács and Stalinism', in *Western Marxism: A critical reader*, New Left Books, London, pp. 61–82.

Parkinson, G. (1970) *Lukács*, Weidenfeld & Nicolson, London.

Stedman–Jones, G. (1977) 'The Marxism of the early Lukács', in *Western Marxism: A critical reader*, New Left Books, London, pp. 11–60.

The Frankfurt School

Crucial works by members of the school considered in this chapter

Aspects of Sociology or one of the readers would be the best starting point; Adorno's *Minima Moralia* is a good source for the 'feel' of the later works.

Adorno, T. W. and Horkheimer, M. (1972) *Dialectic of Enlightenment*, Herder & Herder, New York.

Adorno, T. W. *et al.* (1967) *Prisms*, Neville Separman, London.

Adorno, T. W. *et al.* (1969a) *The Authoritarian Personality*, Norton, New York.

Adorno, T. *et al.* (1969b) *The Positivist Dispute in German Sociology*, Heinemann, London.

Adorno, T. W. *et al.* (1973) *Negative Dialectics*, Seabury Press, New York.

Adorno, T. W. *et al.* (1974) *Minima Moralia: Reflections from damaged life*, New Left Books, London.

Adorno, T. W. (1975) 'The stars down to earth: The *Los Angeles Times* astrology column', *Telos*, no. 19, pp. 13–90.

Arato, A. and Gebhardt, E. (eds) (1978) *The Essential Frankfurt School Reader*, Basil Blackwell, Oxford.

Connerton, P. (ed.) (1976) *Critical Sociology*, Penguin, Harmondsworth.

Frankfurt Institute for Social Research (1973) *Aspects of Sociology*, Heinemann, London.

Horkheimer, M. (1974a) *Eclipse of Reason*, Seabury Press, New York.

Horkheimer, M. (1974b) *Critique of Instrumental Reason*, Seabury Press, New York.

Marcuse, H. (1960) *Reason and Revolution: Hegel and the rise of social theory*, Beacon Press, Boston, MA.

Marcuse, H. (1964) *One-Dimensional Man*, Routledge & Kegan Paul, London.

Marcuse, H. (1966) *Eros and Civilisation: A philosophical inquiry into Freud*, Beacon Press, Boston, MA.

Marcuse, H. (1968) *Negations: Essays in critical theory*, Beacon Press, Boston, MA.

Marcuse, H. (1969) *An Essay on Liberation*, Allen Lane, London.

Marcuse, H. (1971) *Soviet Marxism: A critical analysis*, Penguin, Harmondsworth.

Secondary works

Of the following, Agger is the most straightforward, Held the most complete. The non-Marxist criticisms can be found in Adorno *et al.*'s *The Positivist Dispute in German Sociology* (above); the Marxist criticisms in Anderson and Therborn (below).

Agger, B. (1979) *Western Marxism: An introduction*, Goodyear, Santa Monica, CA (chs 4/5).

Anderson, P. (1976) *Considerations on Western Marxism*, New Left Books, London.

Benhabib, S. (1986) *Critique, Norm and Utopia: A study of the foundations of critical theory*, Columbia University Press, New York.

Brumer, S. E. and Kellner, D. (1989) *Critical Theory and Society: A reader*, Routledge, London.

Buck-Mors, S. (1977) *The Origin of Negative Dialectics*. Harvester Press, Sussex.

Held, D. (1980) *Introduction to Critical Theory*, Hutchinson, London.

Jameson, F. (1971) *Marxism and Form*, Princeton University Press, Princeton, NJ (chs 1 and 2).

Jameson, F. (1990) *Late Marxism: Adorno, or the persistence of the dialectic*, Verso, London.

Jay, M. (1973) *The Dialectical Imagination*, Heinemann, London.

Kellner, D. (1989) *Critical Theory, Marxism and Modernity*, Polity Press, Cambridge.

Ray, L. (ed.) (1990) *Critical Sociology*, Edward Elgar, Aldershot, Hants.

Rose, G. (1978) *The Melancholy Science*, Macmillan, Basingstoke.

Schoolman, M. (1980) *The Imaginary Witness: The critical theory of Herbert Marcuse*, Free Press, New York.

Schroyer, T. (1973) *The Critique of Domination*, George Braziller, New York.

Therborn, G. (1977) 'The Frankfurt School', in *Western Marxism: A critical reader*, New Left Books, London, pp. 83–139.

Wellmer, A. (1974) *Critical Theory of Society*, Seabury Press, New York.

Also mentioned in the text:

Dowling, C. (1982) *The Cinderella Complex: Women's hidden fear of independence*, Fontana, London.

Lasch, C. (1980) *The Culture of Narcissism*, Sphere, London.

Chapter 12

JÜRGEN HABERMAS:
BACK TO THE FILING CABINET

INTRODUCTION

Habermas studied under Adorno for a number of years and is generally recognised as the major contemporary heir to the Frankfurt inheritance. Although there are distinct common themes between his work and that of his forebears, he none the less takes it in a very different direction. I compared Lukács with Adorno, Horkheimer and Marcuse as optimistic and pessimistic representatives of basically the same theoretical framework; what united them was a passionate concern with human freedom, however remote the possibility of that freedom existing in the real world. In the work of Habermas this passion is less apparent, although it is there. He breaks out of the swing from optimism to pessimism and instead devotes much more attention to the analysis of social structures and action than the writers discussed in the previous chapter, returning to something like the analytic model I discussed in the Introduction, breaking the world down into its different parts and suggesting very general relationships between them. He develops another filing system – not as complicated as Parsons's, but nevertheless a filing system: he has a particular penchant for arranging things in threes, from types of knowledge to stages of social evolution.

Habermas is certainly of the Left, but in perhaps unexpected ways, critical of his own tradition and eventually distancing himself from the student movement of the 1960s. He offers a radical critique of Marxism and takes up many of Parsons's themes. In the context of the arguments in this book, he can be seen, first, as trying to hold together conceptions of structure and agency in a totalising theory, and we shall see that this is the source for one of the main lines of criticism of his work. Secondly, he can be seen as a defender of the 'project of modernity', particularly of ideas of a universal reason and morality. His argument is that the project has not failed; rather, it has never been realised – modernity is, as yet, 'unfinished'. Considering his predecessors' critique of Enlightenment reason, this seems to take him in the opposite direction, but he can also be seen as insisting that there is a *dialectic* of the Enlightenment, that it is a double-sided process. One side involves exclusion and hierarchy, as the postmodernist writers claim; the other side at least carries the potential for a free, inclusive society. Postmodernism loses this second possibility, yet postmodernists are trapped in the dilemma that their rejection of reason must actually employ reason: they are as much caught up in it as anybody else.

As we shall see, Habermas takes the 'linguistic turn' and argues that it does not lead to abandoning hopes of achieving a universal knowledge or a universal morality; rather, we can find in the philosophy of language – or, perhaps better, in language itself – the standards for such a knowledge and morality.

HABERMAS'S VIEW OF CRITICAL THEORY

In his earlier work, Habermas distinguishes three types of theory, all of which he sees as necessary to human development. These in turn are based on three 'cognitive interests'. By this he means that we always develop knowledge for a certain purpose, and this purpose provides us with an 'interest' in the knowledge. This idea is not dissimilar to saying that a student develops an 'interest' in a particular type of knowledge through her purpose of gaining a degree, and then a job, by means of it. The interests discussed by Habermas, however, are shared by all of us by virtue of the fact that we are members of human society. His argument is rooted in Marx's early work, and we can find here the beginnings of his major criticisms of Marxist theory. It is not only labour, he suggests, that distinguishes human beings from animals and enables us to transform our environment; it is also *language*, the ability to use signs to communicate with each other – an idea not dissimilar to that of G. H. Mead. These abilities, to work and to communicate, give rise to different types of knowledge. Work, or labour, gives rise to a technical interest, an interest in mastering and controlling natural processes and using them to our advantage. We all, for example, have an interest in the development and employment of electricity, since we can all benefit from it.

This interest gives rise to what Habermas calls 'the empirico-analytic sciences' – what earlier critical theorists might have called positivism, and what both would label 'instrumental reason'. Habermas, however, affirms the place of this type of knowledge in human life – even when it is applied to human beings – since we are all affected by natural processes outside our consciousness, over which we have no control. The earlier critical theorists are much more dismissive of this form of knowledge. Each interest develops through what Habermas calls 'media' – areas in which the interest is put into practice. The technical interest is rooted in and developed through work, and the problem with instrumental reason is not so much that it is in itself wrong or leads to domination, but rather that in modern societies it has gained priority over other forms of knowledge.

The second means by which human beings transform their environment, language, gives rise to what Habermas calls the 'practical interest' which, in turn, gives rise to the 'hermeneutic sciences'. The practical interest is concerned with human interaction – the way we interpret our actions to each other, the way we understand each other, the ways in which we direct our actions together in social organisations. Hermeneutics is the science of interpretation – several of the approaches considered earlier can be seen as hermeneutic: symbolic interactionism, ethnomethodology, the structuralist analysis of culture and post-structuralism are all concerned in some way with making sense of what people say and think, and its connection with their actions. The term itself originated with the practice of interpreting sacred texts, of understanding God's message, but today it is a label attached usually to an abstract form of philosophical argument concerned with what we mean by 'understanding' as well as with how we understand. Hans-Georg Gadamer is generally recognised as the leading hermeneutic thinker, and Habermas has been engaged in a long debate with him around the nature of understanding. The practical interest develops through the 'medium' of interaction, and one of Habermas's central themes is the way in which interaction is distorted and confused by social structures: people can be wrong in their understanding of each other, they can be systematically misled and manipulated, systematically blind. In Gadamer's work, so Habermas contends, such ideological distortion cannot be understood.

The practical interest, Habermas argues, gives rise to a third interest, the 'emancipatory' interest. This is also connected with language, and rids interaction and communication of their distorted elements. It gives rise to the critical sciences, for which Habermas takes psychoanalysis as the model, and it is rooted in our ability to think and act self-consciously, to reason and make decisions on the basis of facts known about a situation and the socially accepted rules that govern interaction. Distortion arises when the facts of a situation are hidden from some or all of the participants, and when the rules, in one way or another, prohibit people from participating fully in the decision-making process. The critical science based on the emancipatory interest reveals and contributes towards correcting distortions in interaction and communication. This is the basis for Habermas's critical theory, and the similarity with traditional critical theory is evident. The medium through which this interest develops is power – the struggle that exists in all social institutions, the eventual end of which is seen as equal participation of all concerned in the decision-making process. Psychoanalysis is taken as the model of a critical science because it attempts to reveal to the patient the unconscious processes which determine her action and bring them under some conscious control in what should eventually become a relationship of equality with the analyst.

In his later work – in particular *The Theory of Communicative Action* (1984, 1987) – Habermas turns to linguistic philosophy to elaborate the basis for critical theory. He presents a difficult argument, which I will try to summarise in three stages:

1. He argues that it is necessary to break free of what he calls 'the philosophy of consciousness', by which he means a philosophy which sees language and action in terms of a relationship between a subject and an object (using Althusserian terms, perhaps, we need to break free of the empiricist problematic). Seeing the world only in these terms leaves us caught in instrumental reason (the subject doing something to the object) and the pessimism which overtook Adorno and, in a different way, Max Weber. From this position, there is no way out.

2. The second stage is summed up by David Rasmussen more clearly than I could hope to present it:

> action could take two forms, namely, strategic action and communicative action. The former would include purposive-rational action while action aimed at reaching an understanding would be communicative. Communicative action is non-instrumental in the following sense: 'A communicatively achieved agreement has a rational basis: it cannot be imposed by either party, whether instrumentally through intervention in the situation directly or strategically through influencing decisions of opponents'. Such an action has implicit within it a validity claim which is in principle criticizable, i.e. the person to whom it is addressed can respond either 'yes' or 'no' based on reasons. Communicative actions are in this sense foundational, they cannot, it is said, be reduced to teleological actions. If they were, one would be back precisely in the problematic of the philosophy of consciousness. (Rasmussen, 1990: 27; quote from Habermas, 1984: 287)

3. A number of things result from giving priority to communicative action. First, rationality in this sense is not an ideal plucked from mid-air, but is there in our language itself, and – most important in the context of Habermas's argument with postmodernism – it implies an inclusive, democratic social system, where the aim is not to dominate but to reach agreement.

Secondly, there is an implicit ethics which Habermas attempts to draw out – a universal ethics, the idea of which has a bad name amongst sociologists: how can we even conceive of an ethics which is applicable across the board to the variety of human ways of living? It seems to me a remarkably subtle solution, although I am not sufficiently experienced in moral philosophy to evaluate or, I suspect, even explain it properly. It is often referred to as a *procedural* ethic which directs not to the content of a norm but to the way it is arrived at. It is arrived at through free rational discussion in which the consequences of the norm are explored primarily with regard to its universalisability: is it something acceptable, through reason, and without coercion, to everybody? The content, as far as I understand it, will depend upon the particular community. This can, once again, be seen as an attempt to save modernism, which demands that an ethic must be constructed on rational grounds rather than on the basis of tradition, which is constantly questioned; what becomes important, however, is not the *what* but the *how* of moral choice.

Third – something I have already touched upon – is the implication of a radically democratic society, in which each has access to the tools of reason, the opportunity to contribute to the argument, to be heard and to be included in the final decision.

Theory for Habermas, then, is a product of and serves the purpose of human action. It is essentially a means to greater human freedom, progressing on a number of different levels, and thus taking us away from the later work of Horkheimer and Adorno and the post-structuralists for whom knowledge is associated with domination and enslavement. It also involves a development of Marx's early work, drawing the emphasis away from labour and towards language and communication. It is to Habermas's critique of Marxism that I will now turn.

THE CRITIQUE OF MARXISM AND HABERMAS'S VIEW OF HUMAN EVOLUTION

For Habermas, as for the earlier members of the Frankfurt School, the productive parts of Marx's work have become buried in an instrumental or positivist concrete. He argues that the responsibility for this can be laid on Marx himself, and his overemphasis that he placed on labour as the distinguishing human characteristic. Although Habermas sees labour, and instrumental reason, as an important dimension of human life, he argues that socially organised labour alone is not sufficient to define human beings; in fact, language and communication are decisive. Habermas suggests, in fact, that the economic level of the social formation is dominant in capitalist societies perhaps only in early capitalism; unlike Althusser, he does not cling on to any idea of the economic being determinant 'in the last instance'. Rather, he argues that we have to look to some other factor, some other level of the social formation, in order to understand the development of human society. It is here that Habermas begins to move closer to Parsons: he suggests, for example, that each type of society is governed by a particular institutional complex: it might be economic institutions for early capitalism, the state in the case of late capitalism, and the kinship system in tribal societies. The institutions themselves, however, may be seen as embodiments of cultural values and norms which he sees as progressing to higher and higher levels of universality.

To make the same point another way: human society is seen as organised around certain ideas – values, norms, or whatever; through history, these ideas are developed to possess more and more general applicability. There is a debt here to Max Weber's notion of the historical process of rationalisation. Habermas uses as a model the development of the individual. As children, we learn first to identify very specific objects and attach names to them: we label the family pet, for example, 'dog'. We progress from this to a stage where eventually we can use the term 'dog' to identify a wide variety of animals, not only those of similar appearance to the family pet but those of very different appearance. Although the application of this model to human society would seem to lead to the directly opposite view to that of Marx, Habermas does suggest that the mechanisms which lead from one stage of social development to the next are not cultural but economic – although critics argue that he does not properly identify these mechanisms. Each evolutionary stage in this process creates a new set of problems and possibilities, and Habermas seems to suggest that change occurs when all the possibilities for human development have been exhausted, yet problems still remain. In fact he refers to some 'unlikely evolutionary thrust' that moves society on to the next stage. However we look at it, that is not a very precise definition of the mechanisms at work.

His most thorough treatment of this process takes us to the ideological rather than the economic level of the social formation, and Habermas employs Freud's work in an interesting way. Freud shows us that social institutions exist not only to facilitate and maintain economic production but also in order to repress desires that would make social life impossible. Rather like Marcuse, he suggests that the degree of repression necessary will vary from society to society and social class to social class. The repression necessary to live and survive in social organisations entails the distortion of communication and interaction, since we are not aware of the unconscious forces affecting or determining our behaviour. The evolutionary trend is towards less repression and distortion, and in trying to trace this he again uses the model of individual development. He deals with this in three areas: the growing independence and autonomy of the personality, the increasing ability to make moral judgements and act on them, and the growing universality of moral and legal systems.

Habermas looks at the evolution of human societies from a number of other points of view, usually producing a threefold classification. I do not want to investigate the detail of these so much as emphasise just how far critical theory has moved, in his hands, back to a more conventional form of action theory. Societies are seen as products of human action in turn structured by norms and values, and it is to the development of these norms and values that we must look if we are going to understand social change. The basis for social criticism lies in the goal towards which social development is moving, a universal rationality in which everybody participates equally, a situation in which communication is not distorted – an 'ideal speech situation' which Habermas attempts to outline. As with Parsons's work, we end with little conception of levels of social organisation beyond that provided by giving priority to the cultural, no grasp of causal mechanisms, and a general classificatory rather than an explanatory system.

HABERMAS'S ANALYSIS OF MODERN CAPITALISM

Habermas's discussion of modern capitalism lacks the passion of that of earlier members of the Frankfurt School. It is seen primarily as a stage in evolutionary development – a stage that might go wrong and lead to disaster, but none the less, for Habermas, a social system rather than an evil. Like the earlier thinkers, he emphasises the dominance of technology and instrumental reason, and we can also see a rather nostalgic look back at the period of early capitalism. During this period, he argues, we can find the beginnings of the formation of a proper 'public opinion': in public places, cafés, and the comparatively large number of magazines and newspapers, a limited number of people could discuss openly and freely public issues about which they shared information. In Britain this period could be dated roughly as ending with the eighteenth century, and it approximates to an 'ideal speech situation'. The operative word, however, is 'limited': the class structure of early capitalism made participation in the formation of public opinion a privilege, and the development of the economic system and class structure upon which such public opinion was based in fact undermined the public realm. Habermas sees modern capitalism as characterised by the dominance of the state over the economy and other areas of social life. Public affairs have come to be regarded not as areas of discussion and choice but as technical problems to be solved by experts employing an instrumental rationality.

For Habermas, state intervention and the consequent growth of instrumental reason have reached a dangerous point, where a 'negative utopia' is possible. The progressive rationalisation of public decisions has reached the point where social organisation and decision-making might be delegated to computers and taken out of the arena of public debate altogether; this is a situation which Parsons might perhaps have regarded as the final confirmation of his theory, but despite his similarities to Parsons, Habermas maintains his critical stance. Classical Marxist economics and sociology, he argues, with their emphasis on class struggle, are no longer adequate to understanding our new situation. Although there are still disputes about wages and conditions of work, the most important conflicts take place elsewhere in the social formation, and if we are to avoid the possibility of surrendering human control over social life, we must understand these new forms of conflict. This leads us on to what might be considered Habermas's most important contribution to the analysis of modern society: his theory of crises.

Before moving on to this part of his work as such, it is useful to make some preliminary points. First, Habermas does not see the relationship between development from one evolutionary stage to another, and the decreasing of necessary repression, as a direct one. Each stage brings itself new problems, new repressions and distortions, and sets in motion new processes of change. His theory of crises tries to trace these processes through the development of capitalism. Secondly, he employs a Parsonian-related terminology of social and system integration. As far as I understand it, social integration refers to the social relationships between people; it has to do with the experience people have of each other and themselves. System integration refers to the systems of institutions in which people are related, the 'steering mechanisms' which hold them together and direct them in their relationship with each other: 'boundary maintenance' again becomes an important term. I will return to this shortly. The word 'crisis' itself is used to refer to a change in the system, experienced at the level of social integration as a threat to one's social identity. These two 'levels', which are in fact the familiar ones of structure and action, should, according to Habermas, be studied together.

He identifies (inevitably) three types of crisis as being endemic to capitalism: each stage of the system's development brings a new type to the foreground, although the previous type has not necessarily been eliminated. His analysis of early capitalism is similar to that of Marx, with economic crises the most important. However, capitalism can be seen as a combination of guess-how-many subsystems – the economic, the political and the sociocultural – and the site of the crisis moves from one to the other as the system develops. Economic crises and the resulting conflict between labour and capital are seen primarily as system crises. The growing intervention and power of the state are a response to and an attempt to manage these crises – on the whole a successful attempt, although Habermas does not claim that economic crises have disappeared; indeed, at the moment it would be difficult to sustain such a claim.

Increasing state intervention produces what he calls a 'rationality crisis'. This, too, is a system crisis which arises because the state has constantly to borrow to fulfil its functions and thus creates a lasting inflation and financial crisis. It is a 'rationality' crisis because the problems are eventually rooted in the state's inability to reconcile the different and conflicting interests of private capital. The basic irrationality is what Marxists usually call the 'anarchy of the market', the idea that we can build an orderly society out of conflicting private interests. On the level of social integration, the rationality crisis appears as a 'legitimation crisis': if the state cannot find the right strategies to reconcile the conflicting interests that it tries to rule, then it loses legitimacy in the eyes of the population; it fails in its task and the justification for its existence becomes blurred. We can see both levels of the crisis simply by following the political rhetoric of the Reagan and Thatcher administrations, both of which justified themselves in terms of decreasing state intervention, state borrowing and inflation, and both of which saw themselves as insisting on the legitimacy of elected authority.

If the rationality crisis can be managed in the political subsystem, then the scene changes to the sociocultural subsystem and the third type of crisis, the motivation crisis. If economic crises are crises of system integration, and rationality crises are crises of system and social integration, the motivational crisis is a crisis of social integra tion alone. The increasing state power and technocratic control necessary to manage the other forms of crisis have the effect of undermining people's motivations for participating in the system at all. The spur of economic competition is steadily removed, together with the 'work ethic', the inner necessity that people feel to work. It disappears because work becomes routinely and bureaucratically ordered and the economic system seems to be self-sustaining. An increasingly powerful bureaucratic state also undermines the possibility of participating usefully in decision-making processes via the usual democratic institutions such as political parties and elections. The label attached to the governing party makes less and less difference to what actually happens. Some modern social movements – the student movement for a while in the 1960s and, more recently, the women's movement and the environmentalist and anti-nuclear-power movements – may be seen as symptoms of a motivation crisis.

In *The Theory of Communicative Action*, many of these themes come together in a slightly different way. Here Habermas elaborates what he calls the 'life-world'; this seems to correspond in part to Husserl's concept of an area of pre-reflective, immediate experience, and in part to the more distinct linguistic conception of a 'form of life' (taken from Wittgenstein). This is clearly connected to social integration, and system integration is now conceived in clearer Parsonian terms. Modernity, for the life-world, is the process through which different areas of our life come to be based on mutual, rational agreement, communicative reason, rather than on tradition. For those more familiar with the critical theory of Adorno and Marcuse, the notion of 'the rationalisation of the life-world' carries the implication of the triumph of instrumental rationality; for Habermas, it is the opposite.

For the social system, on the other hand, modernity is the process of differentiation and reintegration, particularly through the media of money and power, that we have already met in Parsons. The development of the social system works through 'functionalist reason', which, as far as I can understand it, is a form of instrumental reason by which the system imposes itself on individuals. By at least analytically separating the life-world from the social system, Habermas is able to produce a sort of critical functionalism. He regards this distinction as maintaining what is useful in Marx's distinction between base and superstructure, without the deterministic implications and instrumental reason of the latter. The basis for criticism is the way in which the 'functionalist reason' of the social system – which, in terms of the system, involves progress – is colonising the life-world and undermining communicative reason, the way in which we achieve progress in the life-world. This happens precisely through the media of power and money.

An example may be taken from the legal system, which involves power. Habermas makes a distinction between regulative and constitutive law. As I understand it, the former accepts and regulates what is happening in relationships in the life-world, while the latter actually makes something happen. The following are my own illustrations. In our day-to-day life, people come together in sexual relationships and break up those relationships, and sometimes the relationships produce children. It seems to me that regulative laws concerning marriage, divorce, custody, etc., would be concerned with the protection of all parties against different forms of injustice and providing the context for rational discussion and mutual agreement around the division of property, care of children, etc. Constitutive law would actually force a particular relationship into existence where otherwise it might not have developed. It seems to me that the automatic award of custody to one parent – usually the mother – is such a case. Habermas also seems to be getting at something even more profound: the way in which, particularly through the development of the welfare state, whole areas of personal relationships become subjected to legal requirements and thus have to be abstracted from their contexts. One might call this Habermas's 'Foucauldian moment'. He goes on to argue that 'expert cultures' are replacing ideologies: the latter at least enabled us to try to get an overall grasp on what is happening. Increasingly, we are subjected instead to partial frameworks of knowledge in the hands of others. This produces a fragmented consciousness.

This is a very bare outline of Habermas's argument, but I hope it is sufficient to give a general idea of his approach to theory, his view of social development and his analysis of modern society; I want to turn now to drawing the issues together in the light of the criticisms that have been made of his work.

CONCLUSION: THE ADVANTAGES OF AMBIVALENCE

In the light of the general themes of this book, it seems to me that Habermas comes closest to holding the two sides – action and structure – together without turning one into the other, although I suspect that he is rather uneasy about this, and – at least in political terms – seems to imply the priority of the rationalisation of the life-world; he also provides a sociology of fragmentation.

The critical literature aims at a wide variety of targets. I will deal with the two that seem to me most important – the first briefly, the second at greater length. The first is that Habermas does not and cannot establish the priority of communicative over strategic action. I am not convinced that this has to be established in absolute terms; what is important is the notion of communicative action itself and its basis in language: that provides us with the *possibility* of the ideal as a critical standard, and an alternative conception of reason. In fact I shall argue shortly that perhaps the attempt to give it priority takes us back to the old problems of action theory.

The second criticism is summed up and connected to the first very clearly by David Rasmussen:

> From a brief look at some of the more significant criticism of Habermas's work one can conclude that not only is the emancipatory thesis uncertain ... but that the very attempt to locate critique in the distinction between system and life-world undermines the rather insecure status claimed for emancipation. Hence it appears that the overall status of the Habermasian enterprise is at dual purposes. If we were to take the larger project in its best sense it would appear that the attempt to secure the primacy of communication in the philosophy of language is undercut by the distinction between system and life-world – because that distinction restricts major areas of human social experience from formation through processes based on communication ... in terms of the social system only some phenomena can be classified under the rubric of consensus. Hence, the argument which supports the linguistic turn towards social theory, and the argument which supports the distinction between system and life-world, are at odds with one another. The desire to secure the primacy of the emancipatory in the former context (language) is undermined by the attempt to restrict the emancipatory in the latter (society). (Rasmussen, 1990: 54)

This seems fair enough to me, and it confirms a point I have tried to make all the way through this book: that if we give priority to one side or the other of the action/structure divide, then the theory begins to fall apart.

But if, unlike Habermas, we do not attempt to give priority but look at the relationships between different contradictory processes in different areas of the social world, then we can find, using his work, both the basis for emancipation and the basis for the failure of emancipation – that ambivalence that must always haunt any realistically conceived politics, the problem of maintaining conflicting necessities and conflicting values. As White (1988) points out, there are conflicts between the benefits of modernity and our inner integrity. The welfare state simultaneously takes us towards the realisation of universal values but takes away areas where we can exercise our human abilities to create the lives we lead with others. The ever-changing ways in which we need to balance these contradictions seem to me a suitable focus for modern radical politics, and this leaves me feeling more sympathetic to Habermas than I did a decade ago. He is doing more than returning to Parsons's filing cabinet; he is suggesting that the filing cabinet need not include everything: it can be kept in its place. Or – in terms of the previous chapter – he is confirming that there is no way out of here, but suggesting that we might at least keep the walls from closing in (or, indeed, falling to pieces).

FURTHER READING

Habermas's own work translated into English

There is no easy starting point in Habermas's work; it is best to choose the work which deals with the issues in which you are most interested. I have included only the more important of the more recent writings:

Habermas, J. (1971) *Toward a Rational Society*, Heinemann, London.
Habermas, J. (1972) *Knowledge and Human Interests*, Heinemann, London.
Habermas, J. (1974) *Theory and Practice*, Heinemann, London.
Habermas, J. (1976) *Legitimation Crisis*, Heinemann, London.
Habermas, J. (1979) *Communication and the Evolution of Society*, Heinemann, London.
Habermas, J. (1984) *The Theory of Communicative Action Vol. 1: Reason and the rationalisation of society*, Polity Press, Oxford.
Habermas, J. (1987) *The Theory of Communicative Action Vol. 2: A critique of functionalist reason*, Polity Press, Oxford.
Habermas, J. (1989a) *The Structural Transformation of the Public Sphere*, Polity Press, Oxford.

Habermas, J. (1989b) *Moral Consciousness and Communicative Action*, MIT Press, Cambridge, MA.
Habermas, J. (1990) *The Philosophical Discourse of Modernity. Twelve Lectures*, Polity Press, Oxford.

Secondary and critical work

The best introduction is again provided by David Held; the widest range of critical essays is provided by Thompson and Held. Rasmussen is excellent on Habermas's later work.

Held, D. (1980) *Introduction to Critical Theory*, Hutchinson, London.
Ingram, D. (1987) *Habermas and the Dialectic of Reason*, Yale University Press, New Haven, CT.
Keat, R. (1981) *The Politics of Social Theory: Habermas, Freud and the critique of Marxism*, Basil Blackwell, Oxford.
Kortian, G. (1980) *Metacritique: The philosophical arguments of Jürgen Habermas*, Cambridge University Press.
McCarthy, T. (1973) 'A theory of communicative competence', *Philosophy of the Social Sciences*, vol. 3, pp. 135–56.
McCarthy, T. (1978) *The Critical Theory of Jürgen Habermas*, MIT Press, Cambridge, MA.
Rasmussen, D. M. (1990) *Reading Habermas*, Basil Blackwell, Oxford.
Rockmore, T. (1989) *Habermas on Historical Materialism*, Indiana University Press, Bloomington and Indianapolis.
Therborn, G. (1971) 'Jürgen Habermas: A new eclectic', *New Left Review*, no. 67, pp. 69–83.
Thompson, J. B. (1981) *Critical Hermeneutics: A study of the thought of Paul Ricoeur and Jürgen Habermas*, Cambridge University Press, Cambridge.
Thompson, J. B. and Held, D. (1982) *Habermas: Critical debates*, Macmillan, Basingstoke.
White, S. K. (1988) *The Recent Work of Jürgen Habermas*, Cambridge University Press, Cambridge.
Woodiwiss, A. (1978) 'Critical theory and the capitalist state', *Economy and Society*, vol. 7, pp. 175–92.

CONCLUSION: PLAYING WITH IDEAS

INTRODUCTION

As a conclusion, I will try to do three things. First, I will make some general comments about the current state of social theory and what we are likely to witness in the future. Secondly, I want to make a case for the continued study of social theory and some suggestions about how students might best employ theory – in their thinking not only about sociology, but about the world in general. Thirdly, I want to engage in some theoretical speculation of my own about what we can learn by trying to think theoretically about one aspect of one of the themes in this book: the nature of modernity or postmodernity.

The first edition of this book was written after what Christopher Bryant (in Bryant and Becker, 1990) refers to as 'the Wars of the Schools'. It was, if anything, a time of theoretical excess, certainly of excessive hopes for theory on the part of its proponents, and it was a reason for writing this book, as well as the topic for the conclusion. Then I discussed it in terms of pulling the rabbit out of the hat, the final trick of bringing it all together, and I came to what I suppose was a 'postmodernist' conclusion: not only is there no rabbit, there is no hat either. I think I would now revise that: if the hat is the social world, the world studied by sociology, we can pull out not only a variety of rabbits but any number of other animals, many of them weird and wonderful. Very few people now claim to have produced *the* rabbit; of those considered in this book, Giddens offers us a skeleton which we can put together in different ways to produce different rabbits, and Habermas tells us in effect that whilst we may have a hat and we may have a rabbit, what matters in the end is not what we pull out of what, but the way in which we decide what it is. The other approaches would not, I think, be able to maintain any claim that they were the one and only rabbit, and indeed they no longer make such a claim.

One pleasing feature of the last ten years is that the theoretical sophistication of the discipline has remained higher – perhaps much higher – than it was before the wars began; there has been a partial, but not a wholesale, return to 'serious research' where intellectual creativity is seen almost entirely in terms of the development of technical research methods. More than any other single person, we have Anthony Giddens to thank for this; in working out his own approach he has introduced and made respectable many of the ideas considered in this book. What happens now – or at least, one of the things that is happening now, and what I suspect is likely to go on happening – is described by Bryant as a 'new pragmatism'. It is recognised that there is no overarching theoretical framework, even by the partisans of one approach rather than another, and there is a constant process of conversation, of translation from situation to situation, guided by the principle that knowledge is not so much a representation of reality as 'a means of coping with it'. I think it is this and more as well, and the rest of this chapter will be concerned with teasing out what else happens in theory.

WHY STUDY SOCIAL THEORY?

I suspect that it is very difficult to abandon the desire for a rabbit and a hat. The need for there to be a 'point to it all' is very strong, and uncertainty is not always easy to bear. At times, it is perhaps important to argue against looking for certainty; at other times, it is important to argue that some things are as close to certain as they are ever likely to be. In the first edition I clearly felt that the former was appropriate, and I used the example of simplistic sociobiological explanations to argue that apparent certainty is a dangerous thing. Social theory emerged and remains in existence because when people live together they find 'emergent' phenomena – things that happen which do not stem from their biological or physical make-up. These things come to comprise the most important problems we are likely to face together or as individuals: war, economic prosperity or poverty, the ways of life open or closed to us. The first reason for studying social theory, and the most basic reason, is that it addresses these problems, and one reason why theory is so difficult is that the problems are so difficult. If the sociological rabbit is a distant mirage, the sociobiological rabbit comes close to being a fraud.

This is, of course, still true. However, my experience over recent years is that neither my colleagues nor my students need any convincing of the inadequacy of simple sociobiological explanations. Rather, it is difficult for them to accept that there are such things as biological limits on human possibilities. The popularity of 'social constructionist' approaches – which include symbolic interactionism, ethnomethodology, and post-structuralism, as well as certain interpretations of structuration theory and structuralism itself – involves a reluctance or inability to recognise such limits. The fact that, for example, men and women have different genitals, and both are necessary for the species to reproduce itself, has varying but extremely important effects on social organisation; as does the fact that we are born, in comparison with other mammals, prematurely, and the fact that we grow old and die. It is, maybe, too easy to write off these features of our life by means of a theory which apparently goes below the surface and demonstrates that the meaning of all these things is socially constructed. The meaning is, of course, socially interpreted, but however hard we might try to avoid it, we are all still going to die. It is, perhaps, when theory penetrates the surface and shows us something that we do not like to acknowledge that its revolutionary potential is at its greatest.

Although there is no overarching theory, then, it is still true that we can actually know things, albeit with provisos and reservations, and we are talking about knowing an external reality, not simply coping with it. Many of the modern developments traced in this book tend towards or explicitly assert the impossibility of such knowledge, and in my view this is one of the most dangerous trends in modern social theory. To argue that because knowledge is not absolute or final there is no knowledge, only interpretations – that because external reality is mediated through language, that language is the only reality – seems to me akin to throwing a tantrum, a sort of intellectual tantrum: because I can't have it all, then I won't have any of it. It undermines what I still think is one of the most vital contributions of theory: it can offer a deeper understanding of what is at stake in political and social conflicts that have a very real external existence; it provides an opportunity to become what might be called 'better citizens', more aware and with a deeper understanding of what is going on around us. If it does not provide answers to problems, it enables a better understanding of their complexity and difficulty.

There are, however, more personal and immediate reasons for the study of social theory, and I hope I have demonstrated these with some of the examples I have used. There is a sense in which anything new we learn changes us on a more personal level, and we are not always immediately aware of it. If the different theories discussed in this book have been thought about as openly as possible, or if you have become enthusiastic about and followed up one particular approach rather than another, then the change might already be noticeable. Every time your view of the world shifts, however slightly, you begin to see things you did not see before: the connection between such shifts and action might be obscure, but it is none the less there. If, for example, you begin to think of mental illness as a result of social processes; or of strikes as built into the relationship between employer and employee; or of the education system as an ideological state apparatus, then your reactions are different when you come into contact with them. Theory has its effect at a much more personal level than might at first appear; the theoretical thinking I described in the introductory chapters is a way of deepening and extending yourself, as well as one of thinking about the world.

HOW TO USE SOCIAL THEORY

Some time ago Paul Feyerabend, an American philosopher of science, published a book on the natural sciences called *Against Method* (1975). He argued for what he called an anarchist theory of knowledge based on the principle 'anything goes'. What we normally regard as the scientific method is, he claimed, restrictive, and if we look at the history of science we find that all sorts of peculiar things have contributed to its present state. He suggests, for example, that Galileo was able to persuade people that the earth moved round the sun not on the basis of scientific evidence but because he was a more imaginative propagandist than his opponents. Feyerabend is concerned to encourage the wilder ideas of science: no old theory should be abandoned and no new theory rejected; they should be worked with, played off against each other, and played with.

I would like to encourage something like this in the case of social theory, but with some modification. A thoroughgoing anarchism is self-contradictory. If anything goes, then a strict methodology is permissible as well, and Feyerabend would not have written his book if he did not consider that his case was better than others. So it is not quite true that anything goes – some things go better. There is, in fact, a broad framework, but none the less a framework, *within which* anything goes. In Feyerabend's case, this consists at least of rational argument, and his book is well and clearly argued. In the case of social theory, I have tried to distinguish a different type of framework based on the objects we study, a framework which is 'out there' in the world rather than part of our argument. I have argued against too rigid an approach, the attempt to embrace all features of the social world in the framework of one theory and theoretical explanation. Instead I have suggested that the social world is made of different types of phenomena, and each type needs a different theoretical understanding and explanation.

The basic organising division is between social structure or society and social action or agency, and I have suggested that the attempt to move across this divide in the framework of one theory is responsible for much of the fragmentation in the area. Beyond these two areas, I have suggested that there are others on either side of the great divide. Each needs to be understood differently and involves a different type of causal explanation. On the side of society, the most basic level is the underlying structure of the social whole. Of the theories I have looked at, structuralist Marxism seems to me to make best sense of this underlying structure, and it provides us with a way of distinguishing between different types of society (according to different modes of production) and different forms of the same type of society (according to different relationships between the three basic levels). I further suggested that there is a 'surface' level of social institutions: those organisations which we can identify clearly, work in and study more or less directly. These include such organisations as schools, political parties, churches, etc., and although some general features at this level might be explicable in terms of structural analysis, they incorporate human action in a very different way. The functionalist model, with its analogy between social institutions and the biological organism, is likely to provide some insights at this level, since it involves looking at 'congealed' structures of action. The conflict model will offer some insights here, too; despite its general theoretical limitations, it points towards the real complexity of such institutions.

In Part III, I placed considerable emphasis on what I called a level of 'general meanings': networks of ideas or systems of thought, both common-sense and theoretical, which, like language, pre-exist each of us and into which we enter as we grow. Structuralism and post-structuralism can tell us something about the organisation and interplay of such systems, the way in which they form and delimit our views of the world. Whereas the structural analysis of societies employs a structural model of causality, and the functionalist and conflict analyses of surface institutions employ a teleological model, neither structuralism nor post-structuralism seems to employ a developed idea of causality: the former deals with rules; the latter sometimes with rules, sometimes just with the play of meanings.

This takes us on to the realm of social action proper. One level of social action is the deployment and use of general meanings in forming attitudes, intentions and actions, and this involves a clearly teleological explanation. Symbolic interactionism brings us closest to the detail and flow of this process, and ethnomethodology makes some steps towards identifying the rules followed. I suggested, without going into great detail, that there seem to be other levels of agency which are not dealt with by these approaches, and that we might reach these through psychoanalytic theory, and both structuralism and critical theory move in this direction. It is critical theory that comes closest to recognising the distinction between society and agency, but fails to hold them apart properly and eventually collapses the former into the latter. However, it does make explicit the ideal or critical impulse that must lie somewhere behind any attempt at theorising.

How, then, does a modified form of 'anything goes' fit into this as far as the sociology student is concerned? The first point that stands out for me from the summary is that the different approaches come into conflict with each other only when they try to account for something to which they are not suited, when they move into each other's territory. This clarifies the reason why so many arguments between different approaches have been sterile and destructive. Such arguments can be constructive, but only when one side or the other is not laying claim to an absolute validity. When that happens, theory becomes a sort of football league, with onlookers and participants applauding points with varying degrees of dismay and pleasure. The arguments should concern themselves less with which is right or wrong – all theories are, in different ways, both right *and* wrong – than with which aspect of some external situation or event may be understood by which theory in which way. 'Anything goes' in this respect means that we can play with a variety of theories – play in the sense of inventing and reinventing explanations of the same object, picking first this approach, then the other, then something not yet noticed, but drawing on all theoretical sources, even when they are not obviously appropriate.

As an example, I want to look at a particular conception of what we might call the 'modern personality', in a variety of ways, from the approaches we have looked at in this book.

MAKING SENSE OF OURSELVES

It is often observed in the psychoanalytic literature that a different sort of person presents herself for psychoanalysis these days. Freud was concerned with what we might call the 'classic' neurotic, someone who would be in some way disabled in one part of their life but functioning reasonably normally in others: the obsessive, the phobic or the hysteric. From the end of the Second World War, and increasingly in recent decades, people who seek analysis have more often been of a different type. They are often successful in the outside world, and apparently functioning well; however, they are subject to intense feelings of inner emptiness, swings in self-perception from feeling omnipotent to hopeless; they find it difficult to maintain long-term relationships and instead seek parasitic relationships which reinforce their self-esteem; and they tend to have an intense intellectual interest in themselves, perhaps staying in analysis for years without changing.

Now of course this change might not have happened, or it might not indicate any significant wider change. For the sake of my example I am going to assume that it has happened, and that it says something important about what is happening to all of us who live in what are – perhaps euphemistically – known as 'advanced societies'. I am interested here not in the psychoanalytic understanding of this type of character structure, but in various ways we may think about the change. I can immediately think of five possibilities.

1. One approach might be to say that, independently of whether such a personality structure actually exists and whether such a change has happened, there is no doubt that some psychoanalysts say that this is so, and this is what we should look at. In this context, ethnomethodology would direct us not to any sociological explanation of what is going on but to the work that psychoanalysts do in the psychoanalytic session, and we could see this in terms of a range of *ad hoc* rules which enable the session to progress; the categorising – or diagnoses – of patients would be constructed out of these rules as ways of doing the work of psychoanalysis.

No doubt interesting things would emerge from this, but we would remain within the psychoanalytic session. One way out would be to look at the interactions within the session as part of a wider process of the social construction of the personality. Following Foucault, we could then look at it one – or both – of two ways. In the first place, we might see it in terms of the attempt by psychoanalytic organisations to define and extend their power over against, say, psychiatry, behaviourist psychology, etc. It is as if psychoanalysis is carving out – constituting – a realm of psychological reality which is then its own. Secondly, the process of psychoanalytic treatment may be seen as part of a wider process of social control – a sort of 'psychological engineering' by means of which a 'socially desirable' personality is constituted. This is not quite the best way of putting it, since social control implies that there is somebody who does the controlling, and this is not what Foucault is about. Rather, psychoanalysis can be seen as one of a multitude of power centres which might, often in contradictory ways, be involved in the constitution of social control.

2. If we remain with postmodernist theories, there is another way of looking at it. It is as if psychoanalysis is situated at the edge of two discursive practices. The first constitutes individuals as possessing a depth, morality and integrity (Freud's model); the second (a postmodernist discourse) constitutes individuals only as surfaces which are broken up in various ways. This leads to two different conceptions of what we should be looking for. As opposed to the 'old' Freudian model of an integrated personality, we are directed towards a personality which is engaged in a constant process of transformation and reinterpretation of itself, rather as the 'good' literary text is the one that is open to most interpretations. In this sense the modern personality, able to engage in endless self-interpretation, is already there: all that remains is to enjoy it.

Alternatively, one could take up a comment by Lévi-Strauss drawing an analogy between the psychoanalyst and the shaman: both are concerned with enabling people to find the categories which allow them to tell their stories in a way that 'makes sense'. The endless play of meanings could be seen as pointing to some underlying structural flaw – as if each of us lives out our own 'Western' drama, but in some of us the categories get confused and we can't understand what we're doing. If the flaw can be corrected, we are back in a recognisable story.

3. An alternative is to regard the psychoanalytic observation of changing character structure as identifying a sort of social fact, there to be explained sociologically. I do not think this excludes the ways of looking at it that I have just considered. Rather, it adds another dimension. If we start with the action theories I discussed in Part I, we have two alternatives. The first would be to try to look at what is happening in terms of what Giddens calls the disembedding of social practices, our increasing reliance on abstract systems: this can explain the sense of internal emptiness as I become the performer of institutional practices, constantly rationalised and rerationalised, leaving me to seek support only through the confirmation I get when I succeed in performing them. Psychoanalysis – and, indeed, the many other forms of therapy that seem to be flourishing today – can then be seen as an attempt to re-embed our practices in face-to-face interaction.

Or we can see the change as a result of system evolution, a process of continuing differentiation and reintegration that has two consequences. First, values become increasingly open and multi-faceted – indeed, multi-facetedness (if there is such a word) becomes *the* universalistic value; and we are placed in an increasing multiplicity of roles, again with the resulting experience of shallowness, and the need for confirmation (with the implicit swing from omnipotence to despair). Much of this could be traced through by interactionist ideas – a multiplicity of 'mes' and the difficulty in integrating them, combined with more and more demanding problems of emotional management. Psychoanalysis in this context becomes a form of adult socialisation, enabling the integration of roles and values of greater diversity than was permitted by childhood socialisation. Again, we have the idea of psychoanalysis as a means of social control.

If we wanted to add a critical dimension to this, we could do so in one of two, or possibly both, ways. We could see the change as a result of the increased instrumentalisation of everyday life and human existence, the triumph of practical activity over value, of doing over being, and the way this can be 'sealed' by psychoanalysis as a resocialisation which calls on potentially dissident aspects of the personality to enable the individual to survive in an instrumentalised world. Or we could see it as the colonisation of the life-world to which the dialogue of the psychoanalytic process may be an antidote, enabling the development of communicative reason.

4. Next, it might be possible to produce a structural Marxist analysis – not unlike Harvey's analysis of postmodernity – in which the change can be seen as the ideological 'effect' of changes at the economic level, the production of new 'subjects' which in turn provide the conditions of existence of the economic change; in place of the moral agent, we have the flexible performer.

5. Finally, on a completely different tack altogether, we can look at both psychoanalytic conceptions of character structure and at the straightforward fact that people seek psychoanalysis to guide them towards the needs they experience as important and the choices they might make in satisfying those needs. In other words, it can offer us a more complex model of the actor for rational choice theory.

Some of these suggestions are rather brief, but they can all be extended in various ways. I do not think any of them are mutually exclusive: each grasps something that is going on in the social world – perhaps at different levels of analysis, perhaps in terms of relationships between different objects. I do not think they can be combined together to produce some sort of total or overall picture. In the elaborations and arguments that might result from them, the rationalisation process necessary to theory will take place as a matter of course; it will always involve some aspect of the traps I have discussed: crossword-puzzle solving, brain-teasing exercises, and the logic trap. The last is most dangerous; I tried to show how the criticisms of structuralist Marxism disposed of the baby at the same time as the bathwater, in particular by insisting that something must be either this or the other. This sort of insistence originates in any claim to have a clear way of distinguishing between adequate and inadequate knowledge, and leads to a form of intellectual terrorism which manifests itself in the classroom and seminar as much as in the debates carried out in books. It is a way of outlawing ideas and ways of thinking in the same way that those who operate in their moral life with clear criteria of right and wrong would sometimes like to outlaw behaviour that others find quite acceptable and normal.

I want to push this argument a bit further. If we deploy a range of different theories, different understandings, we ourselves change. Understanding changes the person who understands, although not necessarily the situation that is understood. The change consists in being able to entertain a range of possibilities and tolerate their differences – even, perhaps, their mutual opposition. This can be seen as a sort of growth, in the old and clichéd sense that 'education broadens the mind', but it has a very real meaning. Being able to look at the world from a number of different and possibly incompatible points of view is a matter of learning to think against oneself and to open oneself out. It is parallel to a much more difficult process of personal integration that confronts everybody as they grow into adulthood: the experience of holding on to and containing contradictory feelings about the same object and person – love and hatred, attraction and repulsion. In this sense, learning to tolerate theoretical thinking, which might tell us something we don't want to know, and learning to tolerate the useful ambiguities and contradictions of different sorts of theory, is tied up with the way in which we might overcome the feeling of emptiness that I have used as my final example. Misunderstood, theory becomes a way of prolonging that emptiness.

FURTHER READING

Bryant, C. G. A. (1990) '"Tales of innocence and experience": Developments in sociological theory since 1950', in Becker, H. A. and Bryant, C. G. A. (eds), *What Has Sociology Achieved?*, Sage, London.
Feyerabend, P. (1975) *Against Method*, New Left Books, London.

INDEX

Abell, P., 75, 76, 77, 79
Adorno, T. W., 209, 211, 213, 214, 215, 216, 218, 219, 220, 224, 225, 226, 227, 231, 234, 236, 241
Alexander, J., 56, 57, 58, 60, 61, 62, 64, 69, 189
Althusser, L., 28, 128, 132, 138, 139, 149–76, 177, 179–83, 199, 200, 202, 206, 214, 234, 236
Anderson, B., 108
Anderson, P., 118
Archer, M., 121

Balibar, E., 161
Barthes, R., 132, 139, 140, 141
Baudrillard, J., 188, 192
Becker, G., 72, 80
Becker, H., 90, 247
Bell, D., 178
Benjamin, W., 209
Berger, P., 100, 101, 107
Bhaskar, R., 18, 19, 20, 21, 25, 129, 151, 173
Blackburn, R., 167
Blau, P., 70
Blumer, H., 87, 88
Bordieu, P., 190
boundary maintenance, 39, 46, 239
Bryant, C. G. A., 247, 248

Callinicos, A., 183
Carling, A., 73, 74, 77, 79
causality, 21–4, 26, 46, 52, 54, 56, 61, 71, 157–61, 164, 173, 181–2, 184, 192, 199, 251, 252
Chicago School
    see symbolic interactionism

Chomsky, N., 107
Cicourel, A., 105, 106, 107
Cohen, I., 121
Cohen, P., 57
Colomey, P., 57
commodity fetishism, 205–7
common-sense knowledge
    see taken-for-granted knowledge
communicative action/reason, 234, 235, 241, 243
Comte, A., 132, 213
conflict theory, 27, 35, 55, 57–61, 69, 168, 172, 186, 187, 251, 252
Coser, L., 51
Craib, I., 116
critical theory, 28, 29, 57, 203–45

Dahrendorf, R., 50, 57, 58–61, 166
Dawe, A., 16
Derrida, J., 132, 184
discourse, discourse analysis, 183–6
domination (in critical theory), 209–11, 219–22, 224, 225, 226, 235, 236
Dowling, C., 217
duality of structure, 112–14
Durkheim, E., 19, 36, 38, 132, 136, 208

Elster, J., 71, 73, 74, 75, 80
Engels, F., 161
epistemology, 19, 21, 23, 155, 174, 193
ethnomethodology, 10, 27, 29, 35, 93, 97–110, 111, 112, 113, 114, 128, 131, 132, 185, 186, 187, 189, 233, 249, 252, 254
evolution, social evolution, 37, 47–8, 49, 54, 117, 118, 119, 236, 238, 239, 255

259

exchange theory, 70–71
existentialism, existential
  sociology, 28, 97

Feyerabend, P., 250, 251
flexible accumulation, 191
Fordism, post-Fordism, 191
Foucault, M., 132, 183, 184, 186, 187,
  190, 225, 242, 254
fragmentation
  of experience, 16, 26, 29, 184, 191,
    192, 193, 199
  of social theory, 15, 16, 21, 24–7, 35,
    49, 56, 129, 147, 152, 172, 177,
    179, 180, 184, 193, 199, 202, 225,
    243, 251
Frankfurt School
  see critical theory
Freud, S., 9, 25, 56, 113, 170, 219, 220,
  221, 224, 236, 252, 254
Fromm, E., 209
functionlism, structural-functionalism, 9,
  26, 27, 29, 35, 37–55, 86, 98, 100,
  101, 110, 120, 127, 145, 169, 177,
  189, 241, 251, 252
functional prerequisites, 42–5, 59, 63,
  112

Gadamer, H.-G., 233, 234
Garfinkel, H., 104, 105, 108
Giddens, A., 26, 28, 35, 36, 52, 101,
  111–23, 187, 189, 190, 191, 247,
  248, 255
Glaser, B., 92
Glücksmann, A., 183
Goffman, E., 84, 90, 93, 94, 108, 116
Gouldner, A., 16, 37, 50, 51, 63
Gramsci, A., 170

Habermas, J., 28, 202, 227, 231–45, 247
Hamilton, P., 56
Harvey, D., 188, 190, 191, 192, 256
Hegel, G. W. F., 28, 173, 201, 203
Heidegger, M., 116
Held, D., 121, 122
hermeneutics, 28, 29, 233
Heydebrand, W., 55
Hindess, B., 76, 77, 78, 79, 179, 181

Hirst, P., 179, 180, 181, 182, 184, 185
Hitler, A., 209, 222
Hobbes, T., 39
Hochschild, A. R., 93
Holton, J., 62, 63
Homans, G., 70
Horkheimer, M., 209, 210, 213, 214,
  220, 231, 236
Hosticka, C., 92
Husserl, E., 98, 99, 241

ideological state apparatuses, 166, 168–
  70, 171
indexicality, 103, 104, 105, 108
institutionalisation, 40–42, 70, 86, 115
instrumental rationality/reason, 79, 80,
  211–15, 224, 233, 234, 236, 238,
  239, 241
  see also critical theory
Iowa School
  see symbolic interactionism

Jameson, F., 188, 226

Kant, I., 132, 134
Kilminster, R., 27
Kuhn, M., 88
Kuhn, T., 11, 17

Lacan, J., 132, 170, 171, 172, 179, 180,
  185, 188
Lasch, C., 222
Lash, S., 190, 193
Lechner, F. J., 61
legitimation crisis, 240
Lenin, V. I., 159
Levi-Strauss, C., 132, 134, 138, 139,
  140, 145, 255
life-world, the, 241, 242, 243, 256
'linguistic turn', the, 97, 101–2, 111, 178,
  202, 232, 243
Lockwood, D., 53, 57, 64, 115, 127, 145
Löwenthal, L., 209
Luckman, T., 100, 101, 107
Lukács, G., 202, 203–8, 209, 210, 211,
  213, 215, 224, 231
Lyotard, J.-F., 187, 188, 189, 190

Marcuse, H., 209, 210, 211, 214, 216, 217, 220, 221, 224, 231, 236, 241
Marshall, G., 11
Marx, K., 9, 19, 28, 36, 38, 55, 117, 118, 152, 155, 157, 158, 163, 183, 200, 201, 206, 208, 219, 232, 236, 237, 240, 241
Marxism, 17, 20, 21, 24, 26, 28, 37, 57, 59, 64, 112, 115, 128, 132, 190–92, 231, 236–8, 239, 251, 256
  Hegelian Marxism, 203–29
  rational-choice Marxism, 71, 72–4
  structuralist Marxism, 149–76, 179–84
Mead, G. H., 85, 87, 88, 89, 90, 171, 232
Meltzer, B. W., 92
Merton, R., 50, 51, 63
methodological individualism, 69–70, 73, 80, 93
Metz, C., 132
Miliband, R., 167
Mills, C. Wright, 27, 54
mode of production, 161–5, 172, 174n, 180, 251
Morris, L., 72, 74
motivation crisis, 240
multi-dimensional theory, 57

negotiated order, 92–3
neofunctionalism, 26, 36, 56–64, 69
Nietzsche, F., 184, 185
norms and values, 38, 41, 42, 46, 48, 49, 53, 54, 59, 78, 86, 98, 100, 103, 108, 236, 238

Olson, M., 80n
one-dimensional culture, 215–19
ontological security, 113
ontology, 18, 19, 21, 25, 112, 120, 184, 201
overdetermination, 157–60

paradigm
  see syntagm
Park, R., 85
Parsons, T., 5, 10, 13, 16, 26, 27, 35, 37–67, 69, 70, 71, 77, 80, 86, 92, 94, 108, 111, 112, 114, 115, 117,
  121, 127, 128, 146, 152, 153, 171, 172, 177, 188, 202, 224, 231, 236, 238, 239, 244
Pascal, B., 171
pattern variables, 45–6, 55
Peirce, C. S., 136
phenomenology, 98
phenomenological sociology, 20, 35, 97–110, 116, 119
phenomenological reduction, 98, 105
philosophy of social science, 16–27, 154, 212, 251–2
Plummer, K., 85, 93
postmodernism, post-structuralism, 13, 26, 27, 28, 93, 101, 120, 129, 132, 173, 177–96, 202, 203, 214, 215, 223, 225, 226, 227, 232, 233, 235, 236, 247, 249, 252, 254, 256
  and modernism, 178, 181
post-structuralism
  see postmodernism
Poulantzas, N., 128, 149–51, 165–70, 202, 224
praxis, 205, 224
psychoanalysis, 13, 170, 219, 234, 252, 253–7

Rasmussen, D., 235
rational choice theory, 29, 35, 69–83, 86, 93, 100, 114, 116, 256
rationality crisis, 240
realism, 18–21, 173
reflexivity, 104, 106, 108, 113, 116, 120, 189
reification, 207–8, 210, 213
relative autonomy, 158, 181, 183
Rex, J., 56, 59, 64
Reynolds, L. T., 92
Robertson, R., 61, 62
Rocher, G., 42
Rock, P., 85, 90, 91, 92
Roemer, J., 73
roles, 42, 48, 52, 59, 86, 89, 91, 92, 121, 171, 173
rules, rule-following, 101–2, 103, 104, 105, 106, 112, 113, 115, 118, 121, 136, 138, 139, 142, 144, 157, 186, 252

Sacks, H., 106
Saussure, F. de, 132, 134
Schutz, A., 99, 100, 102, 103, 104
self, the, 88, 89, 94
semiotics, 93, 139–44
Sen, A., 75
Serpe, R. T., 92
Sharrock, W., 108
signs, 136, 137, 138, 139, 140, 141, 142,
    185
significant symbol, the, 87, 88
signifier/signified
    see sign
Smith, A., 70, 78
Smith, J., 121
social formation, 156, 157, 165, 174n,
    179, 182, 199
social integration
    see systems, social systems
social roles
    see roles
sociobiology, 248–9
speech/language, 136, 145, 146
Stalin, J., 183, 209, 222
status roles
    see roles
Stinchcombe, A., 117
Strauss, A., 92
structuralism, 26, 28, 29
    127–48, 199, 201, 203, 216, 223,
    224, 226, 233, 249, 252
structural functionalism
    see functionalism
structuration theory, 26, 28, 29, 35, 36,
    101, 111–23, 128, 189, 249
Stryker, S., 92, 93
symbolic interactionism, 9, 21, 26, 27,
    29, 35, 55, 85–96, 99, 108, 114,
    117, 189, 233, 249, 252, 255
syntagm/paradigm, 137–9, 140, 142,
    144, 145, 185
systems, social systems
    structural functionalism, 38, 40–45,

46–7, 50, 51, 52, 55, 59, 63, 86,
    127, **128**, **145**, 177, **188**, 241
structuration theory, 112, 114, 115–17,
    119, 120, 121, 122, 128
system integration and social
    integration, 53–4, 115, 118, 127,
    145, 239, 240, 241
systems theory, 45, 46–7

taken-for-granted knowledge, 99, 100,
    102, 104, 105, 106, 113
teleology, teleological explanation, 23, 90,
    182, 235, 252
theory, theoretical thinking, 3–13, 15–31,
    152–5, 247–57
    dangers of, 10–13
Thomas, W. I., 80
Thompson, E. P., 192
Thompson, J. B., 121, 122
time and space, 115, 116, 117, 118, 119,
    120, 121, 189, 191
totality, 203–5, 215, 226
Toynbee, A., 178
Trotsky, L., 159
Turner, B., 61, 62, 63, 121
Turner, R., 89
Twenty Statements Test, 88

Urry, J., 121

values
    see norms and values
Ventura, R., 190

Weber, M., 38, 59, 70, 75, 99, 208, 213,
    234, 236
White, S., 244
Winch, P., 101, 104, 113, 187
Wittfogel, K., 209
Wittgenstein, L., 101, 187, 241
Wright, E. O., 73, 74, 119, 151
Wright, W., 139, 141–5, 146